Sue,

AFRICAN
QUEEN

I hope you enjoy
the stories

Richard

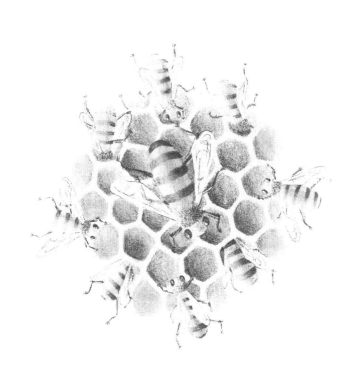

AFRICAN QUEEN

Tales of Motherhood and Wild Bees

RICHARD S. GODFREY

Published by Richard S. Godfrey

First Printing, 2015

Paperback edition printed by CreateSpace, Charleston SC

ISBN: 978-0-9965042-1-8 (Print), 978-0-9965042-0-1 (Ebook)

Library of Congress Cataloging-in-Publication Data
Godfrey, Richard S., 1947–
African Queen: Tales of Motherhood and African Bees.
Includes bibliographic references and photo acknowledgements.

For my mother

Contents

Foreword

by Said Obama

Many things have happened in Kenya, East Africa, long before our people achieved Independence from British colonialism in 1964. As Kenya and Africa continue rising there is still much to be done to create a healthy gender equality. Indeed, this is enshrined in the 2010 Constitution—Global Goals #5. Mama Sarah Obama, the late Mary Onyango, and the late Wangari Maathai each held our country, our cultures, and our world together in a circle of sustenance. Wangari Maathai's contribution was planting trees, Mary Onyango's contribution was being a cancer survivor and fighting breast cancer, while Mama Sarah Obama has dedicated her life to a support system for orphans, mainly AIDS orphans, and impoverished children that need to maximize their potential.

In these three stories the author has been able to reconstruct Kenya's past, however painful or glorious, using accurate information. It is through stories that intertribal friendships are kept alive and burning for the ages. For "Until the lion learns to write the tales, tales of the hunt shall always glorify the hunter"– Ibo Proverb. With more than forty-two plus ethnic groups and forty seven million citizens, there is a multi-faith tradition manifesting itself as Kenya—or a superorganism as described by E. O. Wilson. Three women uniquely define themselves as custodians of Mother Earth, traversing and impacting the larger world.

Through this book Godfrey has laid out the foundations for better understanding of my family experience, age-old Luo traditions and proverbs, and our environment. He helps to destroy wrong notions and false 'facts' authoritatively, with the help of trusted and reliable locals. He establishes much of what must be known by our ever interconnected, interdependent world.

The three Tales of Motherhood, Wild Bees, and Wasps and the poignant fig tree ("tree of God") illustrates the connection of good health and wealth when we're in tune with our environment and nature. This book belongs to my children, and their children's children. Peace. *Amani. "Kwe kende."*

Said Hussein Obama

Monday, September 21st, 2015,
U.N. International Peace Day,
Kisumu City, Kisumu County, Kenya.

Introduction

Biographies and stories describing humanity's journey through time fill the shelves of the world's libraries and perhaps new accounts need not be written. On the other hand, everything changes. When I first met Mama Sarah Obama, it seemed as if she had witnessed all the changes a grandmother could comprehend in the span of nine decades. She had a sharp perspective, as may be true of anyone who has survived through a century of Kenya's cultural evolution. Something else unique, however, kept me returning to her home. It took several years to understand why her life was unusual and why her *dala*, or farm, was so challenging.

I faced limitations in translating Luo, not a difficult language but hard to master if you spend only a few weeks each year working in Kenya. I was helped by family members as well as by the written work of many others, including the autobiography of Sarah's step grandson, Barack Obama. Even so, it became important to also explore the lives of two other women, Mary Onyango and Wangari Maathai, in order to appreciate the larger transformations taking place in women's lives and health care in Kenya. Working in different hospitals and participating in the building of a new women/children's hospital in Western Kenya made it easier to see how these three women were creating social transformation. Witnessing the diverse geography of Kenya made it clear that environment shapes lives.

A fourth female subject in this story is an insect—the queen bee. One explores many territories when writing a biography. My connection with Mama Sarah began with a single colony of bees living high up in one of her mango trees. As a beekeeper, I had an interest in the behavior of the African bee and was led inevitably to the role of the queen bee and her significance in biology and evolution. The parallels between these three dynamic women and a queen bee became more evident to me as I studied the 150-million-year development of bees and their eusocial behavior. Bee colonies exist as superorganisms, and their collective intelligence transcends the capacity of a one-milligram bee brain. Like our human brain with ten billion neurons working synergistically to facilitate thought and behavior, the bee colony uses fifty thousand bees working together to promote survival and reproduction.

Kenya, like its colonial counterpart of the past and its American and Chinese partners of the present, has a strong patriarchal culture that is awakening to the voice of many women. Nowhere is this more apparent than in the voice and actions of Wangari Maathai, Africa's first woman and the first environmentalist to win a Nobel Prize. Professor Maathai's extraordinary vision and actions were well ahead of her time. It is easy to become pessimistic as you look at climate change, population growth, and the loss of diversity now occurring on a planetary scale. Some believe that man is an invasive species. As Leonard Shlain wrote in *Sex, Time, and Power*, "An organism that kills its host ceases to be a parasite and is reclassified as a 'pathogen.' It could be argued that Homo sapiens has degenerated from its beginnings as a symbiotic prey to a symbiotic predator to a parasite and has now transformed into a planet-devouring pathogen." Dr. Shlain, a surgeon like me, wrote prolifically about the re-awakening of matriarchal society, suggesting that a more positive worldview is possible.

Even more suggestive of humankind's evolution towards a sustainable planet is E.O. Wilson's concept of the superorganism. Wilson compares the collective behavior of individualistic humans with instinct-driven bees. We humans are self-sufficient in ways that bees can never be. And yet, our collective behavior has similarities to that of bees. As a spokesman for evolutionary biology, Wilson points to a more hopeful future, even as we and our children approach another process of transformation.

There are lessons to be learned from a ninety-three-year-old grandmother and from those who speak out on behalf of a sustainable environment. In this story of wild bees, I receive some pointers taught by eusocial insects, and many of them were stings! Honeybees have evolved on the planet much longer than Homo sapiens. They have learned how to manage in extremes of heat and cold, how to subsist without depleting the world around them, and hopefully how to survive despite great external stress. How bees connect with African queens and lead into the future is the subject of this book.

1

High in a Tree, the Queen Bee

*The earth is a beehive; we all enter by the same door
but live in different cells.*
—African Proverb

Looking down from the tree, I see an assemblage of family members—and the Bushman, Tom—all being entertained by me, the *muzungu* (white fellow), climbing up towards a large colony of African bees. The tree has a thin, rough, bark, giving traction to some old tennis shoes, and as I pull on the thick branches, they seem strong enough. Perhaps forty feet up, the colony is dense, ominous, and threatening as hundreds of forager bees do waggle dances in front while the sentries wait to fend off invaders. The queen will be well protected somewhere inside the organized comb, and it will take at least a miracle to see her up close.

In the distance, above us, the sky is darkening. Clouds and moisture lift up from the wide bosom of Lake Victoria, or *Nam*

Lolwe, the endless lake. Known also as the "Eye of the Rhino," this largest tropical lake on the planet is endangered, reflecting the activity of the neighboring inhabitants as overfishing, pollution, and eutrophication threaten the aqueous ecosystem. At this moment, I'm more concerned about a sudden invasion of black soldier ants crawling over my veil. I disrupted their nest in a hollow of the trunk, and they are determined to dispel me. There's still fifteen feet to go before I can swing a rope over a branch to hang a collecting box, and it isn't certain who will succeed—the bees or me.

I think to myself, "Why am I here?"

First Meeting with Mama Sarah

Kenya, like many African countries, has an ever-evolving system of government. It has undergone smooth and convulsive changes over the last one hundred years—from a diverse "tribal" social construction, to British Colonial rule, to independence and a single-party republic, and to a multiparty democracy with a recent constitutional reform. This is a short statement to cover transition from humanity's cradle to the political vanguard of East Africa, from rural subsistence agriculture to global industrialism and the cell-phone led information age, complete with government skyscrapers, expanding municipal slums and unrelenting traffic jams. Think of a population bursting from ten million in 1950 to forty-four million today, and you get a sense of the future.

The economic disparity index in Kenya is similar to that of the U.S.A., with much of the wealth controlled by the upper elite. This is a relative measure, and perhaps the more significant difference is the ratio of an average American's income compared to a Kenyan's, which is approximately sixty to one. The difference makes for interesting personal encounters when an American visits Kenya. By far more remarkable for me, however, were encounters with three special mothers and a queen bee.

It's 2007, and we are sliding fast around goats, cows, and bicyclists on the road to Kisumu, in Western Kenya. Our well

traveled van is making good progress when the driver over-
hears us talking about a man named Obama, a young African
American who has the hope (and audacity) to run for president.
We're doctors returning from a busy two weeks during which
we were operating at a government hospital. We are eager to
get to Nairobi and fly home.

"You know, his grandmother lives close to here," the driver
tells us, nodding to his right where a small signpost announces
the *Senator Obama Kogelo Sec. School.* An iron-red dirt road
points south, looking mostly abandoned.

"Will we miss our flight?" Terry Dunn, the Gyn surgeon
from Colorado, asks.

"No, we can make it," he assures us, "but you need to hang
on. I'm taking a short cut."

With that, the van turns south, now rolling between fields
of corn and sugarcane, bouncing along open patches of land
grazed by ubiquitous cattle. Our group, called *Matibabu* (which
means *treatment* in Kiswahili) is small, part of a larger organization that runs a medicine clinic further north. We are buoyant,
having dealt with a volume of hernias, cancers, emergency C-
sections, and other cases that left us tired, but satisfied. In the
burgeoning district, malaise finds its way to the government
hospital in haphazard fashion, more often late than early. The
task of maintaining order amidst the chaos of illness is like
functioning in a crowded beehive: rules of management are
not always explicit, but we know our job.

"It is with profound gratitude and great humility that I
accept your nomination for the presidency. . ."

Eleven thousand miles away and days earlier, Barack
Obama had won the presidential primary and was waving his
hands in victory to the ecstatic audience packing the Mile High
Stadium of Denver, Colorado. He told the Democrats the story
of his childhood, about the impact his mother and her parents
had on him as he journeyed into adulthood. But it was the influence of the Dunhams and his maternal American family that
he spoke of, and little was mentioned about his father's family
or their home in Kenya.

We bounce and slide through a few miles of farmland and arrive at a small tan-colored building surrounded by mango and pawpaw trees. It is the home to six or seven women and children supported by Mama Sarah. They, in turn, help support her. The *dala*, or Luo homestead, encloses cows, goats, chickens, rabbits, and turkeys. Said Obama greets us as we pull in and nods to the back of the building, where his mother works in the vegetable garden. Her visage is the opposite of frail, although she walks up to us slowly. She invites us into the tin-roofed cement house, smiling widely at our spontaneous and self-appointed delegation.

Sarah Onyango Obama comes from a lineage of families extending at least as far back as the Nilo-Sudanic migration of Luo people traveling from the Southern Nile Region of North Africa to the shores of Lake Victoria, five hundred years earlier. Over these centuries, a single woman's role has changed from supporting men in their explorations to being a matriarch in a prominent family.

I wondered why. What was unique about Sarah?

The Luo were latecomers to Kenya, displaced or assimilated into other emigrating ethnic groups, such as the southern Cushites from Ethiopia and the Bantus from Southeastern Nigeria. They found the shores of Lake Victoria conducive to fishing, agriculture, and cattle raising. By raiding the Bantus' cattle and fighting sequential battles, they "won the east," or at least a part of it, and currently they are the fourth largest tribal culture in Kenya, some four million strong. Africa's history, like America's, is a saga of cultural expansion, filled with tales of conflict and balance and the need for new territory to accommodate a growing population. Since independence half a century ago, the growth has accelerated, and many of the Luo men have moved away from the countryside and into the three-million-strong capital city, Nairobi. This was true in the case of Sarah's husband, Hussein Onyango Obama, who left the Nyanza province at an early age to seek employment with the British. In his autobiography, Barack Obama quotes Mama Sarah giving a description of Hussein:

Even from the time that he was a boy, your grandfather
Onyango was strange. It is said of him that he had ants
up his anus, because he could not sit still. (1)

Ochunglo odhi thir, ants up the anus, refers not just to an
attention deficit or wanderlust, but to an endemic migration
of Luo men heading to the big city. Hussein was an early pio-
neer who returned to his homeland after seeing much of the
world. He married at least three times, some say six, and his
third wife, Sarah, assumed the responsibility of raising Barack
Sr., the father of Barack Jr. All three men had a proclivity for
extensive traveling.

"How long have you lived here?" I ask.

Sarah sits down on a hard yellow couch as someone brings
out a tray of fruit drinks. Her visage when among visitors is
both humble and proud; she faces ahead, because avoiding direct eye contact is good etiquette. A headscarf shields the sun
but leaves her ears free, and she hears everything, picking out
subtleties in the conversation in spite of the English. She nods
as we talk, vocalizing the *ehhh* sound that means *yes*, and easily senses the mood of the group.

"Since I was married, which is many years ago."

Fred, the Luo physician in our group, translates, and when
we ask about her health, she points to her knees. Mike Dunn,
a family physician in our group, examines them. Like soft mel-
ons ready to burst, they give claim to eighty years of field and
garden work. When he rotates her legs sideways, she grimaces.

"And what do you think of your grandson? Will he be the
next president?"

She smiles now. "Ehhh. Not of Kenya; maybe America."

We laugh and spend ten minutes asking more questions,
taking photographs, and enjoying the fruit drinks. When we
explain our hope of building a hospital, she quickly offers a
project of her own and passes around a petition for a secondary school. Her forehead is lined with wrinkles, but it relaxes
as she collects donations towards education.

Before leaving, I ask Mama Sarah if she had requested any-

FIGURE 1: Home of Mama Sarah and family – solar panel on roof

thing when young Senator Obama visited her. When Americans come to Kenya, it's common practice to ask if they can return with a gift from the U.S. In turn, they are often offered a gift to take home with them. She says she wanted a television set, which explains an important function of the solar panel on her roof.

"I want to watch the election," she says in Luo, nodding at a Zenith set in the front room. She smiles again and shakes our hands as we hurry to catch our flight from Kisumu to Nairobi. We are running late.

We won't see Mama Sarah for about a year, but it occurs to me that her maternal story is still unfolding and that she's emblematic of the evolving role of women in Kenyan society. A woman who spent most of her life tending fields, carrying water and firewood to the family kitchen, and preparing meals, she now watches television and experiences a new pride as her step-grandson runs for the U.S. presidency. Her role in the family home continues, however, with the same challenges she has faced all her life.

I have challenges myself, having lost my mother when I was relatively young. Like a lot of men, I probably am always in

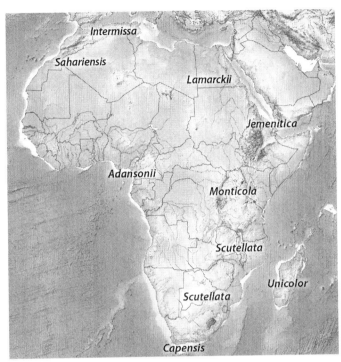

FIGURE 2: Map of the Distribution of African Bees

search of another mother. This thought inspires me to explore the role of other strong women in Kenya's society, focusing on three qualities. First, she must arise from the common people, the *wananchi*. Second, she must provide a special leadership. And third, she must procreate, give birth to successors, or in some way nurture the future. By no coincidence, the same three qualities are found in the African queen bee. If you follow this discourse, you will discover, as I finally did, how they are all connected.

Bee Biology

Man truly became master of the bees, although furtively, and without their knowledge: directing all things without giving an order, receiving obedience but not recognition. For the destiny

*once imposed by the seasons he has submitted his will. He
repairs the injustice of the year, unties hostile republics, and
equalizes wealth. He restricts or augments the births, regulates
the fecundity of the queen, dethrones her and installs another
in her place, after dexterously obtaining the reluctant consent
of a people who would be maddened at the mere suspicion of
an inconceivable intervention.*

—Maurice Maeterlinck, 1901 (2)

As a backyard beekeeper, I'm accustomed to searching for the
queen, who has a unique role in holding together a colony. Think
of the term *superorganism*, defined by E.O. Wilson as "applied
only to colonies of an advanced state of eusociality, in which
interindividual conflict for reproductive privilege is diminished
and the worker caste is selected to maximize colony efficiency
in intercolony competition." (3). Pulitzer-Prize-winner Wilson,
often regarded as the father of sociobiology, describes the cooperative behavior of ants and bees and how it determines their
survival. Eusociality implies three characteristics: cooperative
brood care, overlapping generations in the colony, and division
of labor with reproductive and non-reproductive groups. Fifty
thousand bees specialize in different tasks and leave reproduction to the queen.

Fed a diet of royal jelly for five to seven days as she passes
through the larval stage (worker bees receive a smaller sample
for two-and-a-half days), the queen emerges from the pupae
with long skinny ovaries that can deliver one egg a minute—or
two to three thousand eggs a day. The almost barren worker
bees have to spin cocoons and pupate until they emerge and
start taking care of their mother.

Ovary-challenged workers do the cell cleaning, brood
capping, brood tending, comb building, food handling, pollen
packing, ventilating, guarding (including stinging beekeepers and other interfering animals), foraging, and honey making. Aptly named drones for their idleness, the males make no
honey. Larger than the queen and without a stinger, they shun
all housework except temperature control. They hang around

the hive, and when their easy days are over, they have one purpose: insemination.

In 1790, the Czech priest Josef Janis observed a hive with an unmated queen bee and noted how, lacking the male sperm, she could produce only drones. Her essential role is reproduction, but in order to produce females, or worker bees, she has to mate. Two years earlier, a blind Swiss man named Francois Huber had discovered how this mating took place by relying on the vision of his servant to study the activity of the queen in their observation hive.

"We saw her promenading on the stand of the hive for a few instants, brushing her belly with her posterior legs: neither the bees nor the males that emerged from the hive appeared to bestow any attention upon her," Huber reported in *New Observations on the Natural History of Bees*. (4) After a five-minute test flight, the queen returned to the hive.

"Then, returning to examine the hive, she rose so high that we soon lost sight of her. Her second absence was much longer than the first; twenty-seven minutes elapsed before she came back. We then found her in a state very different than she was after her first excursion. The sexual organs were distended by a white substance, thick and hard, very much resembling the fluid in the vessels of the male, completely familiar to it indeed in colour and consistence."

So, the queen emerges from her birth cell and wanders around the hive for five or six days doing practice runs. She increases her endurance until it's time to meet up with the boys. This rendezvous at the drone congregation area (DCA), a place thirty to forty meters high, includes several hundred to as many as twenty-five thousand drones who wait urgently, scenting out her pheromones. No one knows exactly how the DCA is chosen. The drones have the best developed eyes of the bee family and antennae with ten times as many plate organs as those of the worker bees and twenty times as many as the queen. They can sense pheromones sixty meters away. Using two antennae to stereotactically guide them, they fly and circle with a droning noise, searching like astronauts poised to connect to a moon module. As they follow the queen, the first and most agile grasps her from behind, everting the internal genitals to deliver sperm in a quick explosion before falling away like an expired lover. The next drone takes over, and the romantic tragedy repeats until the queen's spermatotheca is full. She returns to the hive with some five million sperm, enough to maintain a superorganism.

The King Is a Queen

Of all the insects the Bees are chiefe, and worthily to be most admired; being the only things of that kinde, which are bred for the behoote of men.

—Charles Butler, 1623 (5)

The queen is under significant pressure upon returning from the mating flight. If she survives mating in the air, she still has to avoid birds, windstorms, spider webs, and other challenges on the way back to the hive. Hopefully, she has had a fruitful encounter, because it becomes apparent if she doesn't have enough quantity and quality of DNA to pass on.

Her partners expect her to perform within a few days of arrival back at the hive. It's crowded inside, with a lot of activity and noise, but they'll know if she doesn't deposit a few thousand eggs a day or secrete enough of the "queen substance," a primer pheromone released from the mandibular glands and distributed by the workers who groom her and each other while exchanging regurgitated food. Queen substance regulates hundreds of genes and specific bee behavior, such as staying longer in the hive to work instead of heading outside to forage. Above all, the queen has to lay eggs. If unsuccessful, she is superseded. New queens will be bred, and she'll be forced to leave the hive while they fight to the death to become the successor. This is the only time a queen can use her stinger, to sting another queen, and she does this before her competitors have a chance to develop.

Does the queen really "rule" the hive? Early beekeepers and authors of apiary literature believed in a king bee supported by an order of servants and staff, as one should expect in a good

English Colony. Charles Butler destroyed the myth in his 1609 pre-feminist revelation, *The Feminine Monarchie*. "The King is a Queen!" he announced. Even though he regarded the queen as being in full control with a proper hierarchy of staff, it was only a matter of time before the truth was further elucidated: the queen just mates, lays eggs, and goes out on a swarm when she's told to. Here's the rub: all that queen substance, or pheromone, which includes *ethyl oleate*, can help regulate the hive and keep younger workers around longer by delaying their maturing into foragers. However, the chemical finds its way around through the rubbing actions of the worker bees. The worker bees, under the influence of queen substance, are the collective force that determines day-to-day changes in the hive.

Second Visit and the Obama Patriarchy

If you touch them, the skin will remain in your hand because they are very soft. But they will come with thunderstorms and they will burn the people.

—Luo Prophet, describing arrival of Europeans, 1800s

Chance encounters are memorable, and my first contact with Mama Sarah's bees happened well before I climbed into her mango tree.

Riding on the back of a motorcycle, turning the corner of a dirt road leading to the Obama family home, I feel a bee collide with me and plant her stinger into my right lower lip. My pain accelerates and clouds of dust rise up as we head towards the compound and pass villagers walking to the market.

When the dust settles, the view encompasses myriad fields of maize, sugarcane, and lesser cash crops, like papaya, kale, pineapples, and legumes. The roadsides are lined with a profusion of colors, flowering nightshade-blue mixed with the brilliant yellow of Mexican sunflowers (*akech*). They offer nectar to the bees and enough bitter alkaloids to discourage livestock from sampling them. Mothers take the yellow flowers and boil them into a bitter broth which is said to cure children's colic.

"Peace be unto you," I greet Sarah, using the little Arabic I was taught in the Peace Corps. She's from a Muslim family, and it's as correct as saying "*Misawa*," the polite Luo greeting. I've written asking permission to work on her biography and have been given verbal consent. At the same time, post-election violence in Kenya has settled down. Barack Obama has been elected president and the U.S. is immersed in two unpopular wars in Muslim nations, as well as a roller-coaster recession. Her compound, recently broken into by thieves trying to steal the solar panel, is now fenced off and protected by a police guard.

"*Alaikum salam*," she answers, and the conversation switches back to Luo. After hearing about the bee encounter, she laughs while noting my swollen lip and Marlon Brando jaw. Sitting down with us in wooden chairs in the open field and mango orchard, she points to one of the trees where a black swarm of bees has resided for years. It's been causing trouble for the family, and she's all too familiar with bee stings. The colony is almost three feet long, hanging from a secondary limb, and contains a family of some thirty to forty thousand bees—possibly the same one that was in the tree when her step-grandson, Barack, first visited in 1987, and probably the same one that supplied the forager that stung my lip.

At this time, I'm reminded of a passage in President Obama's autobiography in which he describes the recitation of Sarah and a group of women gathered together beneath a mango tree, sitting on straw mats, while braiding hair:

> I heard all the voices begin to run together, the sound of three generations tumbling over each other like the currents of a slow-moving stream, my questions like rocks roiling the water, the breaks in memory separating the currents, but always the voices returning to that single course, a single story. . .
>
> First there was Miwiru. It's not known who came before. Miwiru sired Sigoma, Sigoma sired Owiny, Owiny sired Kisodhi, Kisodhi sired Ogelo, Ogelo sired Otondi, Otondi sired Obongo, Obongo sired Okoth, and Okoth Sired Opiyo. The women who bore them, their names are forgotten, for that was the way of our people. (6)

Saved in oral tradition are the names of the Luo leaders who fought battles, claimed and cultivated land, and sought and married many wives. Around 1600, while religious wars were being fought in Europe, New England was being "civilized" by the pilgrims, Peru and Mexico were being carved up by the Spanish, Southeast Asia was fought over by everyone, and in essence, war and conquest prevailed globally—the Luos would not be left out.

Owiny-Sigoma, with spear and loincloth, assembled a moving army of warriors that, village by village, overtook the land of Alego, beginning in what is known as the Luo nation— now approaching five million inhabitants. How Kisodhi, Ogelo, Otondi, Obongo, Okoth, and Opiyo figured into the expansion is difficult to trace, even with the writings of Bethwell Ogot, Peter Firstbrook, and other historians, but unquestionably there were many women along the way whose history was never recorded. Sarah Onyango Obama's story still revolves around her husband.

She was born in 1922 in Kendu Bay, South Nyanza, and was, depending on the numbering system, the third or fifth wife of Onyango Obama. The surname refers to a breech, meaning "to be bent" at the time of birth. It has another Swahili derivation, referring to members of the Luo tribe who convert to Islam. As Sarah tells Barack Obama, described in *Dreams from my Father*, Onyango was strong-willed, independent, serious, and filled with curiosity. While he was a boy, he sat with herbalists and learned their craft. He left home at fourteen years of age to learn things outside the village. When he returned from the small city of Kisumu, he was dressed in a white man's clothing. His father, Obama Opiyo, was offended and mistrusting of the shirt and trousers. He regarded his second-oldest son as disrespectful of customs and deserving rejection, and Onyango's brothers laughed at him.

Sent away, Onyango went on to work for the British and learned English and the colonial ways. He was put in charge of road gangs and spent some World War I years in Ethiopia, Egypt, and the Eastern world before settling in Tanganyika and Zanzibar. Eventually he returned home to Kendu to claim a piece of land. He pitched a tent rather than building a house (*simba*), much to the surprise of the villagers. Soon after claiming his plot, he set off walking to Nairobi, a distance he could cover in two weeks, fending off leopards, wild buffalo, and snakes—animals that were still prevalent for a traveler in the early 1900s.

Just before this time, the "Lunatic Express," an infamous railroad running from Mombasa to Uganda, made possible the swamp-ridden city of Nairobi. Like Burton and Speke's determined search for the source of the Nile, the British Empire's steel track would not be stopped. It ran its "iron snake" to where Kenya's "capital" and metropolitan center of East Africa now stands. As the train headed further west to Kisumu and Lake Victoria, Indian, and African rail workers were mauled and devoured by the "man-eaters from Tsavo," maneless male lions that roamed the territory. Onyango's eastern journey would never be an easy one.

His travels took him beyond Nairobi to the battles of World War II in Burma, Ceylon, Arabia, and beyond. But not before he returned to his land in Kendu, alongside Lake Victoria, where he married an uncertain number of times. Polygamy, sometimes still practiced in Luo culture, was common in 1941 when Onyango chose Sarah. She was nineteen, he in his mid-forties. It was an arranged marriage in which Sarah's father accepted a dowry of cows in exchange for his daughter, the traditional practice that determines a formal marriage. Onyango lived with many women, but thus far had only sired children with his fourth wife, Akumu. He was allegedly not an easy man to live with: strict, demanding, and tough on those who didn't comply with his rules. When pressed by one of her own daughters as to why she would submit to such a marriage arrangement, Sarah replied:

> Our women have carried a heavy load. If one is a fish, one does not try to fly—one swims with other fish. One only knows what one knows. Perhaps if I were young today, I would not have accepted these things. Perhaps I would only care about my feelings, and falling in love. But that's not the world I was raised in. I only know what I have seen. What I have not seen doesn't make my heart heavy. (7)

She was raising her family during the national struggle for independence while Kenyans were under the yoke of British rule, and her load was heavy enough. After serving the British in Nairobi and in distant countries during World War II, Onyango was allegedly apprehended for an unwarranted charge and placed in detention camp for six months. Sarah is quoted in a newspaper interview:

> "The African warders were instructed by the white soldiers to whip him every morning and evening until he confessed. . . (Onyango) said they sometimes squeezed his testicles with parallel metallic rods. They also pierced his nails and buttocks with a sharp pin while his hands and legs were tied together and his head facing down. . . She said, "That was the time we realized that the British were actually not friends but, instead, enemies. My husband had worked so diligently for them, only to be arrested and detained." (8)

Written records from the Kamiti prison are not available to document this story (such documentation was destroyed every six years in the colonies), but according to Peter Firstbrook, Sarah claimed Onyango never fully recovered after the incarceration. (9) Today, the Obama family expresses doubt that such incarceration ever took place. Nevertheless, the British repressed the uprising of the Mau Mau freedom fighters and created many detention camps, punishing suspected insurgents with interrogation, torture, and often death. From 150,000 to 320,000 native Kenyans are said to have been detained, 1090 rebels hung, and 20,000 men killed in fighting. A State of Emergency was still in effect after Onyango returned home. (8, 9)

Sarah had spoken these words to her step-grandson and to reporters several years before. Now, sitting across from her, I study a face that provides the mystery every human countenance bears. "What makes her heart light?" I wonder.

Like all mothers, she takes joy in the successes and accomplishments of her children and her family. Her community and her country, or nation state, are probably a more distant importance for a woman who is still raising children—the hundred or so orphans who live in Kogelo and come to her *dala* for support, as well as several who stay in her home. In her many decades, she has witnessed the beginning of the AIDS epidemic and still confronts its ravages, manifested by families without parents.

The interview becomes lengthy. As temperatures rise in the afternoon and others arrive to greet and pay respects, we return briefly to the subject of bees. I have brought a jar of honey from my beehives in California and offer it, and she looks up once more at the mango tree.

"Do you know about these bees?"

There is a black colony high in the air, hanging from a branch like an incendiary device. Studying it from a distance, I tell her, "I know about my bees, but not so much about the ones you have here."

"They come down and sting the children," she continues, looking now into my eyes, "and I would like to know if you can remove them, eh?"

2

Home Cubed – A Muslim Family

"Tell her I'd like to learn Luo, but that it's hard to find the time in the States," I said. "Tell her how busy I am."

"She understands that," Auma said. "But she also says that a man can never be too busy to know his own people."

—Barack Obama in conversation with his half-sister and step-grandmother, 1988. (1)

In Kenya, there is a colloquialism, "home-squared," which refers to one's ancestral home. Those who live in Nairobi or other large cities often have a family home in the countryside where they were born and raised, or where their early ancestors lived. It's feasible in a largely rural society that one can return to one's roots, which is not so easily done in agribusiness America. President Obama felt the longing when he made his first trip to Kenya to visit his father's family. In Barack's autobiography, his half brother, Roy, said, "For you, Barack, we can call it Home Cubed." Indeed, when Obama traveled to Kogelo, he left his

American home and went by way of Nairobi, where his father
and grandfather had once lived and worked, to finally arrive by
train and *matatu* (minibus) at the home of his paternal grandfather. His journey was a personal one, embarked on before his
intense political career began. My visit was work-related, but
personal, as well. I wanted to know more of Sarah Obama's life
as a mother. Were her origins humble, as in a citizen of Kenya's
common folk? Did she exhibit a special leadership among her
people? Equally important, did she give strength to new leaders?

Matriarchy and Raising Children

Dhako ema kelo mwandu. It is a wife who creates wealth.

—Asenath Bole Odaga, *Luo Proverbs and Sayings* (2)

An enterprising, attractive young woman from a good Muslim
family, Sarah Ogwel most likely caught the attention of Hussein
Onyango through the orchestration of Saidi Aoko, who served
as the *ja-gem*, or middle man. Saidi attended the same mosque
as Onyango and found him to be "clean, intelligent, and well
liked by the community." No doubt, the final arrangements were
determined by the *mzee*, or male elders, who would decide the
dowry and ultimate suitability of the couple and their respective
lineages. Already experiencing some frustration with his fourth
wife, Akumu, and sharing his compound with Helima (childless
and soon to leave), Onyango was ready to marry again and expand the family. Some claimed that Onyango married in Burma
and brought back a photo of a light-skinned woman that Sarah
still keeps on the wall. But the family denies the likelihood of
this. He intended to live with Akumu and Sarah.

As a child, Sarah enjoyed good health and the status of being the first born to her mother, Mama Athiya. She was the third
child of her father, Omar Okech Abila, and had six siblings after
two of her brothers died young. Her other two brothers were
able to go to school, but despite her own eagerness to attend, she
wasn't allowed. When she attempted to sneak into classes, she
received a hard spanking. Luo girls were expected to develop

homemaking and farming skills, and respectful obedience was necessary for a successful marriage. She was enterprising in her early years and worked with her mother preparing *mandazi*, an East African variant of donuts cooked in hot oil. She sold them in the marketplace and also bought fresh fish to sell at a better price. Like other Luo girls, she had already formed skills by playing games such as *kora*, where pieces of broken pottery are thrown into the air and then caught on the back of the hand, or *bao*, where seeds are moved on a board and you try to capture your opponent's collection. Sarah was adept at moving resources in a communal setting, and Onyango took note of her aptitude.

On returning from the battles of Ethiopia and Burma, well into his forties, Onyango would also have been an impressive figure to a teenager. Elaborate wedding celebrations, however, weren't the order of the day.

"We did not have a big wedding: it was merely the legal registration before I started my life as a wife."

Sarah moved in with Akumu and her children in Kendu Bay and was soon taken to Nairobi, where Onyango worked for the U.S. Embassy. It was 1941, and he had established a village reputation as a strict, no-nonsense man. As described by John Ndalo, who was trained by Onyango:

> Onyango loved to welcome visitors. If his women did not behave well in front of them, then he would beat them right there, right in front of the visitors. He would not wait. (3)

Charles Oluoch, a nephew, confirms that being married to Onyango was not always blissful:

> At mealtimes Onyango insisted that others wait to wash their hands until after he had washed his own. He would then eat his meals alone, "and no one could sit down at the table until he was done." When Oynango visited the homes of his brothers, he instructed their wives on how to cook their food and demanded that only a single measure of water ever be put in a pot, with no additional liquid allowed. (4)

Said Obama, Sarah's fifth child, refutes this description as "complete nonsense," explaining that the reason his father would not allow young persons to wash their hands before elders was simply to follow established custom in Nyanza. Onyango was not a man to eat by himself and enjoyed company. He could, however, be direct—true of most Luos, as well as of patriarchal culture in much of Africa.

Before long, Sarah was brought back to Kogelo, where she was expected to learn the ways of her husband's family and help in raising Habibi Akumu's children. Onyango obtained work at Makere University in Uganda, and Akumu was the first to join him. Sarah was told the two of them would rotate, but meanwhile, she had to till the fields, prepare the meals, and look after Akumu's three children—Sarah, Barack Sr., and Hawa Akuma. She also looked after the mango trees and bananas, which she helped plant and maintain.

"I loved mangoes," she told Daphne Barak, "and ate so many of them during my first pregnancy with Onyango that the fruit became locally very popular: You see, after my Omar was born, mangoes were associated with giving birth to a boy." (5)

Traditionally, Luo husbands visit with the *mikayi* (first wife) and their additional wives as fertility and personal preference dictate. By 1944, Sarah had borne two children and established herself in Kogelo, both at the marketplace and at home. Perhaps Akumu felt less attention, became more rebellious and unhappy, but by 1945, her life became too difficult and she chose to quit her marriage.

"He didn't like anything that is called dirt to be around him," said Charles Oluoch, in recalling the split between Onyango and his *mikayi*. "So that is the number one cause which brought the disagreement with Akumu. There was a fight between Akumu and Onyango in K'ogelo—a quarrel. He dug a grave and he was going to cut her up and bury her there. An old man [a neighbor] came and helped Akumu, otherwise she would have been killed—she was being slaughtered!

"The old man came and wrestled with Onyango, then Akumu escaped and walked all the way to Kisumu by foot [64km]. I think there was some problem because having married the other wife Sarah, it might have put a lot of pressure on Akumu." (6)

Contrary to these assertions, Sarah's fifth child, Said Obama, denies such violent actions ever took place. It was, however, a violent time in history. During that same year, the battles of WWII raged on, Hitler evacuated Auschwitz and committed suicide, and the U.S. dropped atomic bombs on Hiroshima and Nagasaki. Significant for the drive towards Kenya's independence, soldiers serving in the war saw that the white colonialists were imperfect and vulnerable, and future Mau Mau insurgents gained guerilla warfare training and experience.

Meanwhile, Akumu never saw Onyango again. She remarried, had five more children, and only returned to Kogelo for the funeral services of her first son, Barack Sr. Onyango did not insist on a return of his dowry, but he retrieved his children when they ran away in search of their mother. Sarah Nyoke was eleven and Barack Sr. was nine when Sarah assumed their care at Onyango's home.

Hawa Auma, the youngest of the three children, still has stories to tell of the hardships that followed Akumu's departure. She recalls being left behind in a sisal plantation because her sister and brother could not carry her. Somehow the leopards were "sympathetic towards me," she related, and the neighbors found her and brought her home. Three years old at the time, she grew up in the care of Mama Sarah but remained unhappy and felt mistreated. (7) Said Obama states that Hawa Auma's story was both "unbelievable" and "cooked up," and that her siblings would never have abandoned her, anymore than leopards would be "sympathetic." Sarah, who bore the responsibility for the three children left behind, relates a different story.

"Who is Akumu?" she responded to Peter Firstbrook's inquiry about the split in the family. "She left when the father of the President was nine years old. And by that time, he had never started schooling. So it was me—Mama Sarah—who protected and took care of them!" (8)

"Meanwhile, our family was expanding," she said, referring back to the year 1944:

I gave birth to Omar. My husband demanded a very neat household—but of course I still needed to raise the children, look after my vegetables and fruits, not to mention selling them. . . and be alert to any urgent need of Hussein. He expected me to be highly disciplined, and obey his wishes at once. But I understood that he was hard working, and demanded that kind of hard work from everyone around. (9)

Black Swarms and House Hunting

A smart swarm uses its collective power to sort through count-less possible solutions while the mob unleashes its chaotic ener-gy against itself. And that makes it so important to understand how a smart swarm works—and how to harness its power.

—Peter Miller, *The Smart Swarm* (10)

I begin to understand the issues of hard work around the Obama *dala*, but how difficult will it be to move a wild colony? Certainly, the more you learn about bees, the better prepared you are. Looking up at Mama Sarah's dark colony of *Apis mellifera scutellata*, native African bees, hanging from a tree branch around forty feet up, I again assess the size of the colony at about thirty to forty thousand. Left alone, they will remain satisfied, gathering nectar, supporting the queen, and reproducing until a better foraging site is necessary or some foolish animal makes the mistake of coming after them. But who would make that mistake—climbing dense foliage, risking life and limb, or even death by countless stings?

The honey badger might. I've never seen one, but this animal helps explain the defensive ferocity of African bees. Why? The badger loves honey and bee larvae and has hunted them for eons. It's hard to believe that this polecat-like mammal the size of a small dog, that breastfeeds its young, is one of the most fearsome in the animal kingdom. Badgers will take on lions, crocodiles, pythons, and black mambas. A badger can even enjoy a spitting cobra for lunch. If attacked by a Cape buffalo

FIGURE 3: Bee Colony in the Mango Tree

or man, it goes for the scrotum and leaves the victim bleeding to death! But its favorite food is the beehive. The honey badger is reputed to locate hives with the help of the honey guide bird; a symbiotic relationship in which the bird guides with a "churring" sound and a display of white tail feathers, followed by the grunt and chuckling of the badger, until they both arrive at the food source. The badger climbs and approaches the beehive backwards and releases, like a beekeeper's smoker, a noxious cloud from state-of-the-art anal glands. This suffocating odor stupefies the bees, sometimes killing them, and the badger moves in to consume honey and bee larvae until fully gorged. The bird gets the wax.

Anticipating this rear-ended approach to their hives, bees have learned to outsmart their foe. The key is to find a hive location that can't be easily taken. Since badgers are fearless, and have thick skin, protective hair, and noxious anal glands, the bees seek a high, protected location where it's tough for invaders to back up or to avoid the stinging sentries aiming for eyes and face. To achieve this isolation, the colony sends out scouts.

An investigation of the swarm-searching mechanism was done by two researchers and a team on a windy, barren island known as Appledore, off the southern coast of Maine. (11) Thomas Seeley and Kirk Visscher elucidated the scouting and decision mechanism by filming it with video cameras. After labeling and painting four thousand bees in each swarm, their study was to see which of five boxes the bees would choose for a home and how they made decisions. Four of the boxes were too small for a healthy hive, but the fifth was just right. The scout bees didn't waste much time going for the fifth hive. When enough of them agreed and had time to communicate their information by waggle dance, a quorum was reached. A "diversity of knowledge" (as Peter Miller describes this process in The Smart Swarm) is then condensed into information perceivable by the larger colony. Scouts "pipe" their group decision to the rest of the swarm.

"It sounds like 'nnneeeep, nnneeeep!'" according to Seeley. "It's a signal that a decision has been reached and it's time for the rest of the swarm to warm up their wing muscles and prepare to fly."

The bees now have a plan and a place. Having sugared up and rested, and stimulated by the "buzz run" of the scouts, they take off for their new home. I try to imagine a swarm as I look up at the feral colony hanging precariously from the mango tree branch. These aren't Africanized bees. They're native Africans that have evolved in a survival-of-the-fittest struggle for millions of years. Maybe Africanized bees, those that evolved and hybridized in South America, are more defensive or more difficult to work with, but I don't doubt the ferocity of these native African bees. There's no honey badger around to make them move off. So the question remains: what other animal is crazy enough to risk life and limb (or death) in order to chase off a hive of African bees?

That would be me.

Youth in the Colonial Years

Dhako bade boyo. A woman has long arms.
(A woman can do so many things at the same time.)

—Asenath Bole Odaga, *Luo Proverbs and Sayings*

As a mother in a Muslim family, Sarah's duties matched those of most women in a rural area: child rearing and managing the *dala* while her husband was away. At the end of World War II, Kenya was still ruled by Britain, the family was under Onyango's control, and Sarah had four children to care for— Akumu's Sarah, Barack, and Hawa Auma, along with her own Omar. The nearest primary school was nine kilometers away, the nearest health center (with minimum supplies and support) twelve kilometers away, and the market where she took corn to be milled and sold green grams to pay for school fees was a fifteen-kilometer trip. Walking was still the primary mode of travel on dirt and gravel roads. Sarah was the first woman to own and ride a bike in Kogelo.

As the first male child, Barack Sr. took precedence in the family and was treated like the *dhahabu ya nyota* (the gold of the stars) according to his younger sister. His father brought him special clothing and a mosquito net for his crib, and when he began primary school he was given a pair of shoes, a rarity for village boys. By age eleven, when the family moved from Kendu Bay to Kogelo, Barack Sr. started attending primary classes under a large fig tree, where a woman instructor taught him reading and writing. He would have none of it, refusing the indignity of learning from a female. He left the outdoor institution within days.

"He came back after the first day," recalls Sarah, "and told his father that he could not study there because his class was taught by a woman and he knew everything she had to teach him. This attitude he had learned from his father, so Onyango could say nothing."

Sarah made sure that Barack Sr. completed his studies at the Ng'iya Primary School, despite the five-mile walk every morning. At times, she took him there on her bicycle and talked about his goals in life. His father also encouraged him.

> I want you to go beyond where I am. People have
> respected me, so you also will be respected much more
> than me. You must study hard and pay attention. And
> always take care of your appearance. (12)

Barack Sr. followed his father's advice, at least through primary school. In 1950, he scored well in the Kenya African Preliminary Examination, thus qualifying for Kenya's top-ranked Maseno High School, located on the highway to Kisumu. He would continue to dress well and excel in his classes, but he also revealed a contrarian attitude that manifested throughout his life. Did the strict early childhood alternating with indulgent fostering by an English-admiring father somehow predetermine a defiant personality? Or did the abandonment by his real mother at age nine create some insecurity? Much has been written regarding Barack Sr.'s development and challenges, beginning with his son's autobiography, *Dreams from my Father*, and there is little consensus. After three years of successful studies combined with continuous pranks and misadventures, however, the rebellious teenager was forced to leave school. When he reported back to his father, he was caned until his back bled.

As a seventeen-year-old, he was essentially expelled from the household, told by his father that he could work as a clerk in Mombasa. "I will see how you enjoy yourself, earning your own meals." Mama Sarah now had her hands full with two toddlers,

Omar and Zeituni, and continued to bear more children. On-yango may have suffered severely in the Kamiti prison, but he contributed to five successful pregnancies after Omar's birth in 1944. Mama's chores continued—overseeing the children (including the unhappy Hawa Auma), cooking, tending crops, going to market, and tending to her strict husband.

Hard Times

Regardless of whether or not Onyango had been in detention, many men and women underwent harsh discrimination. The British initiated the State of Emergency in 1952 in response to the Mau Mau uprising, and as Caroline Elkins notes in *Imperial Reckoning*, unpleasant events disappeared from the records.

> I found that countless documents pertaining to the detention camps either were missing from Britain's Public Record Office and the Kenya National Archives or were still classified as confidential some fifty years after the Mau Mau war. The British were meticulous record keepers in Kenya and elsewhere in their empire, making the absence of documentation on the camps all the more curious. I came to learn that the colonial government had intentionally destroyed many of these missing files in massive bonfires on the eve of its 1963 retreat from Kenya. (13)

Elkin was concerned about the confusing information that was available.

> Something else nagged at me about these numbers. Except for a few thousand women, the vast majority of the detention camp population was composed of men, despite several files discussing the steadfast commitment of Kikuyu women to Mau Mau and their role in sustaining the movement. I soon realized that the British did detain the women and children, though not in the official camps but rather in some eight hundred enclosed villages that were scattered throughout the

Kikuyu countryside. These villages were surrounded by spiked trenches, barbed wire, and watchtowers. Armed guards heavily patrolled the area. They were detention camps in all but name. Once I added all the Kikuyu detained in these villages to the adjusted camp population, I discovered that the British had actually detained some 1.5 million people, or nearly the entire Kikuyu population. (15)

Elkins described the detention years as follows:

A routine of forced communal labor dominated the day-to-day lives of the villagers. They spent the first several months living outdoors or in makeshift lean-to structures while they built hundreds of huts. With Home Guards chasing them about with whips and clubs, the work was done at breakneck speed. From dawn until dusk women and the handful of men, mostly the elderly and infirm, cut wood, thatched roofs, and plastered walls with mud and thin white clay, giving the structures a whitewashed look. (16)

Ruth Ndegwa, whose husband had been arrested and detained, describes the forced removal from her village and her own detainment.

We had not been given any warning beforehand that our houses were going to be burned. No one in the whole ridge knew that we were to move. The police just came one day, and drove everybody out of their homes, while the Home Guards burned the houses right behind us. Our household goods were burned down, including the foodstuffs like maize, potatoes, and beans, which were in our stores. Everything, even our clothes were burned down. One only saved what was wearing at the time! During the move I got separated from my children, and I could not trace them. They had been in front, leading our remaining cattle, but I failed to find them. I could hear a lot of shooting and screaming. (17)

Bee Territory

The Africanized bee is the pop insect of the twentieth century. Media star of tabloids, B movies, and television comedy, it has been nicknamed the killer bee.

—Killer Bees: The Africanized Honey Bee in the Americas (18)

Killer Bees don't make it into the news as often, and few Americans know of their origin. Twenty-six Tanzanian Queens, brought to Southeast Brazil in 1957 by biologist Warwick E. Kerr, were intended to breed with the local bees to increase honey yields. Coming from the hot climate of equatorial Africa, Kerr believed the bees would flourish in a tropical climate, and he succeeded beyond expectations. African queen bees would not be denied a chance to seek local drone congregation areas and find mates, and shortly after escaping the confines of their cage, a northward ascent began. Moving at the rate of a mile a

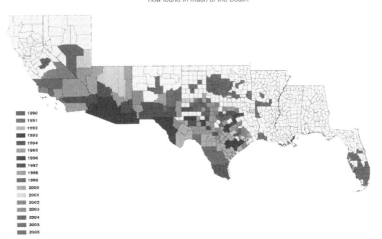

**Spread of Africanized honey bees
by year, by county**
Updated January 2007

First found in southern Texas in 1990, Africanized honey bees are
now found in much of the South.

▨	1990
▨	1991
▨	1992
▨	1993
▨	1994
▨	1995
▨	1996
▨	1997
▨	1998
▨	1999
▨	2000
▨	2001
▨	2002
▨	2003
▨	2004
▨	2005
▨	2006

FIGURE 4: Spread of the Africanized Bees: U.S. Distribution 2007 (19)
See Appendix Chapter 2.

day, they went from Argentina to Central America by 1970, from Trinidad to Mexico by 1980, and from Texas to sunny California by 2000, the new colonies encountered few interruptions.

The African queens have an advantage over their Latina counterparts. They're smaller and hatch a few days earlier. This head start allows them to sting other queens before they emerge from their cells. Every once in a while, an unsuspecting human gets in the way of the colony of "Africanized" bees and is stung to death—thus the nickname "killer bees." In the U.S., it happens approximately once a year.

The queen bee's mission, as explained earlier, is simple—find the men, get the sperm, and then replicate the genetic information as far as it will go. Besides mating, however, African honeybees are notorious for shopping around. They have a greater tendency to abscond, to leave the established hive to look for better forage. When the scouts signal it's time, giving off a "piping sound" to alert fellow workers to start their warm up, they are ready to go airborne. The queen is starved of royal honey until she's slim and trim and ready to keep up with the workers. A flying squadron of twenty to thirty thousand keeps her oriented to the task. Aloft some twenty to thirty feet or so, the scouts find a waypoint to congregate and search from. A tree trunk, a large branch, or sometimes the eaves of a roof will do.

An average European bee can travel from three to four miles in one trip at about sixteen miles per hour. African bees are faster. If a honeybee was human-sized and left Washington D.C. to reach Canada, it would be back in about an hour and a half. Even with bees of normal size, a swarm can halt traffic, stop baseball games, and put crowds of people on the run. The primary goal, however, is just to find a new home. So, back in Africa, after the scouts find a dry, secluded spot in the bright foliage of, say, a jacaranda or mango tree, they return to the swarm and do a waggle dance.

During the 1950s, Austrian Karl von Frisch spent hour after hour in his lederhosen, studying the bees' communication system. There's the round dance: the worker bee goes clockwise and counterclockwise inside the hive, followed as if in a line dance by the others and letting them know there's good pollen within fifty to a hundred meters. The waggle dance is for longer range, and it happens vertically on the comb in a figure eight pattern. In the middle segment, the forager "waggles" her body laterally to indicate good locations relative to the sun when leaving the hive. The duration of the waggle indicates distance. The liveliness of the dance signifies how good the foraging is likely to be.

Von Frisch received a Nobel Prize for his work, but the repertoire of bee dances is not limited to two. Finding a new hive site requires a collective decision to be made before moving on. If there are twenty thousand workers in a consort, an experienced group of scouts will convey their urgency. If the foraging site is capable of producing more nectar than can be processed in the old hive, the scouts do the tremble dance, shaking back and forth with their forelegs held above, like a buzzing hallelujah! Ten to fifteen scouts then make a forum to deliver their message to the thousands—waggling, trembling, shaking, and persuading the colony that they've found the right destination. The swarm travels off. They could find their prize as far away as East Africa: a place high in the shade and amid the luxurious scent of a mango tree. Home-squared!

The End of British Rule

Gima ichuoyo ema ikayo. What you sow is what you reap.

—Asenath Bole Odaga, *Luo Proverbs and Sayings*

Sarah today looks across her *dala* as she recalls raising children during the end of the colonial period. Whether or not Onyango was ever tortured, he survived and came home. The Mau Mau were guilty of terrible crimes, but the fate and the slaughter which befell the freedom fighters and Kikuyu people was a disproportionate punishment that is rarely acknowledged half a century later. The collective memory of colonial repression still shapes the country's development, just as positive forces of economic and cultural input do in a multi-lingual, English-speaking nation.

Life was relatively peaceful in Luo territory. The men were

taxed heavily and conscripted into the King's Army Rifles, but their land was not as choice or desirable for colonial settlers and they were not subjected to mass detention. During and after this time, Sarah gave birth to more children.

"And where were they born?" I asked. "Can you say a little bit about your children?"

"I had six," she told me.

"In the hospital? At home?"

"My first pregnancy took place in the hospital at Kendo, and it was stillborn. The others I gave birth to at home." She referred to Omar, Zeituni, Obure, Marsat, Yusuf, Said, and Razia, without elaborating. Obure died in his infancy.

"With a midwife?"

"For the first four, yes; but the last ones I delivered alone."

Giving birth at home was possible for a Luo woman, although she often had help from others. The process included cutting the cord with a *mirich*, a piece of sharpened cornhusk, smearing butter on the newborn, and burying the placenta within the family compound. Luo tradition requires that one's body at death is returned to the homestead where the placenta is buried. Since the act of birthing is integral to survival, it makes sense that names are given according to the time or place of birth, or according to unusual circumstances, such as the incidence of twins. Onyango, for example, refers to one born in the morning, and Opiyo refers to the first born of twins. Sarah obtained the name Onyango from her own grandfather and Obama from her husband, Hussein.

The State of Emergency came to an end in 1960 as the British realized the futility of holding onto a colony that was in constant revolt. Two political institutions, the KAU from central Kenya, led by Jomo Kenyatta, and KADU, led by Oginga Odinga and Tom Mboya, helped pave the way to Kenyan independence. Sarah heard the stories of sweeping political change and knew the role of education in ensuring her own family's progression. While tending the fields, gardens, and kitchen, she was occasionally visited by Barack Sr., who was still hoping for an education despite his failure at Maseno. His redemption came by way of two American sponsors in Nairobi that helped him gain admission to the University of Hawaii. Even Onyango was impressed that his son gained acceptance to an American university. During this period when Kenyans were beginning to run their own country, Barack, which means "the blessed one," would ask his pregnant wife Kezia and their son Malik to go and live in Kogelo with Sarah. He was destined for higher learning.

The End of the End: Kevin and the Bushman

My own education about bees would require some input and experience from others, and I knew I would have to depend on local knowledge if I was to make any progress in moving Mama Sarah's bees. Help came from a couple of young men who were used to hard work and bad luck.

I first meet Kevin Simbi at the Mwisho Mwisho roadside motel, where I stay while making visits to Mama Sarah and doing medical work at nearby Siaya District hospital. *Mwisho Mwisho* means *the end of the end*. The well-named motel skirts the side of a tarmac highway heading towards Uganda. It has an outdoor bar, a restaurant, and mud-puddle pathways that lead to small rooms with bathrooms, showers, and toilets—plus or minus seats. It's a place where you can lose your computer, a good night's sleep, or freedom from malaria, but I'm comfortable enough and it's a short walk to the hospital. The business center consists of a locked-up 1990s vintage desktop computer. Inside, I meet twenty-year old Kevin, who impresses me with his skills. After an hour and a half of trying to send one email to America, I'm exasperated, but he can accomplish it in five minutes. He's young and bright. I'm old and uptight.

Kevin is also thin and slight—features that don't command respect in a paternal culture. He exudes energy and confidence, however, and it's not long before he has my sixty-two-year-old body on the back of a motorcycle as we race across town and countryside. On one trip to Mama Sarah's, I explain to him that despite our age difference, I have a lot of work to do and need a few more years to do it. It's not easy to communicate, however,

even without helmets, because we travel at high speeds directly into the face of oncoming traffic. There are gaping potholes
every twenty yards. He steers with his left hand and the right
holds a cell phone to his ear. We need to reach a compromise.

"Kevin, slow down!" I yell, as we swerve around another
deep crater. "I want to live."

"Okay, you carry me," he answers, logically.

So, soon I'm young again, steering the motorcycle with
two hands, with Kevin on the back, talking.

The other partner in my quest for wild bees is Tom Mboya.
Tom lives next to Lake Victoria, is well into his forties, and bears
the name of a famed nationalist leader who was assassinated
in 1969. Our first encounter takes place in a coffee shop/cyber
café in downtown Kisumu. Word has gone around town that
I'm looking for a Luo teacher to improve my language skills.

Tom stands at the café doorway and calls out, "Where's
Godfrey?"

"Are you looking for me?" I respond, taken aback by this
tall, slender figure with a voice that demands attention. His
gaunt, angular face has raised cheekbones and coal-dark skin.
He enters using a crutch to support his right leg.

"Are you Godfrey?"

"I am. Who are you?"

"I am Tom Mboya, the Bushman!"

It's the beginning of a friendship and many safaris. Tom
lays out his credentials: multiple scars and the disfigurement
of his right arm, mangled by mambas, spitting cobras, puff ad-
ders and sharp scalpels that cut away dead tissue. Five operations were required to save his arm, he tells me, raising a hand
that delivered snakes to zoos and biologists interested in their
venom and display potential. He announces each viper's name
in Latin, insinuating his unparalleled skills.

"Tom, I'm looking for a language teacher, not a snake
charmer."

He pauses, assessing my worthiness as a Luo speaker. Then
the lessons begin.

"Godfrey, look me in the eye. I teach the language of the

FIGURE 5: Tom Mboya – the "Bushman"

Luo directly, not with a blackboard and letters. You are to repeat after me, and then I will test you for memory."

Everyone around us drinks tea or coffee. Tom's stentorian voice catches their attention.

"Say, '*Adhi e nam Lolwe*.' That means 'I am going to the lake.' And remember, Luo means 'to follow,' and you will follow me along the lake. You must purchase a bible in the Luo language and study it next to your English one. Now, tell me how to say, 'I am going to the lake.'"

"*Adhe e nam*," I answer. It seems to please him.

"Good," he says. "Now say, '*Adwaro ka kechi alot*.'"

I pronounce it, wondering what it means.

"That means, 'I want you to lay down. I want to have sex.'"

At this point, the coffee house crowd is smiling, waiting for the next lesson.

"Good. Now say, '*Hakuna matata,*' and then say, '*Hakuna matiti.*'"

I pronounce both. Everyone knows the Swahili expression for "no worries," while the second expression contains Luo and means "no titties." The coffee house delights in my progress.

Tom's swollen right foot causes him to limp. The injury was acquired (according to him) from an encounter with hippos while he was working near the lake. It slows him down, but it doesn't keep him from leading hikes into rough, wild areas. His boat safari partner, Daniel, however, alleges a barroom fight caused the injury. Either way, Tom has more experience than my young friend, Kevin. Tom's speech has an odd lilt or brogue, picked up from a Scottish high school teacher. He trained for a while in a missionary school before becoming disillusioned and seeking out his career as self-taught naturalist.

"You must read the book I've begun on the birds of Lolwe. There are one thousand, three hundred species here," he tells me earnestly, "and I will take you where you can see each one of them."

Mostly I want to learn the language of the lake.

Children Abroad

All to see a woman who had no blood relationship to the famous American, and was, as one Kenyan put it, nothing more than a historical accident.

— David Maraniss, *Barack Obama: The Story* (20)

Sarah speaks Dholuo along with Kiswahili, but very little English. Talking with her is rarely easy or direct. I rely on a translator, and we encounter issues in a family that becomes more private as public attention increases. She has learned to field questions carefully as a famous grandmother figure, but one can sense her awkwardness when surrounded by Americans and reporters. After the first Obama presidential victory, several books were written describing Barack Jr.'s African roots. They focus, like much Kenyan history, on the men and their achievements and concentrate particularly on Barack Sr. and the challenges he faced transitioning from a small village to the University of Hawaii, then Harvard University, and finally to the upper echelons of the early Independence government of Kenya. They tend to single out his weaknesses and difficulties and hardly put Sarah Obama in a positive light.

I ask her what it was like in the 1960s, when she and her husband were hoping for a better world and encouraging their children and peers to rise above the domination experienced under colonialism. Barack Sr. was at the forefront of bright, determined young men who would step into positions of government and business, filling the vacuum the British left as they slowly, progressively surrendered land and authority. His letters from Hawaii arrive home almost a month after they are written, and Sarah had to rely on Onyango to translate them.

"Some of them described what Hawaii looked like, the people he met," Sarah said. "He was studying hard, and getting great grades. I was happy. He had gone there on a scholarship; I heard that this white woman, Elisabeth Mooney, had also contributed to financing his studying. Barack was getting so close to our dream.

"It was after more than a year that I saw my husband reading a letter and throwing it away with such anger. I asked: 'What is wrong with Barack?' My husband was so furious that he could hardly spell it out." (21)

During the summer of 1960, well ahead of the Woodstock generation, Barack Sr. met Anne Dunham in a Russian language course, and their romance flowered overnight. By November, Anne was pregnant, and by the following February, they married. When Onyango received news of these events, he was upset with Obama Sr. for not looking out for his Kenyan wife, Kezia, and her offspring. What happened next, however, impacted

Anne more than Kezia. Barack Sr. chose to accept admission to Harvard in order to pursue a master's degree in economics. After arriving in Cambridge, he struggled to financially support himself and both of his families. He eventually managed to send some funds to his first wife, who enrolled in school in Nairobi. His treatment of Anne, however, was not as supportive. Right before the Civil Rights Act of 1964 was passed, she filed for divorce. By mid 1965, Sarah learned through letters that Barack Sr. was returning to Kenya. "Bigamy" was not a familiar word, nor was it really an issue in Luo or Muslim culture, but she knew her son had encountered problems.

Forced to return home before completing his Ph.D., Barack Sr. began working in Nairobi as a management trainee in the finance department of Shell Oil. Ruth Baker, his most serious Cambridge girlfriend, soon followed him to Kenya. They married and settled into an upper-end province. First wife Kezia did not move in, and it was awhile before Ruth learned that he had also been married in America and had a child named Barack Jr. By 1965, he had left his first job with Shell Oil and joined Kenya Central Bank as an economist. The new job lasted only nine months.

The letters to Mama Sarah were now replaced by visits from her stepson, who would arrive in a red 1955 Ford Fairlane, bearing gifts of food and clothes. He would bring along Ruth, who was by no means a Jewish American Princess; she carried pots down to the river to get water and cooked meals with Sarah. She was not well appreciated by Onyango, however, even though he had married out of his own religion several times. Sarah received news and visits of Barack Sr.'s wives with equanimity and accepted Kezia's children to raise along with her own, always happy to see her grandchildren.

While selling *mandazis* (spicy fried donuts) in the marketplace and talking with Onyango, Sarah heard about the eventual dissolution of Luo participation in Kenyatta's mostly Kikuyu government. This coincided with Barack Sr.'s downhill slide, one that continued as he wrote a critical article for the East Africa Journal, which espoused a more socialist and communal agenda for the new government.

The Zig-Zag Life

Piny agonda. The world (life) is zig zag.

—Asenath Bole Odaga, *Luo Proverbs and Sayings*

The 1970s continued as difficult years for the Obama family. Mama Sarah's children were in their teens and older. Her first son Omar had traveled to Boston in 1963 and remained in America, where he lives today, having recently been granted citizenship. Zeituni, her second child and Onyango's favorite, went to school and found work as a computer programmer in Nairobi. Barack Jr. describes her as fun-loving and sisterly in his autobiography, but she chose to leave Kenya for political asylum. After obtaining U.S. citizenship in 2011, and amidst a swirl of controversy on immigration in America, she recently passed away due to advanced breast cancer. Said, Sarah's fifth child, continues as an investor and farmer in Kogelo, while Yusuf and Marsat also made their way through school and work in Kogelo and Nairobi.

Sarah squints into the distance from her white plastic lawn chair. The chickens peck into the dirt in front of her, and two turkeys, a black and a white, parade by as she contemplates the decade when few things went well.

It was a difficult period for me, as well. My own mother died, followed by my sister, and I confronted an alcoholic father who had the same problems that Sarah recognized in her stepson, Barack Sr. Was I searching for a mother again? I scrutinized a face lined with furrows of nine decades of travail. Having listened to and counseled thousands of different visitors while raising a family, maybe she saw into my unrest. Or perhaps I represented one more American looking for a photo opportunity. Survival alone deserves respect and wonder, but of the three maternal qualities I searched for, Sarah struggled most with the second and third. In a Luo marriage, she was required to concede dominance to her strong-willed husband. While trying to foster leadership in her progeny she had to recognize the frustrations of her stepson, Obama Sr., who struggled even more on the path of professional and political ascendancy.

Sarah sat and shucked corn for hours in the back of her compound. Children and friends came and went as the kernels gathered on the yellow straw mat in front of her. Shooing away chickens and ducks was easy compared to fending off memories of her husband's last year. She was always preparing meals, which gave her time to reminisce. Onyango became weaker as his vision declined until he could barely see in front of himself and needed a crutch. She bathed him and helped him to mobilize, but for a proud man who had been self-sufficient throughout life, there is no easy decline. When he passed away in 1975, he had spanned eight decades and seen the rise and collapse of the British Empire, fought in two of their wars, and acquired their strengths while remaining a traditional Luo. Barack Sr. came home to arrange a Muslim burial and funeral for his father.

Barack Sr.'s life became more difficult. He was plagued by disappointments in his professional career, political alienation, and a heavy drinking habit. Jomo Kenyatta, now in his eighties, was nominally overseeing a Kikuyu-dominated government that tolerated no dissent. Yet another assassination occurred. The body of J.M. Kariuki, member of Parliament, was discovered. He was known for his declaration, "We do not want a Kenya of ten millionaires and ten million beggars." The outspoken Barack Sr. lost Kenyatta's favor after espousing a socialist and egalitarian direction. But he found new work in the finance ministry after encountering the Minister of Finance, Mwai Kibaki, who recognized his skills and potential as an economist. As the oldest male in the family and with financial burdens that included five school-age children, he would share some of his concerns with Sarah, who in turn encouraged him to drink less.

Barack Sr. must have acknowledged his mother's advice, because he made progress in the assignments he was given. By 1980, he was a lead negotiator for Kenya in development projects involving Ethiopia and other countries. He made several trips to Europe and Sudan, and he contributed to the newly developing markets as well as to international tourism. In 1981, he married young Jael Otieno, his fourth wife, and found more stability, but the following year would be his last. After an

FIGURE 6: Family portrait in Mama Sarah's home. The portrait was taken during Barak Jr.'s visit to Kenya in 1987.

evening of drinking with friends, he was driving home alone when he collided with a tree stump. Given the political climate of the day and the repeated assassinations, many Luos believed he had been poisoned.

Five more years would pass before a son of Barack Sr. with the same name would visit his father's graveside. Sarah's life remained busy with homemaking, gardening, and tending to her older children as well as the first orphans of the Aids epidemic. She earned a small amount of income through selling goods at the market. In 1977, the visit of Barry Jr. caught her off-guard. It also made her immensely happy.

"Halo!" she greeted the twenty-five-year-old American as he arrived at the *dala* with family members from Nairobi.

"*Masawa*," Barack Jr. answered. Connecting with his father's family was the final leg of his African journey. A photo of young Obama hangs on the wall of Sarah's living room. He visited her twice more, but his first visit was instrumental in the formation of an autobiography, a work which preceded his trajectory into the American political stratosphere. His second visit in 1992 was with Michele Robinson, and his third visit was in the year 2006, after he had been elected senator. Sarah was more comfortable accepting Michele as a new family member than she was with the news that Barack had decided to run for presidency in the U.S. She worried that his ambition might carry him into calamities similar to what Barack Sr. had experienced on his return to Kenya. But as her fame and recognition spiraled upwards, propelled by that of her step grandson, it was difficult to argue with success.

"I am happy to use my popularity," she told me, "if I can do something to help my people. All these visitors, they bring attention, and I try to use my position so others can benefit."

National and international attention would pull her closer to the political realm, where mothers and grandmothers rarely have a front seat. (See Appendix—Chapter 2.)

Meanwhile, like the bees up in the swarm of the mango tree, attending to the flowers, pollinating, taking nectar and pollen, visitors arrived in multitudes to visit with Mama Sarah. They brought gifts, shared stories, laughed, and joked, but sometimes they captured Mama Sarah's words and used them to sting her or her family. Likewise, the mostly friendly bees above would occasionally get agitated and sting the children. I wanted to know if Sarah was the kind of ideal mother I sought. She still wanted to know if I could capture the bees.

3

Deep Wounds – A Christian Family

Mary Onyango

For whosoever desires to save his life shall lose it,
but whoever loses his life for my sake shall find it.

—Matthew 16:25

Sarah Obama rose up from the ranks of the *wananchi*, or common folk, having contributed indirectly to the fostering of an American president and manifesting the qualities of a strong mother. She was less prominent in leadership due to honoring traditional Islamic and Luo culture by respecting her husband, but her opportunities to lead would increase.

    In 2006, I was introduced to another woman who led others by trying to improve the level of breast cancer care in Kenya. We were connected through email by an oncologist who thought the two of us could learn from each other. Mary

Onyango had Stage IV breast cancer, and it turned out I would learn much more from her.

We met in person in 2007 at a popular Indian restaurant in Nairobi as part of a mixed group of Kenyans and Americans. As we sat around a large table, sampling dishes of highly-spiced delicacies buffered with Basmati rice and *naan*, our conversation focused on healthcare and political issues. Differences surfaced like the curry chiles, forcing us to reach for water or wine and then chase our topics with hard-formed opinions. Mary, regal in appearance, was openly assertive about the passiveness of Kenyan politicians and medical providers. A bright-blue scarf covered her bald head, and a natural glow accentuated high cheekbones, large laughing eyes, and immaculate dress. It was easy for her to command a group's attention.

"These guys," she announced disparagingly, referring to the politicians, "are always waiting for someone to come in and do their work. And why do we always need NGOs to take care of our problems?"

Hearing this, we silently recognized the irony of her comment and our own intrusion; after the gourmet dinner, we would be starting another medical mission. While Mary supported our group, she expressed pervasive frustration about Western dependency and sniffed in some air before emitting a gentle snort.

"I mean, where do you guess all this money goes, that is supposed to reach the villages? Do we see any villagers driving around in a Mercedes Benz like the government officials?"

Christine

Understanding Mary begins when we meet her mother. It is a journey that requires hiring a vehicle and traveling several hours into a rural, verdant village in Nyanza District. We leave the Siaya Government Hospital in a small Toyota designed for better roads and head twenty miles into the countryside. Once off the disintegrating asphalt, we hit the mud—long gullies of water combined with particulate matter as fine and treacherous as quicksand. Encountering rain here is like encountering snow in a ski resort. There's moist discomfort but joy in the gift from above. Villagers walk or run home in torrential downpours that happen just before dusk without smiling, but happy with the water for the fields and crops. The skies are saturated as a result of temperature changes and pressure differentials over Lake Victoria. If you're among the lucky ones in an automobile, you accept roads with two-foot-deep gullies. Kenyan drivers negotiate them with the skill of downhill racers. When a car slides off, everyone disembarks and pushes for a semblance of traction, while wheels spin and mud flies in all directions.

Fortunately, Musumba, the driver, is a master. Walter Adero nd I are packed like skiers in a small gondola, looking out at the farmland and thin forests of the Ugenya District. We stop often to ask directions because there are no maps, and even if there were maps, there are no signs or markers. The dirt roads are primarily for driving cattle from one farm to the next. Walter is a Luo, soft-spoken and polite. Perhaps because he's very tall, he is even more reticent. I first met him at the "Russian Hospital" in Kisumu, where our medical team was struggling with patient problems in an unfamiliar operating room. Built by the Russians, it's an imposing, three-hundred-bed government compound that is short on sanitation, water, and electricity. We have permission to take care of patients we bring in from our clinic thirty miles away. I could say kind permission, but the administration also requires forty thousand shillings in exchange for the privilege of working there. Walter, a "medical officer" fluent in five languages (including Russian), was completing his med-school training on the surgical service, and he helped guide us through small and big problems that arose on the wards.

"Every monkey sees things from his own tree," he comments whenever we get frustrated.

Frustrations are pretty frequent. Early on at the hospital, we encountered a young woman named Christina, who had just turned twenty. Her right breast had been removed and the exposed raw muscle was covered with tumor nodules. One doctor suggested they were an infection or possibly granulation tissue and asked if I would do a skin graft. We ordered a chest x-ray, and it showed explosions of cancer cells, small cumulus clouds spreading across the darker image of air-filled lungs. Christina most likely had AIDS, with a "triple-negative" tumor which is biologically very aggressive. She couldn't afford chemotherapy, let alone antiviral therapy. In another ward were older women with cancers rising slowly from the chest wall, as if to defy gravity in their rock-hard eruption, visible from a distance. The ward was filled with other patients who suffered from AIDS, malaria, or TB, and they were hopeful that their family members would bring enough money to cover the costs of treatment.

An older patient had waited to have treatment for weeks, maybe months, hoping someone would remove a cancer that had taken a few years to replace all the healthy cells in her breast. We could have been in the late 1800s, when Halstead perfected his radical mastectomy at the Johns Hopkins Hospital. We watched as she was given general anesthesia and then aseptically prepared for the procedure. William Halstead had been an early proponent of sterile technique and designed the first surgical rubber gloves, wanting to protect the sensitive hands of a scrub nurse, who later became his wife. Now, repeating his radical operation, my scalpel found the last remnants of the patient's skin that were still cancer free, just below her clavicle and above the seventh rib. It cut precisely away from the cancer as an ancient diathermy machine cauterized bleeding vessels. Like extirpating a rogue volcano from the base of the earth, kilograms of solid tumor were lifted and swept laterally off the chest, including the underlying muscle and lymph nodes that extended sideways and remained like boulders in the axilla. By the time the specimen was handed off, there remained a gaping platform of ribs and fascia barely concealing a pulsing heart below. Linda Waters, a plastic surgeon from Stanford, harvested swaths of skin from the left leg and this served to cover the wound, after which the woman recovered from anesthesia. She slid onto a bare metal gurney and was rolled to a recovery area. Without Dr. Adero, we would never have found her again.

Now, three years later, Walter is able to stretch his cramped legs as we slide into the home compound of Mary Onyango. It is surrounded by the tall euphorbia and bougainvillea vines that provide a living fence for many Luo households.

"*Amosi!*" we greet Mary and her mother when they meet us at the gate. Tall and still strikingly beautiful, Mary's countenance exudes strength, even though she's in the mid-cycle of her second course of chemotherapy. Her wide smile is matched by her mother's, who seems small standing next to her. But when Christine moves, it is with the quick energy of a seventy-year-old who runs a farm. Mary's father died from complications of hypertension, leaving behind many acres of well-tended land to his *mikayi*, or first wife. We're immersed in a yard filled with cows, goats, turkeys, and most notably, the sound of weaver birds. The birds occupy a jacaranda tree next to the main house and make a gregarious racket that drowns out Christine's voice. She leads us on a small tour before inviting us inside for tea and an assortment of bread, jam, and sweets, and as she prepares the main meal, I ask Mary how about her health.

"I am feeling okay," she says. "You know I always bounce back. The last treatment was rough, making my feet and hands quite numb. But I'm fine."

I ask her about Abbi, a woman I met a few months earlier while visiting Mary in the Nairobi hospital. The two of them were receiving chemotherapy in opposite beds and carried on a discussion in Luo and Kiswahili as I sat silently in a chair struggling to decipher the different tongues. Both had advanced cancer, but they laughed and shared stories and included me in the discussion whenever they switched back to English.

"She is no longer with us," Mary now announces — to three men in her mother's small but well-furnished living room. The windows are open and admit the unending clamor of weaver birds. "You know, I don't know what happened. Abbi was taking coumadin and she kept having this bleeding from her kidneys. She had several episodes and the doctors couldn't take her off the medicine, and then something went wrong and she died, quickly. Just like that."

We wait silently as she looks out the window. Hundreds of carefully woven bird nests hang tenuously from the jacaranda.

"I suppose she might have had a blood clot. Something of that sort. Did you know? I had received a phone call from her before she died? I told her at the time, 'I knew you were going to call me, because I was just thinking of you,' and this was just before her death. That's a strange thing, isn't it? She called me to say goodbye, right before she left. I really miss her."

I know from earlier conversations with Mary that she loses companions frequently. In 2003, she and Julia Mulaha founded the Kenya Breast Health Programme. Julia passed away the same year. Now, as executive director of the program, Mary comes in frequent contact with patients, the majority of whom have advanced breast cancer and short survival times. It's clear that she and Abbi were close as neighbors and as Luo partners in the chemotherapy ward.

We wait for her to speak again.

"So, I didn't attend her funeral. I have been to so many and, you know, now these funerals are such a political process. I just couldn't bear to go."

Mary is silent. I say something awkwardly about synchronism, the Jungian concept that related events happening simultaneously indicate a subconscious connection.

She returns the subject to politics and mentions another friend, Ida Odinga, the wife of the Prime Minister of Kenya.

"Ida went to Washington D.C., where she received the Global Recognition Award from the Susan Komen for the Cure Foundation. She was presented the award for being an advocate of women with breast cancer, and raising political awareness. I really support her. I mean she doesn't have that much experience with breast disease, but she can influence policy and represents Africa. There are too many women with this disease!"

Unspoken is her own contribution. As a founder and driving force for the Kenya Breast Health Programme, she was also invited to attend the ceremony, but only at her own expense, which was impossible. She then relates how some members of parliament once came and asked for figures on the incidence of breast cancer in the country. Her voice is determined, incredulous.

"How do these guys have the audacity to ask me this question? I mean, I have to turn around and tell them, 'This is your responsibility to find out the information! And to know it! Do you think that I have the access to hospital records? Do you think I have a budget to learn these things?'"

She pauses, expelling a short burst of air as if her lungs are under pressure.

"And so they go through their records and they tell me there are 'sixty-seven' cases of breast cancer in the year 2007, so it's not really an issue. Can you imagine that? Sixty-seven cases in all of Kenya?"

We're careful not to smile. What she has helped make the country aware of is that breast cancer is the most common malignancy among women, causing 23 percent of cancer-related deaths. HIV/AIDS may be more prevalent, but many women suffer both diseases. The actual incidence of breast cancer is five hundred times greater than 'sixty seven.'

She sits comfortably in the meticulously furnished room. Finally, she smiles, recounting phone calls and the requests she gets from politicians just before election time. They want her friendship, she explains, because it's always good to be connected with women's support groups when election time is close.

I'm aware that wasps have flown into the room; they fly past us, circling, as we sit and listen. They're similar to California hornets, around the same size, and not to be swatted at. On the Justin Schmidt scale, a wasp sting might rate a 2.0 score, described as "hot and smoky, almost irreverent. Imagine W.C. Fields extinguishing a cigar on your tongue!" Schmidt, an entomologist who subjected himself to the stings of 150 insect species, should probably know. The bullet ant gets a 4.0-plus (like fire-walking over flaming charcoal with a 3-inch rusty nail grinding into your heel). Meanwhile, one of the wasps comes too close to Mary's right arm, which is swollen from lymphedema, and my distraction gives Mary a pause. She notices the insects but seems comfortable, so I ask her how we should proceed with our hospital project.

"As the new hospital organizes, what do you think are most important things to concentrate on?"

"I would suggest you work on outreach," she says.

I continue watching Mary's right arm and the wasps. In the States, more people are reported to die from wasp stings than from venomous spiders or snakes.

"Don't worry so much about all the high-tech medicine stuff," she continues. "You have to work with public health, education, all those things. It's not so easy here. But you have to reach the women. They need to be in charge of their health, and the government initiatives need to start acknowledging this."

Mary's mother, Christine, calls us to lunch. On a large dining table is a cornucopia of Kenyan staples—*ugali*, a traditional millet-based starch, along with *sukuma wiki* (specially prepared kale), rice, chicken, and *chapattis*. Portions are generous. The conversation switches to lighter topics. Christine, besides managing a busy farm, spends much of her time doing community work and oversees the building of a new church. Seeing her next to Mary helps explain the daughter's international image, highlighted in *Time* magazine. I wonder how important it is that neither of them have living husbands and now devote their time to communities? For the moment, we're happy that Christine finally sits with us at the table; traditional culture would not have women eating at the table with the men, and the first wife will only join after the men have finished eating. After tea we make our way outdoors. I notice a nest of smaller bees in the ceiling of the screened porch.

The Earliest Breast Cancer and the First Bees

Kich ithodho to kecho. Honey is harvested while bees sting.
(Success comes with hard work and perseverance.)

—Asenath Bole Odaga, *Luo Proverbs and Sayings*

A debate exists among paleopathologists as to whether cancer existed or was infrequent during prehistoric times. While the Edwin Smith Papyrus documents the first written descriptions of breast cancer, at around 1600 B.C., earlier evidence of cancer is based on x-rays and DNA analysis of recovered skeletons. Cancer was likely present in early history, but not nearly as much

FIGURE 7: Gathering Honey – Mesolithic Rock Art

as today, since humans had short life spans and less exposure to carcinogens. The Marlboro Man has been around for only sixty years. Compared with starvation, infectious disease, and warfare, cancer might have been a less traumatic disease for those fortunate enough to have longevity. In addition, women were accustomed to having children early and often, so if they weren't pregnant, they were breastfeeding, activities thought to reduce breast cancer development. Prior to the Renaissance and Enlightenment periods, breast cancer was considered incurable, and one punishment for treating a recurring disease was amputation of the hands. No surprise that patients often went untreated.

The earliest treatment of breast cancer was also barbaric, utilizing cautery, guillotine amputation, and worse. When William Halstead introduced radical mastectomy, the survival rate went from 10 percent to 50 percent, and today there's a 90 percent survival rate due to multimodality therapy and early detection. Mastectomies today are much less frequent and can be corrected with reconstruction. But with all these improvements, most notably in survival, breast cancer incidence is still high and remains the most common, solid cancer among women in both the U.S. and Kenya. Besides longevity as a risk factor, research points to genetic disposition and exposure to hormonal influences and toxins. The genetic pathway of breast cancer has been elucidated in exquisite detail. Likewise, the entire genome of honeybees has been traced out. Nevertheless, we can only predict a minority of the women who will develop breast cancer, and we don't know why so many bees are dying off.

Who knows when the first bee was born? When the first angiosperms raised their flowering heads one hundred thirty million years ago, they invited the winged insects to develop tongues and fine-haired appendages so that pollen could be spread across the earth. Did the carnivorous wasps come first, sampling pollen and honeydew until a sweet tooth was perfected? This Cretaceous Period deliverance of floral colors, eusocial flying insects, and sweet nectar was, if you count all of earth's history as one hour, about one-and-a-half minutes ago. Compare that to man's divergence from the apes by taking an upright position about five seconds ago, and more recently, the appearance of homo sapiens about half a second ago.

Switching back to real time, we think that man's hunter-forager years date back to 40,000 years ago, when the symbiotic relationship of man, bees, and flowers became possible. In the DNA shuffle, plants saved some reproductive energy by letting the bees collect pollen (sperm) from anthems of attractive flowers, speeding its coordinated transfer to ovules in distant parts. The bees, for their part, also gained the nectar they needed to make honey, sometimes referred to as the "elixir of sex." (2) Traveling back in time in Africa, where much of this started, the next trick is how humans found the honey and what they did with it.

We are familiar with the expression of making a beeline for some object. Imagine the early honey hunters studying the flight of bees as they return to a hive hidden deep in the forest or jungle. By following that line of flight one is likely to arrive at the source of sweet and rich liquid nutrition. You may overshoot the target at first and need to observe a few more bees, but persistence leads to the home colony. Unless a honey badger has done advance work, however, one still needs to access the hive to capture the prize. The original honey hunters had a high tolerance for stings, but eventually they discovered smoke, which for reasons not fully understood causes bees to retreat to the hive, gorge on honey, and become passive. A rock drawing from a limestone cave in Spain dated between two and eight thousand years ago shows a man or woman reaching deep into a pot of forager's gold (see illustration). The ancestors of President Obama were expert at finding hives as they migrated south along the Nile River and then east along the shores of Lake Victoria. Today, the Ogieks, Potoks, Maasai, Hadzabe, and Dorobos still use these hunting and foraging techniques.

Just as humans evolved from small groups of hunter-gatherers to organized farmers living in large colonies, so the carnivorous wasp changed into a nectar-gathering, eusocial bee. Some of the newer species stopped using stingers, ergo the "stingless bees." The advantages of making and storing honey influenced eusocial behavior; the bees formed larger colonies that functioned from a hive and became what Wilson first described as "superorganisms." My traveling ten thousand miles from home to treat breast cancer and chase after wild bees is another example of eusocial behavior, but I'm not sure if it reflects superorganism activity or is just a lack of intelligence, as my son suggests.

Tropical Bees

Every time a bee species goes extinct, the jigsaw puzzle of life loses another important piece. Every time a bee's species goes extinct, the world becomes a simpler place—and one that is less suitable for our continued existence.

—Laurence Packer, *Keeping the Bees* (3)

Why follow bees? Quite simply, they are part of the search for motherhood. The queen bee is a quintessential biologic expression of matriarchy. Granted, queens don't command their colony; the reverse is true. But they determine genetic direction and outlive all the other bees. It impressed me that Christine and Mary were comfortable with wasps flying throughout their house. Likewise, Mama Sarah had no problem with some of the bees around her compound because they were stingless bees and didn't attack her family.

Secured deep within an old tree trunk, predating the mango trees planted by Onyango Obama in the early 1900s, is a colony of stingless bees, which are quite distinct from wasps. Nelson Ochieng led me to them. He helps oversee the *dala* and tells me these bees are not threatening like the ones in the higher branches. Of the nineteen thousand or so species of bees in the world, about five hundred are social, belonging to the *apidae* family. The stingless bees of the *trigona* genus have only vestigial stingers, but they can still defend their nest by biting, landing in mass on an intruder's face, or just irritating intruders in any way that protects their hive. Nelson assured us that these bees have not stung or bothered anyone, so the family leaves them alone.

If you live in a warm climate and wait patiently close to the flowers in your garden, you will discover a number of smaller bees buzzing beside the common honey bees. Stingless bees are native to warm tropical regions, including Africa, Mexico, Central America, Brazil, India, and parts of the U.S. Prized for their honey, they produce only small amounts, one kilogram being good production for a *meliponine* colony as compared with seventy-five kilograms for an *Apis mellifera* colony. The honey of stingless bees was considered sacred to early Mayan

FIGURE 8: Tropical Bees on Concentric Hive

cultures. In fact, the Mayan name for bee was *xunan kab*, "royal lady." After having been raised for thousands of years, many species face extinction. Nevertheless, in Central America, one can still find honey specific for kidney, liver, and eye disease, as well as for fertility and aphrodisiacs. Like common honey, African stingless bee honey is good for burn treatment. The cost is less than Silvadene, a topical burn salve, and since honey is hyperosmotic, inhibits bacteria, and contains the enzyme glucose oxidase, which produces hydrogen peroxide, it can be useful for large and small wounds.

David Roubik, an expert on tropical bees, has focused concern on the possible extinction of stingless bees in Central America due to the expansive spread of *Apis mellifera scutellata*, or Africanized bees. (4) In an email exchange, he foretold problems as a result of the immigration scenario:

> As the remaining forests of Central America and South America recede, Africanized bees particularly threaten the sensitive tropical bees. On the other hand, the

invading species of African bees actually help the environment through pollination of more plants. Central
American beekeepers have been able to adapt to their
aggressive nature and the honey industry has held up.
But Nature will have her way; not always in a predictable fashion.

I convince my friend Kevin that our first mission should
be to relocate the large colony at Mama Sarah's *dala*. We will
transfer it into a more distant wooden hive where it is easy to
collect honey and eliminate the problem of bees stinging children. That the swarm is forty feet up remains a logistical problem, however, so while at home I consult more experienced
beekeepers in Northern California. Most are reticent when I ask
for advice, perhaps because they've never had to deal with African bees. There's one who says he worked in Africa for several
years and even gave lectures on the bees of Kenya. I'm excited
to get his insight, and he assures me that his lecture is short.
On the phone, he also lets me know that he is dying of prostate
cancer and doesn't expect to live much longer. As I drive on
the freeway, I listen to a story of life in Kenya, and then, after
half an hour, he finally returns to the subject of African bees:
"It's simple," he says, "whatever you do, stay away from them!"
    My determination to help Mama Sarah by moving the col-
ony of bees is solid—but my experience in the field is limited. I
contact another experienced beekeeper named "Mr. Bee," who
has worked in South America and retains extensive knowledge
of Africanized bees and apiaries. Just before a trip to Kenya,
Mr. Bee helped me capture a swarm from my own hive. The
exercise was challenging, as the bees were thirty feet up in a
pine tree. Trying to capture bees in a cardboard box attached
to a long pole is like fishing for minnows with a bucket—while
standing on an extension ladder and lifting the bucket ten feet
above you! Somehow we succeeded, and he assures me I will
do fine in Kenya.
    How should I accomplish this task in a tree branch forty
feet high with a more aggressive species? "You need a better

technical maneuver," he tells me. The simplest solution seems to be a "trap out," where you hang a small box near the desired colony or swarm and hope the bees will choose the more optimal place as a new home. According to the literature, this has the advantage of safety. Eureka!

Back in Kenya, with the help of Kevin and a beekeeper named Philip, we prepare all the needed equipment. It includes bee suits, a special cardboard box, a long rope, lemon grass tea, queen pheromone, and honeycomb. The idea is to lure the bees with the scent of the tea, pheromone, and comb. We will hang the box in the mango tree, near the swarm, hoping the bees decide to move to a nice, rain-protected box. So, with a small crowd watching, I'm the first up the tree. As I reach the higher branches, however, I sense the first insect invasion. It's not bees. A large colony of black ants rush over my white suit. They cover my veil like flecks of mud obscuring a windshield. Swiping them away in order to see where the colony is, I manage to get a rope over a selected branch and head back to terra firma—rapidly.

Mammography

If you start screening later and screen less effectively, more women will develop advanced disease and more women will die.

—Robert Smith, American Cancer Society

Mary was diagnosed with breast cancer in 1999. A year before visiting her and her mother at the family home, gynecologist Diane Sklar and I had interviewed her in her Nairobi office.

"In '97, I felt ill," she told us, sitting at her desk in the Kenya Breast Health Programme headquarters. Wearing a blue dress, accented by pearl earrings and a scarf, she looked strong, despite a cough that had developed after her last course of chemotherapy. "I felt off-balance. 'Something is off,' I told myself at the time. My youngest daughter was ten years old, and I had been using birth control pills. I decided to have a tubal ligation. And finally, in '99, I decided to keep a yearly medical appointment."

I made notes as she went over her history. Diane and I had walked for an hour and a half to get to Mary's office in a remote section of the city. She seemed more comfortable speaking to Diane.

"I was just turning forty. Dr. Nyongo said I should have a mammogram, but it cost three to four thousand shillings (forty to fifty dollars). The doctor told me it would be a good thing to note in my file, so I went ahead. And then we were both very surprised. At first, he wouldn't read it to me. 'I don't like what I'm seeing,' he told me, when the results came back. He referred me to a plastic surgeon who did a fine needle aspiration (a skinny needle biopsy that sometimes misses the cancer cells). That test was negative. Then, I had a larger biopsy, which led to a diagnosis of breast cancer. It was very upsetting, but I was fortunate to have a doctor who helped me understand that having this disease was not really a death sentence. There were many choices to make in the treatment, and I needed to educate myself."

As we listened, I thought of the many times I've had to give bad news. Ideally, physicians are well trained to communicate a difficult diagnosis, and with breast cancer, it's often possible to give the message that the disease is curable when first detected by mammography. Unfortunately, Mary presented with Stage II disease. In Kenya, most cancers are detected even later. Impoverished women are reluctant to reveal a breast lump, knowing that the cost of medical care will put their husbands and families in jeopardy.

In 2010, Mary told a news reporter:

> My work involves challenges including stigma attached to breast cancer, access, and the high cost of treatment. Some of my lowest moments have been meeting women who have been kicked out of their matrimonial homes, thanks to breast cancer diagnosis. My worst experience, however, was dealing with women who completely refuse to take treatment and choose to die with their breasts for fear of losing their spouses should their breasts be removed. The stigma is real. It is fuelled by lack of access to accurate information.

When surgeons obtain a first diagnosis through biopsy, they become the messengers of bad news. If they are anxious or inexperienced, they sometimes present a very negative—even if realistic—prognosis. As she was often the second person to explain to a patient what she faces with breast cancer, Mary shared with us her frustration with fatalistic doctors. She chose to undergo her own treatment in South Africa, and her care plan was more extensive than that offered to most women in Kenya.

"I had a modified radical mastectomy. My tumor was ER-positive, and the nodes were positive. And then I was told to have radiation therapy. But I went for a second opinion and was told to do chemotherapy, first. I did six cycles of CMF, followed by cobalt radiation—without any simulation (targeting the area for therapy). I was also placed on tamoxifen."

When her cancer was first noted, she wanted to know the cause. The usual risk factors were considered, including: family history, exposure to oral contraceptives or estrogen-replacement therapy, age of menarche, number and timing of pregnancies, breastfeeding, high-fat diet, use of alcohol, and smoking. She'd had none of these, other than use of birth control pills. But much has changed, especially in developed countries like Kenya. Women no longer have one baby after another right after puberty, with breastfeeding in between. Thus, hormone levels in the breast differ from historical trends. In the past, the average women's longevity was fifty years or less, and breast cancer was thus relatively infrequent. Today in Kenya, it occurs in thirty thousand women each year (far more than the "sixty-seven" women first suggested by the government). And Mary was unusual in that she'd had a mammogram—and that she could afford one.

"I stopped taking the pills and had a tubal ligation in 1998. I don't know if the hormonal dosages were that much stronger in those early birth control pills. Another year went by before I had the mammogram and the calcifications appeared. It's difficult for me to say how it got started."

Cancers can start when a single cell loses self-regulation and uncontrolled growth takes place. The exact genetic pathway varies for different parts of the body, and each breast cancer may have a distinct origin and behavior. Diane and I, while walking the five miles to Mary's office, had seen the urban changes of Nairobi—ascendency of automobiles, crowded slums, a rapid pace of industrial life, and the stress of poorly controlled growth. It was a macrocosm of what might happen in an individual body. A modern, high-pressure lifestyle, a difficult divorce, perhaps some deep depressions—do these psychological factors contribute to breast cancer? Comparing Mary's life with her mother's (or with women of earlier times), the physical and psychological differences seem both subtle and obvious.

A Luo woman raised in traditional fashion would be well-rehearsed in the art of cooking and care of cattle, in addition to dancing and singing. Since early culture involved warfare with neighboring tribes, the women had to manage the cattle when men were away, and they had to have babies when the men were at home. With a more settled pattern of living, agriculture took on more prominence. They did much of the field farming, as is still true today. "In more recent periods of the Luo development, digging has become the most important of female agricultural tasks. Her ability to dig was the symbol for agricultural knowledge." (5)

Christine's environment required constant exercise, and she was nourished with unprocessed food. She had minimal exposure to toxins, and experienced early and frequent childbirth. Her children had this early environment, too, but Mary left for Nairobi at age sixteen to train to become an accountant. When Mary set off for urban life, her mother continued to farm and exercise. Her mother's automotive experience was limited to rare trips in a bus or *matatu*. Pesticides were rarely used, her cows and chickens received no hormones or antibiotics, and the fish were all native and flourished in unpolluted waters. She worked from the crack of dawn until dark, and her wildest parties were church socials, weddings, celebrations of birth, and funerals. Mammography was not in Christine's vocabulary until Mary was diagnosed with breast cancer.

Delivery

Christine gave birth to Mary in 1959 in a small hospital located in a remote area of the Nyanza District. Back then, just one physician served the larger community, supported by midwives. The health system of Kenya included many mission hospitals, with the largest in Nairobi. It was an irony of colonial expansion that Christian missionaries and their attention to native disease and suffering preceded repression. Then when the repression ended, the hospitals remained, not unlike our health care system for indigenous tribes of America.

Luo women were expected to give birth early and often. Jared Diamond has written of how menopause changed the feminine role, in that beyond reproducing, a woman could expand the mammalian nurturing instinct and use that liberated energy to advance the culture, along with her own life span. Her primary role, however, was still reproduction. At night, Luo fathers would visit their youngest wife—the one most likely to conceive—and before daybreak, they would return to their own *duol* (hut), probably to catch up on some needed sleep. Once pregnant, a woman continued working in the *dala* and fields until labor came, and the baby was born behind her hut. As with Mama Sarah's deliveries, the *mirich* (sharp corn cob) was used to cut the umbilical cord, and the baby was smeared with butter to help keep it warm. The placenta would be buried somewhere in the compound area, thus defining the ancestral home.

Tradition required that the mother keep the newborn in her hut for three days (four days for a male), after which the baby would be placed outside the hut for careful observation in a ceremony called *golo nyathi*, which means removing the baby. (6) A celebration would last several days, requiring large amounts of local beer and sometimes accompanied by debauchery. Another cultural event was *kalo nyathi*, jumping over the child; three days after delivery, the parents make love with the child placed between them. It was private and was considered necessary for cleansing and making sure the mother remained fertile. After a few weeks, the baby's head was shaved, something still practiced in the current culture. Luo children never underwent circumcision or clitorectomy, and they no longer have their bottom six teeth removed.

The above description assumes that childbirth proceeds without trouble. In Christine and Mama Sarah's time, and still today, if a bad problem develops in pregnancy, the outcome is often disastrous. Midwives have few tools with which to intervene, and arrested labor can lead to poor development for the child and long-term suffering for the mother, or. . . death.

High Risks

Chandrouk medo rieko. Suffering increases wisdom. (Experience is the best teacher.)

—Asenanth Bole Odaga, *Luo Proverbs and Sayings*

There are few insects with sufficient venom and ability to kill humans. A rare exception is when a small amount of venom causes an allergic reaction, which can result in obstruction of the airway due to swelling, hypotension, and loss of oxygen. This, in turn, leads to heart failure. Anaphylaxis disasters occur around 1,500 times per year in the United States, mostly from food allergies, and around forty times a year from the stings of insects of the Hymenoptera order—bees, wasps, yellowjackets, and hornets. Fortunately, severe allergy to bees is quite rare; only around one in five million people will develop a systemic reaction. It may start with local swelling, but if it proceeds to wheezing and difficulty breathing, then shock and loss of consciousness can occur within minutes. It's rare, however, for a first sting to cause such a massive response. A person with a hyper allergic reaction can be treated with venom therapy to decrease the chance of systemic reactions. Beekeepers with such allergies must be treated or give up their work.

When insects combine forces, as bees do in large colonies, the odds of death increase. Humans can withstand around twenty stings per kilogram, or ten stings per pound, but after that their chances sink. Eighty-two-year-old Lino Lopez of South Texas was reported dead from only forty stings, suffered when he took a smoking burlap bag and tried to eliminate a cluster of Africanized bees. Curtis Davis had not recognized his place in the odds either, when, in a Good Samaritan effort, he went after a bothersome hive with a partial bee suit that covered only his upper body. Neighbors called the fire department after he was discovered collapsed on the ground. He died within a few days—covered with bee stings in just a few exposed areas. Around seventeen deaths have been reported in America since the arrival of Africanized bees in the 1990s. This means that the odds of dying from these bee stings are similar to being trampled by a circus elephant.

Bee sting mortality in Africa is harder to assess. It's greater than in America, as the bees are more defensive, and rural hospitals are few. Recently, a child was brought to the Siaya District Hospital, barely breathing and his body covered with stingers. His treatment was similar to that for a major burn—large volumes of intravenous fluid and placement on a breathing machine—but it was to no avail. There are even more fatalities for animals than humans, since both can wander into the wrong place at the wrong time.

A legend in Kenya relates how one-time member of Parliament and political leader, Argwings Kodek, was fatally attacked by a swarm of bees through his car window while driving to Nairobi. The discovery of bullet injuries to the head from a police-issued rifle raised a further question of how the bees got hold of the gun, aimed it, and escaped the scene without a buzz.

Chemo

It is not the strongest of the species that survives, nor the most intelligent that survives. It is the one that is the most adaptable to change.

—Charles Darwin

After undergoing a modified radical mastectomy, Mary needed chemotherapy. There was no detectable sign of disease in her body, but her lymph nodes were positive, so she was offered adjuvant (additional) therapy to control any systemic disease. She elected to receive Cytoxan, Methotrexate, and Fluorouracil (CMF), the most commonly used regime. Although she and her husband were divorced, he was supportive through the treatment, as were her three daughters and her physician. She missed her father most of all. He accepted her diagnosis with difficulty, and only as she began chemo, did he finally decide to visit her. The day before his trip, he died.

"It was a very trying time for me, dealing with his death and the treatment at the same time. I had just had my first chemotherapy treatment. Before the funeral, I was washing my hair, and it all fell off. It was too much for me to handle."

Mary completed her chemo and went on to adjuvant radiation. Although her tumor was not large, she had six positive nodes, more than enough to mandate both chemotherapy and radiation. Herceptin received FDA approval in 1998, but HER2/neu testing was not available in Africa at the time. HER2/neu is a protein receptor that helps regulate cell division, and when it is overexpressed, patients are treated with Herceptin, at a cost of around $70,000. In Kenya, there was only one radiation unit to treat all the cancer in the country, and it would be awhile before Herceptin would reach the medical market. Mary could afford to take tamoxifen, but unfortunately she manifested with systemic disease a few years after her first chemo and had to go on to other regimes.

I met her in January of 2010 at the Nairobi Hospital, while she was being treated with Xeloda and Taxotere, hormonal management having failed. She was dressed in a loose, cloth gown. Her face was swollen, making her cheeks more prominent and causing her to appear almost childlike. Her scarf was off, and I could see that she had only a few hairs remaining, but she still wore her pearl earrings and her eyes still lit up with intensity. Through the open windows of the tightly spaced room, I could see a green lawn, a hedge, and the morgue just behind.

"I really think they could have picked a more encouraging location," she insisted.

A few feet away was her friend Abbi, who was still alive

at the time and receiving an infusion. Dr. Abinha, one of three oncologists in Kenya, had started an IV in Mary's port, but it stopped working. He searched for a vein in the left arm since the right was swollen with lymphedema. Both hands now had peeling skin and Mary's nails were falling off.

"You know, Richard, it's really mental. I have these side effects, and there is the fatigue when you get through the chemo. They reduced the dosage from 1800 milligrams to 1500 and now to 1300, but I will finish it. It's not something I can disregard."

I brought some alternative medicine products from a health food store—ginger drink compound and a small bottle of bee pollen. She smiled as she received them; we both felt they were token palliatives. We discussed various alternative therapy methods for a short while. She knew of a local center that offered reflexology and massage.

Then the conversation turned to symptoms of constipation, and Abbi, in the adjacent bed, said she had the guaranteed cure. "You take a few ripe mangos and eat them with all the skin!" she announced brightly. "It cures your constipation every single time!" We burst out laughing.

Our conversation switched over to special laboratory services available in South Africa. Mary had by now tested negative for HER/2neu, the blood marker indicating responsiveness to Herceptin. She was estrogen-receptor positive, however, so she could still be treated with Arimidex. Now, breast cancer is viewed as a chronic disease—not an acute, life-threatening death sentence, and survival has improved steadily with new treatments. Arimidex works to block the synthesis of estrogen in the body, which in turn slows down or "turns off" the cancer. Good information and emotional support are also essential, and Mary almost single-handedly made this possible to others through her Kenya Breast Health Program.

As we talked, her cell phone vibrated every ten or twenty minutes. Her lunch arrived, and then her brother, Peter, appeared in the room. He was moving with great difficulty. I learned that he had been randomly shot in the stomach while attending a party in Nairobi. The bullet ricocheted off his spine, causing a partial Brown Sequard syndrome, a hemiplegia from hemisection (partial division) of the spinal cord. It had resolved enough that he was able to get around with a walker.

Mary's faith was tested from many sides. Although losing her father had been the most difficult, going through a divorce and then facing cancer and its recurrence had created a need to help others. As she told one reporter,

> Supporting women diagnosed with breast cancer is one of the positive highlights of my journey with cancer. Seeing a woman on the verge of dying put up a spirited fight for her life lightens me up. Some of these women have become pillars of support to newly diagnosed women. Knowing that I have put a smile on a woman's face has been particularly rewarding. I have always refused to dwell on self-pity. Instead, I prefer to look at the positive side of life. My faith in God has also kept me going.

"If you think about it, even Jesus cried when he was on the cross," she said to Abbi and me as we waited for their chemo to run in. "There are many families that don't want their loved ones to know that they have cancer. They hide the reality, which doesn't make it easier. And the patients don't understand at all when they first talk with the doctor. They are in the shock of discovery, and this is when it is so important to help them come to a good realization so they can make the right choices."

She switched over to a conversation in Luo with her brother and Abbi. I had slept little the night before, and my attention drifted. I was immediately awake, however, when Mary's daughter, Adele, came into the cramped quarters. Adele had the vibrancy of her mother and her grandmother and entered the room with a full-toothed smile. Young, thin, and attractive, she is a recognized poet in Nairobi and broadcasts on a radio show. Like her mother, she has taken on a cause for the women of her community. After experiencing an assault, she now speaks out against date rape— a new phenomenon in the modernizing culture.

Mary still had a half-liter of chemotherapy to receive when my ride showed up. Dr. Reuben Misati, a surgical resident who helped us on our first medical missions, coincidentally worked at the Nairobi Hospital. Reuben's ability to think on his feet impressed me when, during the post-election violence period, he solved a difficult problem. Called from home by his wife, who was threatened along with her children by an angry mob of youths with gas cans and machetes, Reuben told her to just wait inside her house. Then, he arranged an ambulance, sped to the back door, and made off safely with the family. Now, he had stopped by just to say hello. Young and dynamic like Adele, Mary knew him well and counseled him.

"You can't be thinking of doing cardiothoracic, Reuben. You know you have to make yourself available to the poor and the disadvantaged. That's why I know you'll become a famous breast surgeon. Tell me that you understand that!"

Reuben smiled at her request. We bid farewell and I left the hospital in his old, weather-beaten Toyota. Bulges on the sides of the tires protruded like small tumors as we hit a cobblestone driveway. Still adjusting from jet lag after a thirty-hour flight to Kenya and a previous week spent operating at Siaya District Hospital, I fell asleep in the back of the car.

Recovery

She who has not carried a load herself
does not know how heavy it is.

—Ugandan Proverb

I thought about Mary and the attributes of motherhood. She seemed as remarkable as Sarah Obama. She came from the common folk (*wananchi*) of rural Kenya, and she set an example as a leader—an example her children, friends, and breast cancer survivors would want to emulate. But I wasn't sure if anyone could follow in her footsteps as director of the Kenya Breast Health Program. Walter, Reuben, and other doctors said she would be irreplaceable.

After Mary recuperated from her last course of chemotherapy, she needed to respond to a new crisis. Violence between competing tribes erupted throughout several regions of
Kenya just after the disputed 2007 presidential election. It created a lingering tension and concern that the next big election
would result in political explosions. Anticipating more post-
election violence the government created the National Cohesion and Integration Commission (NCIC), and Mary applied
for a position. The commission's role was to promote lasting
peace, sustainable development, and harmonious coexistence
among Kenyans. President Kibaki appointed her as vice chair. As
spokeswoman for the Luo community and a recognized leader
in Kenya, Mary's role was to identify hate speech and steer the
referendum process towards a peaceful beginning and conclu-
sion for the 2013 election. Coming to another crossroads, torn
by tribalism to the point of near dissolution, Kenya's citizenry
needed to hold democracy together. In her own words,

"At the end of the day, you are a Kenyan. Whether you vote
yes or no, you are a Kenyan. At the end of the day, we will have
to laugh together; we will have to cry together."

4

The Environmental Wound – A Traditionalist Family

No tribe could long survive without the meaning of its existence defined by a creation story. The option was to weaken, dissolve, and die. In the early history of each tribe, the myth therefore had to be set in stone.

—E.O. Wilson, *The Social Conquest of the Earth* (1)

It was an unplanned encounter: she was trying to catch an international flight, and I was headed for Kisumu, near Lake Victoria. Accompanied by an aide, she wore a conservative long dress with sandals and carried a large briefcase. She seemed absorbed in purpose. Dan Ogola, who had brought me to the airport, recognized her immediately.

"Richard," he nudged, as we approached the two women ahead of us, "that's Wangari Maathai!"

In the past few decades, women have been breaking barriers and achieving goals in every segment of society, but few have been as prominent as this woman. Having met only one other Nobel Prize winner, I wanted an opportunity to shake her hand. Like most Kenyans, she was courteous and accommodating.

"Hello, Dr. Maathai. I've read your books," I announced, although at the time I had read only two. She acknowledged us quietly, but with a friendly smile. That she would live to write only one more book, and that she would be impossible to meet again, was not yet clear to me.

Wangari traces her own beliefs and past in her autobiography, *Unbowed*, in which she recounts the Kikuyu creation myth of Gikuyu and Mumbi, primordial parents created by God and given the land west and north of Mt. Kenya for settlement. (1) Together, this primeval couple had ten daughters but no sons. When these daughters were ready for marriage, Gikuyu prayed under a holy fig tree, *mugumo*, hoping God would grant him sons-in-law. God responded that he should instruct each of his daughters to cut a stick as long as they were tall. With these sticks, Gikuyu set up an altar under the *mugumo* tree and sacrificed a lamb. As the fire consumed the lamb, nine men walked out of the flames. From the marriage of the daughters and these nine men (the youngest daughter did not marry), the ten Kikuyu clans originated, and each was known for a trade or quality. In the case of Wangari, her clan is associated with leadership.

Jomo Kenyatta elaborates further in his narrative on Kikuyu culture, *Facing Mt. Kenya. Kirinyaga, place of brightness*, refers to the mountain where Kikuyus still turn to when they pray. In Kenyatta's version, Gikuyu and Mumbi's daughters and sons marry, and many children are born into the ten clans, which are known as Rorere rwa Mbari ya Mumbi, or Mumbi's tribe. This matriarchal tribe did fine for a few generations, but with time, the women became domineering. They practiced polyandry and, out of sexual jealousy, many men were put to death. Since the women were stronger fighters and always subdued their partners, the men covertly planned a way to overthrow them. By inducing the women leaders into a simultaneous time of sexual intercourse and then waiting six moons, they anticipated a collective weakness. When it arrived, they easily overcame the pregnant women. Polygamy replaced polyandry, patriarchy overcame matriarchy, and the rest is history—at least until Wangari.

The "Prof"

During the season of long rains, on the first day of April 1940, the third of six children was born in a mud hut beneath the towering crown of Mount Kenya. She would be a strong, healthy, quick learner. Like her brothers and sisters, Wangari grew up during a time when the British were determined to maintain strict control of their remaining Imperial colony. Her parents worked hard on a settler's farm near Nakuru in order to pay the government taxes. A man of legendary strength, her father also learned to read and write, and he was referred to as *athomi*, one who reads. Since he never went to school, his reading was limited mostly to the Bible. Wangari's mother was able to save a one-and-a-half shilling tuition fee to send her daughter to primary classes after they moved to the mountainous area above the town of Nyeri, while her father stayed near Nakuru working for a British landowner in order to support the family.

Before school years, Wangari lived in the still pristine farmland and forests of the Aberdare range. In her autobiography, she describes the transformation of the mountains when the colonial government took over the forest to establish commercial plantations. There were massive bonfires of the native trees prior to the planting of monoculture pine, eucalyptus, and black wattle that would cover the water tower area. The new trees grew fast, and provided building timber for the colonials as they expanded their new territory—once fertile land for the Kikuyu. The trees also created havoc with the ecosystem, eliminating the plants and animals and a water holding system that had once prevented erosion and floods.

She describes her childhood pastime of walking alone up a river that began at the base of a large fig tree with roots planted deep into the earth. As she went looking for firewood, she would often return to a nearby stream, the beginning of one of many rivers in the Aberdare range. Exploring this verdant oasis, she spent hours in a thick patch of arrowroot, playing with and studying the large collection of frog's eggs, which she wanted to gather and use for a necklace—but they always came apart. Freed from their jelly as she tried to pick them up, they swirled and cascaded downstream. In time, she noted thousands of tadpoles that filled the edge of the stream, and eventually she discovered full-grown frogs. She was too young to make all the connections, but her fascination with the natural environment pointed towards a career in biology.

There were no school buses in Ihithe. Like Barack Obama Sr., Wangari walked barefoot with her classmates for three miles each day to primary classes. The distance would lengthen to a full day's hike when she transferred to the more elite St. Cecilia's Catholic primary, but by then she moved into a dormitory at the school. She relates her fear of walking alone in areas distant from home, since people still encountered wild animals at that time. Stories abounded of children disappearing into the gaping jaws of crocodiles. Hyenas were particularly feared. Occasionally, a man would collapse on the trail late at night, having become intoxicated on locally produced beer, and the hyenas would attack his buttocks and face—a savage cure for alcoholism.

Her mother helped her conquer her fear of big cats by telling her the meaning of her name. In Kikuyu, *leopard* is *nagari*, and the possessive form of *leopard* is *wa-nagari*. She was told that if she should encounter the tail of a leopard on the trail while walking, she should step over it and explain to the leopard, "You and I are both leopards, so why would we disagree?"

Working in the forests and fields with a hoe and machete, Wangari was as much at home in the wilder countryside as she was in the more restrictive and protected Catholic school system. She would return home to her mother after cultivating crops and happily watch the stars come out at night as the family shared a meal and talked about their work. These were the early experiences that made her feel close to the land and close to the soil.

The experience of learning with the Consolata Missionary Sisters from Italy differed widely from life in the Aberdare Mountains and traditional Kikuyu culture. In place of learning through storytelling in their native language, the students were restricted to speaking English. If they were caught in school, conversing in Kikuyu, they would be required to wear a badge that said, "I was stupid. I was caught speaking my mother tongue." At the end of the day, whoever wore this monitor badge received a punishment of work. Wangari described the greater punishment—the embarrassment one felt for talking in her mother tongue and the undermining of self-confidence. In spite of this she expressed admiration for the nuns. She found them nurturing, encouraging, and compassionate. They were women with youth and beauty who had sacrificed having families and living in comfortable surroundings and instead "committed themselves to God and had come to serve strangers in a remote part of the world". (2)

While at St. Cecilia's primary school, Wangari converted to Catholicism and changed her name to Mary Josephine. She was associated with the Legion of Mary, whose members espoused following Christ by serving others. After finishing at the top of her class, she went on to the only Catholic high school for girls and excelled, finishing in the top tier and awarded with a Cambridge School Certificate. In 1959, the Kennedy airlift project was proposed to assist Kenyans in the transition from colonial rule to self-government, and she was one of three hundred Kenyans selected to attend college in the U.S. Contrary to some accounts, Barack Obama Sr. was not among this initial group that traveled in a DC 7. The long-term results of Wangari Maathai's airlift and Barack Senior's subsequent travels to America, however, were profound for both individuals.

While studying biology in Kansas, and receiving a master's degree at the University of Pittsburgh, Wangari witnessed the tumultuous era of the civil rights' struggle as well as the early rise of a feminist movement in America. Of equal significance, she was exposed to the environmental movement in Pittsburgh that focused on local air pollution control. By the time of her return to Kenya, where she had been offered a position in the university as a research assistant, she had born witness to the assassination of JFK but also developed a strong sense of a woman's role in society.

In 1966, graduate degree in hand, Mary Josephine arrived back in Nairobi, changed her name to Wangari Muta, and sought out her new academic position. She met with her family, who she had not seen in seven years. Because of the new independence of Kenya, they were able to stay at the New Stanley Hotel—once the exclusive domain of whites only. In her own words, "After all the troubles that Kenya has had since independence, it is difficult to convey how exciting that time was. We felt that Kenya's destiny was in our hands. It truly was a whole new world, and yet. . . "

She came punctually to her first day of work in the department of zoology on January 6th, and was just as promptly informed that her job had been given to another individual. The letter of acceptance was not official, she was told, because it was handwritten. Stunned and disappointed, it took her a while to realize that she was from the wrong tribe, the wrong sex, and would not be guaranteed anything in the university. Forty years later, in her autobiography, she relates how those conditions have continued to challenge Kenyans and an opportunity for independence and equality gave way to tribal adoption of colonial subjugation and control of resources.

Every person who has ever achieved anything has been knocked down many times. But all of them picked themselves up and kept going, and that is what I have always tried to do.

—Wangari Maathai (3)

After losing her job, she acted in a manner characteristic of her throughout her life—she moved on with greater determination. Within a year, she found another position working for a German professor in the department of anatomy. She was sent to Germany, where she acquired the skills and knowledge of electron microscopy, and in 1969 returned to the University College of Nairobi as an assistant lecturer. She was twenty-nine when, celebrated by the ululations of her Aunt Nyakweya and the happiness of her family, she married Mwangi Mathai, a devout Christian businessman. There were two weddings, one in Kikuyu tradition at her father's home, and the other a Catholic ceremony at Our Lady Queen of Peace in Nairobi.

In *Unbowed* Wangari describes the long, white Western-styled wedding dress and veil she adorned with a beaded necklace of nine strings. The necklace, later stolen from her home, represented the married daughters of Gikuyu and Mumbi, primordial parents of all Kikuyus. At critical junctions in her life, Wangari would return to the mores of her first culture. While acknowledging the importance and depth of her Christian upbringing, she reflects often on the experiences that were unique to her family and Kikuyu background. Having been forced into a detainment camp by the British when she was walking to school as a young student, she recognized the strengths of her people as they adapted to harsh conditions, and she went on to change them. Her work, like so many others who have suffered repression and discrimination, was strongly motivated by a sense of justice and a "positive attitude toward life and fellow human beings"—qualities she attributed to both her western education and Kikuyu heritage.

The Task Continued

The life of bees is like a magic well. The more you draw from it, the more there is to draw.

—Karl von Frisch

More than a year goes by from the time I tell Mama Sarah that I will manage the bee situation in the orchard in front of her house. After climbing the mango tree in her yard and hanging a rope near the rogue colony, we tie our "trap out" box and suspend it in a position conducive to relocation a few feet away. I return to my regular work in California, and it becomes a common occurrence to receive a phone call from Kevin, usually between three and four a.m.—right around his lunchtime.

"Hallooo. . .?"

"Yes, yes, Kevin, what is it?"

Years of receiving late-night phone calls while on call as a surgeon condition you to get to the root of the problem, even as your wife is waking up.

"It's Kevin. . ."

"Yes, Kevin. What is it?"

"How is your family?"

"Kevin, they are fine," (and coincidentally wide awake). "How is your family and why are you calling?"

Call after call, once a few more pleasantries are exchanged, Kevin tells me that the bees have not moved. And then, finally, they move. The queen, at the behest of her workers, makes the ten-foot journey to our box with its pre-made comb and protection from the rain.

"Halloo. . . ?"

"Yes, Kevin. What is it? Everyone's fine!"

"We are fine, too. The bees are in the box. You should come, and we will move them."

Three months after hanging the trap-out box from a rope, I return to Kenya and look up into the tree at the telltale sign of dark bees circling in front of their new home. It's late in the afternoon on the day chosen to make our transfer. I have just finished a busy week of operating in the District Hospital, the rains are due to fall any minute, and there's a flight leaving from Kisumu airport in a few hours. Unfortunately, Kevin has not prepared any of the requested equipment. We lose an hour getting ready as we search for Philip, the only experienced beekeeper nearby, who also has the only smoker. We're slowed down once more when Kevin drops his cell phone from the back of the motorcycle. After turning around to retrieve pieces scattered widely over tarmac, we're finally at the *dala* and contemplating the challenge.

"Philip, you start the smoker. I'll climb the tree," I suggest, pointing forty feet up. The box has to be lowered down by the rope, but it's stuck on one of the branches.

"No, I climb, you catch the bees," he counters. He's much younger.

"Okay, time's running out, and we need to get moving!"

As I look around, I see Mama Sarah and her family standing outside, keeping a watch. Nelson Ochieng, a bright, new-age relative, wants to help, and stands nearby without a bee suit. Storm clouds are approaching, and it's still the rainy season. I've always been told that one should not work with bees in bad weather, but that's for European bees. These are African bees and the stakes are even higher. My next thought is of future headlines: "Doctor Murders President's Grandmother with Killer Bees," but Philip is now halfway up the tree.

When he reaches the branch from which the trap-out box is suspended, he loosens the rope enough to begin lowering the entire assembly. I slip the rope upward, two feet at a time, and the buzzing box comes down in equal measure. So far there's light activity, manifested by fifteen or twenty sentries flying in front of the entrance hole. The plan is to cover this opening with duct tape.

"Get ready!" Kevin and Nelson urge. They're unprotected, watching from a short distance. I think I'm ready, but the things you hear about the versatility of duct tape are exaggerated. If you tear duct tape with thick leather gloves, it doesn't go easily; and meanwhile, there is a rapid exodus from the bottom of the trap-out box.

"Hurry up! Hurry up!" the spectators warn. The bees have discovered that their home is not only in motion, but is also being invaded by their worst enemy—man.

The fifteen or twenty sentries have multiplied and are emerging as fast as possible through the semi-taped hole of the box. These are guard bees, hard-wired to attack, kamikaze style—to die for the hive. They seek out any weakness, stinging through socks and chasing Kevin and Nelson. I elect to carry the box as fast as possible to the chosen site of our new hive, a few hundred yards away. Still new to this work, I don't anticipate the need to travel at least three miles distance from the original site if the bees are to be prevented from returning. Philip has descended from the tree and follows me, and at least we're relieved to see that Mama Sarah has gone indoors and closed her front door.

The art of transferring bees from one box to another has a shallow learning curve. I'm low on the trajectory. Philip is not in the least nervous, however, and he's ready to proceed with the maneuver, which consists of banging one box onto a larger box below. He asks if we really need the smoker in order to do this. The necessity is equal to that of having water in the middle of a raging fire. I start the smoker while he transfers the largest pieces of comb, hopefully including the queen, into our wooden box. Smoking as though our lives depend on it, we bang the rest of the bees into the new home and place a lid over it. Suddenly, we're done, seemingly successful. We shake hands just as the rains start. Climbing onto the back of the Kevin's motorcycle, I find it easy to tolerate the acceleration while knowing I'm late for another flight to Nairobi. The trip will be wet, but we aren't being pursued by tornadoes of bees.

Next Steps

Faith is taking the first step, even when you can't see the whole staircase.

—Martin Luther King, Jr.

Justice would become an elusive goal for Wangari in the following years. The American tragedy of Martin Luther King's death in 1968 was followed by a devastating murder that Barack Sr. witnessed in Kenya. In 1969, Tom Mboya, a Luo political leader who helped lead the struggle for Kenya's independence, was shot in the streets of Nairobi by a single Kikuyu assassin. Mboya had spearheaded the Kennedy Airlift and was a likely candidate to replace Jomo Kenyatta as president. The tension between Luos and Kikuyus built up dramatically, and when Kenyatta banned the Kenya People's Union, led by Luo leader Oginga Odinga (father of Raila Odinga), multiparty democracy ended for twenty-three years.

Pregnant with her first child, Waweru, Wangari continued working on her dissertation and doctorate while helping her husband run for Member of Parliament. These were fertile years. Although Mwangi did not succeed in his first bid for Parliament, Wangari gave him two more children, Muta and Wanjira. During this time, while raising the children, teaching at the university, and becoming the first woman in Kenya to receive a Ph.D., she began raising tree seedlings in her house and backyard. Determined to support the unemployed, she formed a small enterprise called Envirocare Ltd., which planted trees for environmental restoration. This created work opportunities for low-income individuals, particularly Kenyan women. Mwangi also helped her husband win election to Member of Parliament in 1974, but by this time their relationship had become strained.

Whether Wangari's first efforts to reach out to the women of Kenya contributed to her painful divorce is speculation. She describes the early years of marriage, when she began to fill the yard and inside of their home with tree seedlings and to question her husband as to his real commitment to find work for the unemployed. What was certain were the facts of gender status in Kenya. Economically, women make up more than half the country's work force; their labor is primarily focused on household chores (like fetching firewood and water, collective care of children, and field work), and is never captured in national statistics. A quarter of rural households are headed by women who live on less than a dollar a day. Reported cases of rape and attempted rape more than doubled from 1997 to 2003, and the incidence of HIV and AIDS is markedly higher among women than men. Wangari was well in the forefront of working on gender rights, and her efforts were not appreciated.

Unannounced, Mwangi left Wangari and the three children in 1977. After a two-year estrangement, he began a difficult and adversarial court process. Press reports, which made their trial a public event, stated that he considered his wife "too educated, too strong, too successful, too stubborn, and too hard to control." She was not the first Kikuyu woman to be accused of such behavior, but her public image was large. After telling a reporter that the judge was either "incompetent or corrupt," she refused to retract her statement and was given a six-month prison sentence for contempt of court.

Wangari never looked back. She was released from prison after a few days, although she would enter jail many times again. While her Envirocare program, collocated with a government nursery in Karura Forest, was not sustainable, a concept realized during her scientific work—the interconnected health of all species to the biologic health of the environment—remained a principle of her efforts from that time on. One of her research assignments had been to study the impact of the brown ear-tick on cattle. She spent countless hours doing microscopic study of the insect, but it was her field work in farms that revealed to her that native cattle were no longer thriving, and for a simple reason: foraging had been decimated by tree-cutting, destruction of the forests, and loss of habitat. Despite increased grazing land, the soil was washed-out and eroded and no longer provided substantial grasses and nutrients. While visiting the location of the fig tree she had marveled at as a child, she found the area had been replaced by a tea plantation. It was no longer the land of her memories—

> We lived in a land abundant with shrubs, creepers, ferns
> and trees . . . Because rain fell regularly and reliably,
> clean drinking water was everywhere. There were large,
> well-watered fields of maize, beans, wheat and veg-
> etables. Hunger was virtually unknown. (4)

Now the trees were gone, their roots no longer stabilizing the steep mountains, and landslides became common. Sources of clean water became scarce and the fig tree she remembered from her childhood had vanished leaving behind a bare patch of ground.

She changed her name a final time, adding an a to her husband's surname, which he had denied her after the divorce. *Mathai* became *Maathai*. As a single mother, she confronted new academic and economic challenges. Always an activist, she ran for chair of the National Council of Women of Kenya (NCWK) and took a position with the Economic Commission of Africa through the United Nations Development Programme. The work required frequent travel, and out of concern for the children's welfare, she took them to Mwangi's home and left them in his care.

In 1982, she decided to run for member of Parliament in her home district, Nyeri. By law, she had to resign from her position as professor in the university, and when she resigned, she was soon informed that she could not run for office because she had not registered and voted in the last election. While contesting this, and in a last-minute decision, the court ruled her ineligible on a technicality. When she attempted to regain employment with the university, she was denied and given eviction papers, forcing her to leave her campus living quarters. The president of Kenya, Daniel arap Moi, was chancellor of the university and did not favor her environmental goals or campaigns on behalf of women's academic rights. Suddenly, Wangari notes in her autobiography, "I had no job or salary". At the age of forty-one she had ". . . nothing to do. I was down to zero."

After moving into a small home that had been purchased years earlier, Wangari spent the following five years dedicating her time to the Green Belt Movement (GBM). Critical support came from the Norwegian Forestry Society. The United Nations Voluntary Fund for the UN Decade for Women provided a $122,700 grant that allowed her work to span throughout Kenya. In addition, she developed deep friendships with supporters such as Peggy Snyder, who would come to her aid over subsequent years. Over time, the GBM reached out to fifteen other African countries, addressing desertification, deforestation, and both urban and rural poverty. For this work, she received awards and international recognition, but it wasn't long before the government forced her to separate the Green Belt Movement from the NCWK, isolating her efforts.

The Moi government reinstituted a colonial-era law that banned group meetings of more than nine people without an official license to proceed. The GBM had already been registering voters and advocating constitutional reform, and Wangari was considered a troublemaker. She gained much more attention when she opposed government plans for a sixty-story skyscraper to be placed in Nairobi's Uhuru Park. Along with parking for two thousand cars, the building would house the headquarters of KANU, President Moi's party, and, of course, a large statue of the president. She wrote public officials in Kenya and England, stating that erecting such a building would be equivalent to hoisting a skyscraper in London's Hyde Park or New York's Central Park. She was denounced by the government as "a crazy woman" who was working with a movement made up of "a bunch of divorcees." When she sought an injunction to stop the building, Moi followed with the suggestion that those who were against the building had "insects in their heads." The GBM was evicted from its Nairobi office and had to move into Wangari's small home. Against all odds, however, she succeeded in her protest against the skyscraper, and the construction never commenced. By 1992, after fifteen years of organizing, the Green Belt Movement had employed more than fifty thousand women and had planted ten million trees. Meanwhile, in the same year, Wangari learned of a "hit list" of pro-democracy activists. Her name was included, and a government-sponsored coup, including assassinations, was imminent.

Kevin's and Tom's Business Ventures

In all the people I see myself, none more and not one a barleycorn less, And the good and the bad I say of myself I say of them.

—Walt Whitman, *Leaves of Grass*

I'm not much closer to getting a good view of the African queen bee. I want to see her in action, dipping her ovariole-engorged abdomen into the waiting hexagonal cells while attended by a host of workers feeding her royal jelly. On a more plebeian level, I wonder about Kevin, who still calls at night, but earlier now, to let me know his status. A few months after our venture with Mama Sarah's bees, he calls with a solemn request.

"I am thinking of starting a motorcycle business. Would you lend me some money to get off the ground? I just need a few *piki pikis.*"

"Off the ground" doesn't depict a happy vision. The *piki piki*, a motorcycle taxi, is not to be confused with the *boda boda*, a bicycle taxi. As an inexpensive mode of transportation, it's not unusual to see an entire family en route on a motorcycle—children sandwiched between the parents. The country roads and smaller cities are filled with young men hoping to earn a living by carrying passengers. They maneuver through traffic on imported Chinese machines that cost less than five hundred dollars. Young and restless, they drop out of school, save, and borrow money to purchase a *piki piki*, and never have more than a half-liter of fuel in the gas tank. A few of the rougher ones steal money and motorcycles, leaving the honest to try and compete with them. The motor vehicle accident rate in Kenya is steep, thirty to forty times that of most industrial countries, and averages three thousand deaths per year, which approaches the mortality of HIV/AIDS, malaria, and TB combined. (5) Helmets are required by law, but many riders, including Kevin, can't afford them. Compound fractures are more common than head injuries and fill hospital beds. Having performed amputations for limbs beyond salvage, and seeing young men die of sepsis and blood loss, I'm not eager to jump at Kevin's suggestion.

"Why don't you start a honey-making business?" I suggest. Kenya is known for its honey market and may provide an ecologically sound way for a young man to take risks and make some money. Also, such a choice on his part will give me a better chance to see the queen bee.

"Okay, I can do that."

He purchases a few hives. Imitating the trap-out procedure we used at Mama Sarah's, he gets a piece of rope and hangs two boxes from trees in front of his family compound. Soon, a swarm inhabits one of them, and he establishes it behind the houses. The bees seem content to breed and leave everyone alone, and soon a new swarm fills the second box. It dangles from a branch with the telltale cluster of bees flying in front. Forager bees return from the fields loaded with pollen and nectar; it seems that Kevin's front yard is a popular spot. I'm optimistic for him. Kevin feels good about it, too.

The Bushman, meanwhile, convinces me that he's going to earn some healthy profits raising chickens in his compound near Hippo Bay on the eastern edge of Lake Victoria.

"Godfrey, these NGOs are all the same," Tom laments, as we drink coffee in the Cyber café in Kisumu. "They come once to make videos of the lake and say they want to help protect it from pollution. And then they never return."

Tom looks discouraged. He's lost weight, not easy for a man who was already bone-thin. At the time, the lake around Kisumu is literally choked by hyacinth plants, making it impossible for the fishing boats to come or go. His business is taking people out in outboard-driven launches to view the rich diversity of bird life along the marsh and mangrove-lined shore—but even the tourists are staying away.

"Where do you think all this pollution comes from?" he asks me, and I'm guessing it is all the villages next to rivers that feed the lake. "It comes from the fish factories that send all the fish to the NGO countries. We (Kenya) have only a small part of Lake Victoria, which is fed by our rivers, and where the fish breeding ground is most concentrated. So all this sewage goes right into the lake and feeds the hyacinth plants. Then there's the Nile perch!"

Ugandan colonials introduced Nile perch to Lake Victoria during the 1950s. The three to four hundred pound perch is a huge predator of native cichlids that once kept the lake in balance. E.O. Wilson considered the impact of the perch as "the most catastrophic extinction episode of recent history."

At first, there was little appetite for Nile perch in Europe, but between 1992 and 2004, it was discovered that the fish has a high Omega 3 content. Fish factories were built in a fortnight, and soon five cargo planes with a hundred tons of fillets were headed weekly for the European market. Boats plied the lake, carrying home twenty tons of fish, while fisherman and middlemen pocketed $132,000 annually. Today, there are more fishing nets in the lake than there are perch, and the boom economy is beginning to collapse. Tijs Goldschmidt, in his memoir, *Darwin's Dreampond*, wrote:

> Ethical or aesthetic arguments for the preservation of
> fauna have no chance at all in the face of short-term
> economic perspectives. Certainly not in poor African
> countries, in which populations barely manage to
> survive. Conservationists are being compelled to express
> the value of an area in terms of money and if they refuse
> or are unable to do so, such an area is doomed. (6)

Tom stares at me as if I'm the culprit. There are several contributing factors to the eutrophication of lake waters, the elimination of Nile perch, and the loss of local income, but they all spell trouble for the Luo community. So, the bushman has decided to leave his job as a nature guide. Even though he knows all the local and Latin names of a thousand bird species in the area, he will now specialize in just one.

"I need you to give me some funds for antibiotics," he tells me. "I'm raising chickens. They aren't doing well and I have to control an epidemic!"

Wangari in Prison

During 1990-1992, the one-party state's edifice of central control cracked apart, and the rules of the game of Kenya's politics since 1969 were transformed by a resurgence of open political conflict. Deeper tensions were exposed, based on ethnic interests but catalysed around individuals, which had simmered for decades, held in check by the power of the single-party state.

—Charles Hornsby, *Kenya: A History Since Independence* (7)

In February of 1990, a popular foreign minister, Robert Ouko, considered a successor for President Moi, was murdered on his farm near Kisumu, precipitating several days of rioting. On *Saba Saba*, or July 7th of the same year, a pro-democracy rally was held in Nairobi, and security forces killed dozens of demonstrators. Bishop Alexander Muge, soon after speaking out for civil rights in Kenya, was murdered in a mysterious car "accident." This political climate prevailed while Wangari was working with the Green Belt Movement and also successfully fought a plan of President Moi's business investors to build a 60-storey skyscraper in the middle of Nairobi's Uhuru park. In January of '92, soon after learning that her name was included on a list of dissidents threatened with assassination, she brought together others supporting a multiparty system and was placed in jail for violation of meeting laws.

Her second incarceration was traumatic enough that she had to be carried into the courtroom for her hearing. Arthritis and hunger rendered her too weak to walk and when she was finally released to Nairobi Hospital she saw a sign from a group called Mothers in Action.

"WANGARI, BRAVE DAUGHTER OF KENYA, YOU WILL NEVER WALK ALONGE AGAIN."

Letters from eight U.S. senators helped to free her and many others who were undergoing court trials. She then joined with a group of women known as Release Political Prisoners and supported them in their effort to free their sons from incarceration and torture. They encamped on the intersection of Uhuru Highway and Kenyatta Boulevard, which was given the name "Freedom Corner." After several days, the gathering increased to hundreds of participants. When police told them to disperse, they locked arms instead. Tear gas and batons came raining down on them. Wangari was knocked unconscious. Other mothers left behind in the tent refused to leave and stripped, showing the police their naked breasts. Doing so invoked an African tradition that says that a woman old enough to be a mother must receive the respect of a mother. Nevertheless, they were forcibly removed and taken to their homes, accused of threatening the "security of the citizens and the nation."

Wangari and the mothers of the imprisoned sons continued their efforts to stop state-sponsored torture and random political imprisonment. In the Anglican church, they held a vigil and subsequently were surrounded by soldiers. The women refused to leave, and for almost a year they stayed in the crypt of the church, sleeping on hard pews, without showers or home comfort. Ultimately, they succeeded, and fifty-one of the fifty-two sons were released. In 1997, the last of their sons was set free.

The Trees in the Forest

Courage. I guess that the nearest it means is not having fear. Fear is the biggest enemy you have. I think you can overcome your fear when you no longer see the consequences. When I do what I do, when I am writing letters to the president, accusing him of every crime on this earth, of being a violator of every right I know of, especially violating environmental rights and then of violence to women, I must have courage.

—Wangari Maathai, Speak Truth to Power, May, 4, 2000 (8)

During 1993, Wangari spent months in Nairobi, moving from one safe house to another. She traveled at night, lying flat in the bottoms of cars to avoid detection. Then, after an invitation to attend a Green Cross International convention on global environment issues in Tokyo, arranged by Mikhail Gorbachev, she was given the green light to travel. President Moi, insisting that he knew nothing of her persecution or underground status, responded positively to Gorbachev's request that she be granted traveling papers. She was unable to attend the Tokyo convention in time, but she did go to Scotland, where she received a medal at the Edinburgh International Science Festival. Several more awards were offered internationally. By this time, the Green Belt Movement had supported the planting of ten million trees.

Planting trees was not only a means to ecological restoration in Kenya; it was a symbolic tool to create cultural and political change. Wangari's unsuccessful attempt at running for office in 1982, which resulted in the loss of her faculty position at the University of Nairobi as well as her campus lodging, accelerated her passion for democracy and political activism as she became more active in promoting an opposition party to President Daniel arap Moi. Her efforts, which included forming the Middle Ground Group, organizing large and illegal meetings in her home (which was small and had to accommodate eighty Green Belt Movement workers), and her repeated arrests and incarcerations in the 1990s, were often punctuated and announced by the planting of a tree.

She ran for member of Parliament again in 1997 and was sabotaged a day before the election by false press rumors that she had decided to support another candidate, causing her to receive only a few votes. It was a fiercely contested election. President Moi and KANU won again, and although thousands of deaths did not occur as they had in 1993, tensions remained high throughout Kenya. One year later, Wangari learned of a critical privatization plan for a unique forest that served as a 2,500 acre pristine catchment area for four rivers. The government intended the Karura Forest area to be used for executive offices, private houses, gated communities, hotels, and golf courses for political allies.

She quickly mobilized a group of strong supporters and began planting trees inside the forest reserve and later at the gates. The group confronted angry young men and construction workers, and for months, altercations took place that were initially softened by teaching sessions and non-violent planting of trees and seedlings, but then hardened by explosive attacks. In December of 1998, ever mindful of the international attention, Wangari brought hundreds of supporters from Europe, the Americas, and nationally, and continued to plant trees. By January 8th, a final clash developed. The group faced off with two hundred guards armed with machetes, whips, bows and arrows, and swords.

> You know, when they attack me, I say this is violence against women. When they threaten me with female genital mutilation, this is violence against women. When they attack me, I attack them back. A lot of people say, "They could kill you." And I say, "Yes, they could, but if you focus on the damage they could do, you cannot function. Don't visualise the danger you can get in. Your mind must be blank as far as danger is concerned." This helps you to go on. You look very courageous to people—and maybe you are courageous. But it is partly because you cannot see the fear they see. You are not projecting that you could be killed, that you could die. You are not projecting that they could

cut your leg. If you do that, you stop. It's not like I see danger coming, and I feel danger. At this particular moment, I am only seeing one thing—that I am moving in the right direction.(9)

Wangari also knew how to dramatize the effects of violence and when her head was slammed violently with a panga she responded wisely. After walking a few miles to the nearest police station, where she and others were scorned, she dipped her finger into the blood welling on her scalp and signed a formal complaint with a red X. Video footage of the incident was widely publicized, and within months, universities in Nairobi were closed because of riots. International pressure along with national protest led President Moi to issue an edict banning allocation of public land. The Karura Forest was saved.

Her activism may have been influenced by experiences in America—such as witnessing the civil rights era—or perhaps it was uniquely Kenyan, but it is difficult to dispute the success and efficacy of her non-violent techniques. In her autobiography she denies recklessness and describes methods of protection—singing and dancing. Singing and dancing don't pose a threat, and as with the civil rights movement, they gave the participants strength and minimized violence. "It is wonderful when you don't have the fear, and a lot of the time I don't," she would note. "I focus on what needs to be done instead."(Jeffries, *the Guardian*)

The Tree of Bees

In late August, I return to Kenya, just before the long rains. I reunite with Kevin to visit Mama Sarah's *dala*, surprised by the news that the bees are back in the tree. Nelson, the grandson, suggests that they might be a new swarm, since the colony we transferred to a Langstroth box was still active. We go to inspect the hive, and indeed it's filled. African bees (*mellifera scutellata*) are notorious for absconding, meaning the entire colony picks up and leaves the old hive, taking along the queen. Swarming, as opposed to absconding, happens when the old queen leaves with half to two-thirds of the workers. After laying one to two thousand eggs a day (weight wise, the human equivalent of having twenty babies a day for a year or so), the queen is entitled to a short vacation.

We're pleased that our newly established hive is still present. Maybe rather than absconding, it swarmed, but there's no way to know for sure. As far as Mama Sarah is concerned, however, a colony remains up in the mango tree, and I haven't finished my work.

"This is good," Kevin tells me. "We have at least one hive for collecting honey. So now, we can go and move the bees that are up in the tree by my house."

The Tree of Peace

Psychoanalysis sees in the tree a symbolic reference to the mother, to spiritual and intellectual development, or to death and rebirth.

—Herder Symbol Dictionary

Wangari was taken to prison a few more times in 2001. Her final arrest was for planting a tree in Uhuru Park. She was celebrating the Seventh of July, or *Saba Saba*, which commemorates the mass demonstration for democracy in 1990, when police fired live ammunition into the crowd.

A more peaceful period of her life ensued when she was invited to return to America as a visiting fellow at Yale University. From January to June of 2002, she taught a course on sustainable development, focusing on the work of the Green Belt Movement and environmental action. But politics pulled her back to Kenya.

Making one last run for office, she succeeded on her third campaign for member of Parliament, receiving 98 percent of the vote. December 2002 was a time of change and celebration in Kenya as Mwai Kibaki assumed the presidency. "There was an electric atmosphere as the country anticipated the end of

FIGURE 9: Wangari – Winning the Prize, Paul Ng'auru Muguro photo

repression and looked forward to the beginning of a new era," Wangari noted in her autobiography.

She was appointed assistant minister in the Ministry for Environment and Natural Resources and began to make changes for her own constituency, as well as nationally. Compared to her days of imprisonment, the progress was encouraging, but her voice was to gain even more recognition. In October of 2004, her cell phone rang as she traveled towards Nyeri, near Mt. Kenya, and she learned that she had been awarded the Nobel Prize. Namalunda Florence, in her detailed biography of Wangari,

reveals a character trait of the prize winner, who reacts by closing her cell phone and announcing to accompanying friends:
"We won it!"

Overcome by emotion, she could not contain the tears of
happiness and celebrated with staff and friends by performing
one more tree-planting ceremony to recognize the long journey
and significance of trees in her work. As Florence relates in her
biography, Wangari was able to balance a tight, grass roots connection with less advantaged women to the large international
community and her higher echelon supporters. Quoting Wangari's own words, from the epilogue of *Unbowed: A Memior*:

> Trees are the living symbols of peace and hope. A tree
> has its roots in the soil yet reaches to the sky. It tells us
> that in order to aspire we need to be grounded, and that
> no matter how high we go it is from our roots that we
> draw sustenance. It is a reminder to all of us who have
> had success that we cannot forget where we came from.
> It signifies that no matter how powerful we become in
> government or how many awards we receive, our power,
> and strength, and our ability to reach our goals depend
> on the people, those whose work remains unseen, who
> are the soil out of which we grow, the shoulders on
> which we stand. (10)

5

Matibabu

Matibabu and the First Mission

That the poor are invisible is one of the most important things about them. They are not simply neglected and forgotten...What is much worse, they are not seen.

—Michael Harrington, *The Other America* (1)

In 2004, the same year in which Wangari Maathai became the first African woman and environmentalist to win the Nobel Prize, an eleven-year-old Evan Otieno received an injury. A small stick had cut open his face. He developed a high fever and, after one eye began to swell and close, his crying stopped—and his caretakers knew it was time to find a doctor. Like many AIDS orphans, he was under the care of neighbors. Children exposed to HIV are susceptible to infections, and this condition had the potential to blind him and take his life. So, his guardians walked twenty miles to a medical camp staffed by Americans who had come from a city called Hayward in the United States. The camp, organized by Dan Ogola, was named *Matibabu*, which in Kiswahili means *treatment*.

A pediatrician named Amanda Schoenberg recognized the acuity of the illness and that Evan was not responding to tetracycline, which had been prescribed by a Swedish nurse at another infirmary. The nurse told his surrogate mother and father that he would need daily injections of a stronger antibiotic, as well as possible treatment for HIV. The people of the region were also facing the onslaught of Slim, or AIDS, a disease that caused more than twenty million Africans to become thinner and thinner until they died. Somehow, Evan needed to get the right treatment.

The Matibabu camp moved every day, reaching out to a half million people with minimal access to health care. Even though the location of the camp changed daily, Evan managed to arrive each day for an injection of Ceftriaxone. His guardians walked thirty kilometers the first day, thirty-five kilometers the next, and so on, since there was no hospital or facility at which they could stay. They started as early as three a.m., determined to follow the doctor's instructions. It took several days, but when Evan's eye slowly began to heal and the swelling decreased, his eleven-year-old spirit returned as well. Everyone felt a sense of joy and appreciation, especially his guardians, the ones who had carried him more than a hundred miles.

The volunteers worked steadily, seeing five thousand patients on their first trip. They examined as many as possible before the late afternoon rains arrived and halted the process each day. Hundreds of patients waited and then left without being seen, walking down dark, muddy roads to their homes. Some of the villagers, like Evan, did well, and some did not.

Two surgeons, Ram Ramachandra and Dick Thompson, worked at the nearby Siaya District Hospital. They took care of hernias, burns, cancers, and other problems referred by the medical camp. There was never enough time to finish. Why these medical workers traveled ten thousand miles to provide care in Western Kenya motivated my own effort to understand eusocial behavior and superorganisms and the work of several determined and dynamic women.

Dr. Gail Wagner has a youthful smile, which is somewhat ironic given the profession she chose. An oriental crease in the linear tails of her eyes seems to stretch further when she laughs—a reminder to casual observers of how close the link between laughter and tears can be. Despite her profession, she likes to have fun. But she can become serious in an instant. Her mind works quickly—quickly enough that friends try not to argue with her. She is decisive.

As an oncologist, she's accustomed to bringing organization and support to patients with cancer. The oncologic discipline helps people with difficult, often incurable diseases, and there's a need to work with a host of other specialties. Her time with Kaiser Permanente gave her extensive experience working in an integrated care program. Kaiser serves around six million patients in California, focusing on prevention, quality, and affordability—a system similar to others such as the Mayo Clinic, the Cleveland Clinic, and the Harvard Plan, which offer large populations what was once denigrated as "managed care." These programs are now increasingly recognized as a remedy to spiraling health care costs. Intrinsic to the plans are large-scale delivery of health services, keeping enrollees healthy from start to finish, patient education, managing chronic diseases proactively, and computer access for providers and patients that is integrated with an electronic medical record system. Would it work in Western Kenya?

In July of 2003, Dr. Wagner, while considering a medical mission to Eastern Europe, traveled to Kenya and walked through the Kibera Slums. This impoverished area that once was designated for Nubian soldiers who served in the King's African Rifles now shelters close to a million inhabitants in an area smaller than Central Park. Surrounded by a golf course and a railroad track leading to Uganda and more substantial buildings, the thirteen villages of Kibera are packed tightly with lean-to shelters and rudimentary structures that lack plumbing

FIGURE 10: Dan Ogola in Kibera

and safe electricity. With less than one toilet per thousand inhabitants, it is not surprising to encounter *flying toilets*, a term that describes feces collected in plastic bags and then tossed into the distance. Dr. Wagner had never seen flying toilets or experienced living in a twelve-by-twelve-foot space with a family of six or more but she was given an introduction by Dan Ogola, a self-trained social worker who had left his home in Western Kenya to work with the urban poor.

Dan has a knack for taking visitors through Kibera and introducing them to levels of poverty that strain the imagination. Like a Cheshire cat, he smiles as he walks you past shelter after shelter, going deep into the center, where crowded dirt paths coalesce into dead ends and the idea of finding your way out begins to seem impossible. Visitors step and climb over trails of wastewater that flow into litter-covered cesspools, all the while wondering how landlords can charge rent. It takes one heavy rainstorm, common enough during the long rains, for unstable soils to give way and for the shelters to collapse. Fires are even more devastating as there is little access for firefighting equipment other than hand buckets.

Unable to afford college, Dan still gained recognition as a person who cared about the poor. He felt that he could make a difference. He and his wife Edwina invested their honeymoon dowry in a small sanitation system.

Wandering with him through Kibera into a cramped room that offers shade and respite from the hot sun outside, I am surprised to discover a working television set. It's supplied with current from a rat's nest of loose electrical wires that run over the Quonset roofs. A few residents have acquired TVs, and favorite programs include Spanish-speaking soap operas with subtitles in Kiswahili. The community of Kibera is highly entrepreneurial; at least one millionaire has risen from its ranks. I ask Dan about theft and crime in Kibera and he shakes his head.

"There is almost no crime here. Gasoline neckties take care of it."

"Gasoline neckties?"

In vigilante justice, anyone caught stealing is collared with a discarded tire filled with gasoline and razed on the spot. When the police arrive, there's nothing to do other than clear the bony remains.

Unfortunately, Dan was not accurate about the incidence of crime. A few years later, he himself was kidnapped. One night, he was held up by a group of thugs who put a gun to his head and forced him into their car. Using his necktie as a blindfold, they took him to an ATM and forced him to empty his account, and then they ran him off after opting not to kill him. Dan jokes about *kikohozi*, the Kiswahili word for *cough*, which signifies a bribe. Then he laughs and admits he had a bad case of pneumonia, meaning that he easily could have been murdered.

Kenyans don't lack for courage or humor. Equally so, they have a wish for security and freedom from the crime that has afflicted Nairobi. Although they left the challenges of farming and an impoverished countryside, they still have reverence for a more peaceful and natural world. As Barack Obama would come to visit "home-squared" and his grandfather's *dala*, so Dan and other Kenyans often return to their family's place of origin. When Dan met Gail Wagner, he asked her to lend him the book she was reading, *Where There Is No Doctor*, and he stayed up all night reading it. He asked for some copies, and when she sent him twenty from the U.S., he decided to ask her if she would bring a group of American doctors to his homeland. Wagner had been planning to do a medical mission in Uzbekistan, and when it was cancelled, she instead organized a group to work in Ugenya, Nyanza Province, where Dan assured her they would have plenty to do.

The Second Mission and an Epidemic

It all started as a rumour. . . Then we found we were dealing with a disease. Then we realized that it was an epidemic. And, now we have accepted it as a tragedy.

—Chief epidemiologist in Kampala, Uganda

The second mission into the Nyanza Province took place in 2005. Dan Ogola was committed to having American doctors return to Nyanza Province and had the ability to move the project forward. Dan had spent his post-school years walking seven or eight miles from Kibera to a pharmaceutical industry, where he earned a dollar and a half a day—an average salary in Kenya but hardly enough to support a family. Coordinating high-energy, altruistic Europeans and Americans came naturally and without the burden of walking to work down a traffic-clogged, air-polluted highway. In Nyanza Province, the average wage for more than half the population was less than a dollar a day. American doctors were caring for patients who earned only a thousandth of their customary wages, and sometimes less.

Dr. Wagner believed she could make a significant impact on health care by working with Dan.

As the team of doctors and nurses traveled to the countryside once more, they focused on the district of Ugenya, where Dan had grown up and expanded his community support group from Kibera. He was hopeful the American team would be more useful in the rural area; many groups were already working in

Kibera, but none in his hometown. They would work out of small clinics, staying until the sun went down and it became too dark, when they would have to leave behind a host of patients until the next day.

Instead of treating common U.S. conditions of diabetes, hypertension, heart disease, obesity, and chronic cancers, the medical team encountered malaria, TB, dysentery, and HIV/AIDS. They saw a preponderance of AIDS, which was known to the surrounding community as *Slim*. The retrovirus had invaded like a dark cloud, overshadowing the young and strong first. In the polygamous culture located along the Kinshasa Highway and the shores of Lake Victoria, promiscuity was common among truck drivers and those in the fishing industry. It took only a decade for the vector to spread through sexually active adults until it had penetrated up to thirty percent, and in some places forty percent, of the population. How could this have happened so suddenly?

Genetic research indicates that the Simian immunodeficiency virus (SIV) appeared one hundred thousand years ago in small monkeys. The monkeys were hunted by chimpanzees, which in turn were hunted by humans. Strains of the SIV virus were identified in chimpanzee colonies in southeast Cameroon but on no other continents besides Africa. Around 1931, a single infected man may have traveled downriver from southeast Cameroon to the Congo, and by 1960, as many as two thousand humans had the virus.

The first epidemic may have occurred in Kinshasa, Democratic Republic of Congo, circa 1970, probably through a wide urban sexual network. The wave of opportunistic infections detected in Kinshasa flowed down the "Kinshasa Highway" as the virus spread through Uganda and Kenya. With widespread labor migration, lack of circumcision (known to help facilitate transfer of the virus), and a plentitude of sex workers, the epidemic accelerated in East Africa, particularly around the area of Lake Victoria. By 1986, 85 percent of Nairobi sex workers were infected with HIV, and by 1993, nine million sub-Saharan Africans had been ravaged by the disease.

The mechanism by which SIV converts to HIV and human infectivity is more complex than consumption of bushmeat and promiscuity and has taken years of research to unravel. Beginning with the isolation and co-discovery of HIV by Robert Gallo and Luc Montagnier, an explosion of scientific studies occurred in the 1980s. Allegations emerged that Gallo had obtained his virus sample from Luc Montagnier, and the awarding of the Nobel Prize went to Montagnier, but Gallo and other scientists continued solving the puzzle of how to diagnose and treat AIDS. Uncovering the retrovirus pathway revealed a step-by-step process, with virions fusing to human host lymphocytes, to genes encoded in single-strand RNA that multiply into double-strand DNA provirus, to more transcription of RNA into new virus particles that invade new lymphocytes, and then to the gradual destruction of the immune system. Unlike the wildly contagious disease of the Ebola virus, which kills its victims within days, HIV-infected patients can survive and transmit for many years, making outbreaks more difficult to isolate and control. But therapies emerged, and between 2001 and 2004, global funding increased from $1.8 billion to $6.1 billion.

Sue Jacobson, an infectious disease doctor in the Matibabu group, had been treating HIV/AIDS for more than a decade. When examining patients in Nyanza District, she might not have heard the common prodromal history, "I had some fever; I lost my appetite," because early symptoms that may have occurred five to ten years earlier were rarely remembered. Instead patients looked "slim" and wasted, their body reserves emaciated by a host of infections. Sometimes the skin was afflicted with small tumors known as Kaposi's sarcoma, with malignant fungal infections, or with wart-like infestations.

As the viral titer, or number of viruses in the body, climbs higher and higher, the immune system collapses. Most often, this occurs in the wage-earning, heterosexually active segment of society. Young women are especially at risk, with double the incidence of HIV/AIDS, and their chance of passing the virus on to their newborns is substantial. As one Kenyan doctor pointed out, referring to the Nyanza fishing industry community,

> Men still believe that it is only women who can be a
> source of HIV in the family, and most of them turn
> very violent on realizing their HIV status. It is interest-
> ing that even those men who are known to be in the
> business of inheriting widows still turn around to blame
> their wives for their predicament. (2)

As with breast cancer, women bear the stigma of disease in an unforgiving way.

Dr. Jacobson knew the complicated nature of getting patients tested and the challenge particular to this population, where poverty and lack of basic education were pronounced. Along with Gail Wagner and another internist, Norma Bozzini, she went to meet with the CDC representative in Siaya to discuss management of HIV-positive women at the time of delivery. It was not a friendly meeting. Competition between NGOs in the fight against AIDS is predictable, even with the extensive U.S. and international funding to help 1.6 million patients carry-ing the virus, and Kenya ranks fourth worldwide in incidents. Through PEPFAR, the President's Emergency Plan for AIDS Relief, fifteen billion dollars was allocated during the Bush presidency towards fighting AIDS in Africa, and forty-eight billion dollars was subsequently allocated for 2008–2013. As one of fifteen countries initially targeted by the largest health initiative in history, Kenya received more than a half billion dollars in 2011 alone, yet each year another hundred thousand patients would be diagnosed with HIV. Like the CDC, Mati-babu was dedicated to health care, but their work would have to include an independent struggle for resources.

Centurions and the Black Messiah

The real religion of the world comes from women much more than from men—from mothers most of all, who carry the key of our souls in their bosoms.

—Oliver Wendell Holmes

FIGURE 11: Miriam Odhiambo

Miriam Odhiambo, at age 104, did not earn any wages. Her function was to oversee her family, which had been reduced by AIDS until there were no members left except great grand-children. Her two sons passed away in their seventies, and she inherited the orphans of their children when the grandchildren died of AIDS in midlife. Miriam told Gail she was happy her sons were old enough not to have been exposed to AIDS during their sexually active years, but now that they were dead from other causes, their grandchildren were her responsibility. Miriam, a survivor of multiple epochs of disaster, was impressed by the medicines and technologies that the American team offered.

A member of the Legio Maria sect, she gained strength and communal support from a religion that broke away from Catholicism in the 1960s. The origin of the Legio Maria is attributed to two founders, Gaudencia Aoko and Simeo Ondeto. Gaudencia was a grieving twenty-year-old mother who, after losing two infant children, was told in a dream by Jesus and the Virgin Mary to start a new church. Simeo, a year prior to this, had had prophetic dreams that he would be the Black Messiah and that his role was to liberate Africans from the oppression of colonialism and to "heal and protect [them] from the evils of witchcraft." It was a period of Luo history almost as devastating as the current AIDS pandemic. Drought followed by heavy rains and flood caused widespread famine, outbreaks of cholera, and a phenomenon known as *lango*, or spirit possession. Simon Ondeto and his followers banded together to overcome the trials of their day, just as Miriam and her orphans attempted to do a half century later. Emblematic of the struggle for a healthy existence, Miriam Odhiambo was just one of the multitudes of patients Matibabu encountered.

Today, children die mostly of malaria, dysentery, trauma, and AIDS. One in five children will acquire the HIV virus when born to infected mothers, and there are 220,000 such children living with the virus in Kenya. In Nyanza District, infant mortality is more than two hundred per one thousand births, and average longevity is around forty-four years.

The Matibabu team confronted these problems, and sometimes things went well. On her second trip, Dr. Norma Bozzini, an internist, helped a young woman deliver her first baby. Lying on a metal gurney with no blanket or sheet, the woman grimaced and moaned quietly as her labor pains increased and she began to push. Norma held the woman's head and hands and comforted her through the ordeal. When it came to an end, she heard the triumphant cry of a baby boy. A Polaroid photo was taken and presented to the mother. She, in turn, was thrilled and asked the name of the American doctor who had assisted her. Word traveled quickly that the child had been named "Norma," which in Kiswahili is masculine enough, signifying "troublemaker."

Newborn and mother might find troubles in the days that followed but Matibabu pointed to progress as patients received testing and treatment for malaria, TB, and HIV. The second mission saw 3,200 patients and began classes for community workers to expand healthcare to distant villages. A school project for deworming children would reach twenty thousand children, vaccines were introduced, and a team of surgeons worked in the nearby Siaya District Hospital performing urgent and non-acute operations. Gail and Dan were collaborating and it seemed that nothing could go wrong.

Creeping Insects and a Donkey's Hind Kick

Ruoth ok yiere e kom kende. A good leader doesn't impose himself on the people.

—Asenath Bole Odaga, *Luo Proverbs and Sayings*

The third medical outreach happened in 2006. It had a strong surgical component including six surgeons, three anesthesiologists, and two nurses assigned to work at the "Russian," a 450-bed hospital in Kisumu. The Soviet financed structure was built as a government facility that could provide advanced care for the million or so inhabitants living in Nyanza province. Its opening in 1969, known historically as the "Kisumu Incident," brought five thousand Luos to hear President Jomo Kenyatta dedicate the hospital. Kisumu had been chosen as the best site for this hospital because, as one Member of Parliament put it, "the only people who are very conversant with the Russian way of life and, for that matter, the Russian policies and politics are around Kisumu. So, if this hospital went to Kisumu, I think it is just a question of putting a round peg in a round hole."

He was referring to the independent, socialist leaning Luo constituency, led by Oginga Odinga, who was considered a political threat to Jomo Kenyatta. As Kenya's first president, Kenyatta had the ribbon-cutting privilege. Oginga had supported Kenyatta during his imprisonment and was instrumental in backing him to be the country leader at Independence. He, in turn, was selected as vice-president in 1964. How different Kenya's future might have been if socialist-leaning Odinga had become president? But he split from Kenyatta in 1966, unhappy with the ruler's right-leaning policies, support of private investors, and bias towards the American military.

Tension between the Kikuyu and Luo cultures was greatly exacerbated when Tom Mboya was assassinated by a Kikuyu, possibly under the direction of a "big man" in July of 1969. When Kenyatta and Odinga met in front of the Russian Hospital a few months later, there was already a growing mistrust and division between the two. Kenyatta was infuriated by the chants of the Luos, who called out, "*Dume, Dume* (Bull, Bull)!" celebrating the brave Oginga who was their preferred leader. Kenyatta responded to the crowd in terse Kiswahili:

> Before opening this hospital, I want to say a few words: and I will start with the Kiswahili proverb which states that "The thanks of a donkey are its hind kick." We have come here to bring you luck, to bring a hospital which is for treating the citizens, and now there are some writhing little insects of the KPU (Kenya People's Union), who have dared to come here to speak dirty words, dirty words.
>
> I am very glad to be with my friend Odinga, who is the leader of these people here. And I wish to say, if it were not for the respect I have for our friendship, Odinga, I would have said that you get locked up today... so that we see who rules over these citizens, whether it is KANU (Kenya African National Union), or so many little insects who rule over this country... On my part I do say this, if these people are dirty, if they bring about nonsense, we shall show them that Kenya has got its government. They dare not play around with us, and you Bwana Odinga as an individual, you know that I do not play around. I have left you free for a long

time because you are my friend. Were it not so you yourself know what I would have done. It is not your business to tell me where to throw you: I personally know where. Maybe you think I cannot throw you into detention in Manyani (previously a British deten-tion camp) because you are my special friend... And therefore today I am speaking in a very harsh voice, and while I am looking at you directly, and I am telling you the truth in front of all these people.

Tell these people of yours to desist. If not, they are going to feel my full wrath. And me, I do not play around at all... They are chanting, "*Dume, Dume*, Bull, Bull." Your mother's c**ts! This *Dume, Dume*... And me, I want to tell you, Odinga, while you are looking at me with your two eyes wide open: I have given my orders right now: those creeping insects of yours are to be crushed like flour. They are to be crushed like flour if they play with us. You over there, do not make noise there. I will come over there and crush you myself. (3)[1]

For a new hospital it was not an auspicious opening. Riots erupted as Kenyatta's troops opened fire on the crowd, killing forty-three. Odinga was imprisoned without trial for fifteen months and the tension between Luos and Kikuyus has never fully resolved. The explosive violence of the 2008 election was a renewed expression of built up tension, happening once again in Kisumu. And it would continue.

Post-cold war, and thirty-eight years after the visit of Jomo Kenyatta, our group of doctors and nurses stood outside the four story expansive Russian hospital contemplating the work at hand. Tall concrete walls and a labyrinth of trails led from

---

1　Encouraging today is the onset of devolution—a shifting of national funds from the central government to the districts. Forty-six years after Jomo Kenyatta's infamous Kisumu speech, his son and current Kenyan president, Uhuru Kenyatta, returned to the Nyalenda slum of Kisumu to declare support for roads, ag-riculture, and health care throughout the Western region. It was a major appeal for friendship between Luos and Kikuyus.

the Administrative offices, where we were dutifully welcomed, to the third floor Operating Theatre. Not, however, until a payment was negotiated. It came as a surprise when the request was made for $40,000. This was to allow access to the OR facilities needed for patients we brought in from the Matibabu Clinic, located thirty miles away. We were not the first nonprofit Medical team to come to the hospital, and precedents had been set by larger organizations that could handle such sums easily. An understanding was met when acceptance of a donated ophthalmology machine matched the relative value of using OR facilities—financial disparity determining visitor charity. It was difficult for us to understand this requirement, but we had already brought patients from a distance to a busy district hospital. If such an arrangement were to be attempted in the U.S. a $40,000 charge for two weeks of OR access might seem paltry.

The first day for a surgical team consists of a long clinic to screen and prepare patients for the ongoing week. We went through three hundred evaluations in multiple languages, diagnosing hernias, tumors, cancers, goiters, and burn deformities. The first day of surgery began as a three-year old boy rolled into the waiting area on a metal cart, speechless with apprehension. His barely legible consent indicated one hernia, although he had two, and no parents were around to clarify or consent. Running water was on short supply. While scrubbing in we noted old scalpel blades and needles at the bottom of the scrub basin, not too reassuring in a district with one of the highest HIV rates in the world.

The day's operations continued well into the evening, coordinated by Dr. Nehra, a smiling anesthesiologist with strabismus. He studied us through a single eye, his other fixed on some distant process, and it was never certain which activity amused him more. Dr. Nehra had two signs next to his office in town, one indicating he was an internist, the other a surgeon, but we were impressed with his anesthesia skills.

The OR manager, Ruto, rarely smiled as he endured continuous requests for instruments and nonexistent equipment, as well as an American-styled time schedule. Operating rooms in Kenya are referred to as *theatres* and while most American surgeons are accustomed to *cutting time* by 8:00 a.m., it was a challenge to get a case going before 10:30 a.m. Anxiety and tempers built, requiring retreats to the break room to take *mandazis* (sweet deep-fried dough cakes) and *chai* (tea with milk and sugar). Dr. Nehra joined us, smiling beneath his tangential gaze and tried to sooth our time-obsessed minds with stories of his years at the Russian. Besides being the first anesthesiologist trained in Kenya, he had once worked as an administrator until his Indian background interfered with promotion.

Most difficult to anticipate were the wards. Described in detail by Cindi B. Brown in *Poverty and Promise*, the Russian Hospital accommodates a large influx of indigent patients suffering the afflictions of low-income. (4) The medical ward was crowded with single wooden beds sometimes accommodating three patients; two laying on the sides with a middle individual facing the opposite direction so the others would not roll off. The surgical wards carried more macabre surprises—a patient with necrotizing fasciitis (a.k.a. "flesh eating bacteria" disease) appeared and disappeared within twelve hours. Necrotic odors from advanced gangrene wafted through the orthopedic ward. A seven-year-old boy gazed back at us stoically as a basketball-sized sarcoma expanded each day, invading his right thigh.

In the female ward tumors rose up like small volcanoes, making it possible to diagnose breast cancer from twenty feet away. We weren't encouraged to attend ward rounds with the medical officers, but we visited our own patients and observed silently. Was there reason to believe that Kenyan surgeons were not dutiful or well trained? This was not the case. They are competent in what they handle—orthopedics, urology, plastic and neurosurgery—the range of problems that renaissance general surgeons in America and Europe have managed for decades and still do in remote areas. This large swath of disease requires discipline and experience, but most surgeons are paid a minimal salary and have minimal supplies and equipment outside of private practice. They work long hours after passing through a rigorous residency that includes frequent nights on call. After paying the costs of tuition for residency they must still qualify through written and oral exams. Like all surgeons, they're independent, proud of their craft, and accustomed to balancing a patient's needs with the limits of human endurance.

We worked hard managing patients we thought we could help and the coordination between our team and the staff surgeons of the hospital was friendly enough—they tolerated our intrusion and monopolizing of operating rooms for two busy weeks. Taking care of non-acute patients that had been sent from the Matibabu clinic in Ukwala was balanced with helping sicker patients discovered on the ward. The boy with the basketball-sized sarcoma underwent a high amputation and some months later his parents sent a letter announcing that he was getting around on crutches and attending primary school again.

Starting from Scratch

Healthcare is the mother of all development.

—David Otieno, District Commissioner, Nyanza

During the third mission the idea of a new hospital began to emerge. Dan Ogola, the inveterate organizer, flashed his Cheshire smile and arranged a breakfast meeting with the Chiefs from his home district. They came to Kisumu to meet with us during a weekend break from surgery.

"After the 2004 and 2005 missions it was a difficult situation," Dan commented, pronouncing 'shun' at the end of his sentence like a soldier. He breaks into laughter, remembering that directing a large group of doctors is like herding cats—difficult enough that he sometimes wandered off himself. "We were facing this challenge of medical 'follow up' after the first two visits and there was always confusion. The community appreciated the care, but when the teams packed and went home after each visit, it could be a year before the patients were seen again. The residents wanted continuity."

Fourteen Luo chiefs and delegates arrived at the Kisumu hotel, dressed in Sunday attire. They appraised the more casually attired, hospital-weary visitors while an Afro-English meal of eggs, potatoes, and sausage was served and a discussion of community medicine took place. The chiefs drank tea, unsure why they had left their villages to meet with these more distant visitors. The Americans drank coffee, wishing they could have slept in. As conversations began, it became a pleasant exchange of different experiences and cultures. Dan had planted a seed of hope in the meeting, anticipating the interests of both groups by arranging a tour of the Kisumu museum, an outdoor display of Luo culture. The Westerners got a day of rest on a local *safari*, and the chiefs saw an exhibit of their own culture that they were proud to share with the visitors. Out of this short gathering, the idea occurred to the chiefs that continuity of care and harnessing good will from medical missions could be more meaningful if there were a hospital. Siaya District Hospital was overburdened and struggled to accommodate more distant villagers. The Kisumu hospitals were farther away, both in distance and cost, so the chiefs suggested building a new one.

But hospitals need land. Dan spent the next several months exploring options with the chiefs, who offered eleven acres in a site that once served as a marketplace, next to the village of Ukwala. Dr. Wagner gave legs to the project—an architectural vision and a funding mechanism. She participated in an administrative team that blended Kenyans and Americans, not unlike the missionary hospital model, but carrying a unifying theme. It would be a women and children's hospital. Private philanthropy and a 1.5 million-dollar grant from USAID and the President's Emergency Program for AIDS Relief underwrote the initial clinical work in Ukwala. Yvonne Hobbs, a lead architect for Kaiser Permanente, offered pro-bono architectural planning and designs for the new buildings. The work had begun.

Women in the Workplace

In the past, men derived their advantage largely from size and strength, but the postindustrial economy is indifferent to brawn. A service and information economy rewards precisely the opposite qualities—the ones that can't be easily replaced by a machine. These attributes—social intelligence, open communication, the ability to sit still and focus—are at a minimum, not predominantly the province of men. In fact, they seem to come more easily to women.

—Hanna Rosin, *The End of Men* (5)

Dan Ogola did what worker bees do in a hive; in this case several hives. He rubbed elbows with worker bees on many levels, trying to establish goals and move forward with a collective project.

"You have to work with the community leaders," he once told me, "and that means they have to believe in your goals."

He and Dr. Wagner began making contacts with key government officials that set directions for health policy and as each contact became a friend, each new friend was part of an expanding brood.

They met with local leaders of Ugenya, the current home of the Matibabu Clinic, and they discussed continuity issues and how a hospital would serve as a nexus. They met with district leaders of Nyanza Province to discuss the impact of a new hospital that would extend the health umbrella through public-private partnership. Finally, they met with leaders in Nairobi, which is equivalent to a Washington D.C. in East Africa. As non-drinkers in social settings where informal meetings often include alcohol, they still connected easily with both men and women. It took three days, however, and the help of a Nyanza District schoolmaster to manage an appointment with Minister of Land James Orengo. When Dan and Gail Wagner walked into the minister's office he looked up from his desk in quiet surprise.

"I'll bet you have no idea why we're here," Dr. Wagner offered. Orengo agreed, taking in the two bespectacled visitors.

The minister also wore glasses and was a bit bemused. As an early defender of multiparty democracy in Kenya, James Orengo was willing to hear the details for a community-integrated women and children's center and hospital. Like Wangari Maathai and Raila Odinga, he had spent time in prison, fighting for the second liberation and confronting the autocratic forces of President Daniel arap Moi. He warmed to the idea of community outreach clinic and a two hundred-bed hospital in Ukwala.

"You must meet my wife, Betty," he suggested.

Educated at the University of Nairobi and Harvard, Betty
Orengo had twenty-five years' experience as an attorney and
legal advisor in the realm of ethnic violence, women's rights,
social justice, philanthropy, and, relevant to Matibabu, the national and international role of NGOs. She and her husband sat
down with Dan and Gail to discuss Kenya's health care problems.

The idea of a state-of-the-art, ecologically designed hospital in an underserved region was well received. It aligned with
six of the eight Millennium Project goals and with the Second
National Health Sector Strategic Plan. It also came with some
support from philanthropy. The limits of this support were being tested, however, and the discussion of a Kenyan fundraiser
was the focus of the meeting.

As the group sampled dishes, they outlined a local plan—a
benefit would be held in the Kenyatta International Conference
Center (KICC), one of the most prominent buildings in Nairobi.
The social and financial elite would be invited and the goal of
building a hospital for Kenyans, paid for by Kenyans, and supported by Kenyans would guide the process. The president and
prime minister would be invited.

Harambee refers to "pulling together," a celebratory process introduced during Kenyatta's early period of establishing
independence and national government. Donors come together
from the financially strong side of communities and cities to
support schools, hospitals, and other institutions throughout
the developing nation. Although meant to express the best of
community service and untainted generosity, through the years,
the activity has become associated with honoring social status
and patronage. The Matibabu benefit, however, had a positive
appeal, and on the day it happened, a sunlit Saturday afternoon,
there was a packed audience—attendees of all incomes and
from all walks of life.

KICC is a centerpiece of Kenyan independence, rising
twenty-eight stories to the acclaimed "one-mile" mark, if measured from sea level. On clear days, now uncommon, Mt. Kenya and Kilimanjaro can be seen from its height. Dedicated to
Kenyatta, who laid the foundation in 1967, the circular NARC
party headquarters' building once boasted a revolving restau-

rant at the top level with a helipad for a roof. The restaurant no longer revolves or serves as a symbol of modernity, but the huge conference center ranks with those in South Africa and Egypt for hosting international meetings and events. The Matibabu conference was held in the amphitheater, a spacious African hut-shaped theater with three balconies seating seven hundred attendees.

I spotted Amanda Schoenberg, the pediatrician who helped start Matibabu and who had treated eleven-year old Evan for his eye infection. We were small *wazungu* (wandering white people) in the assembly of well-to-do Kenyans making their way into the high-tiered seating arrangement. It seemed colossal compared to medical practices in the rural provinces, and looking up and down, we saw hundreds of well-dressed doctors, attorneys, headmasters, bankers, and businessmen— so-called gatekeepers, according to Dan. Many had come from Nyanza Province, and they were in a festive mood.

A band of musicians played flutes and pounded out Luo rhythms. Brightly costumed dancers shook hips and shimmied, and while the elaborate sound system made the massive "hut" pulsate, the auditorium filled with the energy of a rock concert. When the program started, I spotted Reuben Misati, one of the surgery residents who had helped us in Kisumu, sitting with all of his family. The celebration reached into everyone's pockets, all tribes invited, and then suddenly, it became quieter as Lands Minister James Orengo took the microphone to announce the reason for the benefit. He handed the mike to Gail.

"You're probably wondering what I'm doing here," Gail Wagner said once more, a bit shyly, as she stood before the audience. "I'm a doctor from California. Why am I trying to help build a hospital in Kenya?"

Tailoring her message, she explained what she and seven other doctors from California had discovered on their first mission. "We found people who were incredibly sick, but who were incredibly well informed and really motivated to get better. This is not an American project. This is a Kenyan project. This is a community project. The hospital is going to be a community project."

Good for a start, but why Nyanza? Why not somewhere else in Kenya? As she sat down Dan took the emotional lead. Never shy, he paused briefly, tilted up his spectacles, and leaned into the mike. After a youth spent farming in Ugenya, followed by community organizing in the Kibera slums and coordinating American doctors for medical missions, it was a rare opportunity for him to be at the podium.

"Siaya County has fallen behind most national health indicators in Kenya," he said, without script. "And our women and children bear the heaviest burdens of malaria, HIV/AIDS, and other preventable diseases. HIV rates in the poorest subdistricts are over 40 percent."

He described the relatives, friends, and countless members of the Luo community who had faced early deaths, although he did not mention his own father and younger brother who had died from malaria. Kenya's overall percentage of HIV had dropped below the ten percent range, but Nyanza district had reached almost 40 percent.[2]

"The maternal mortality ratio is 456 per 100,000. The infant mortality rate is 77 per 1000 live births. There are twenty-two health facilities in this region and only three Level 3 facilities. That means 10,000 patients per doctor."

He leaned further into the mike, his words echoing off the high, sunlit ceiling.

"There is no facility able to conduct comprehensive emergency obstetric care, blood transfusions, or neonatal care in all of Nyanza District! Do we need to see young mothers hemorrhaging to death in hospitals? Let me ask you this—without any medicine? Do we need to watch burials of children who have never walked? Do we need to see our young people die because there are no doctors and nurses? Allow me to ask you—do we need this?"

The audience squirmed. "No," a few whispered.

"No! We need to have a hospital," he went on, "and we need to begin health services for all of our community in Siaya District. Matibabu is the community-focused health system

---

2 It is closer to 20 percent today.

that will provide health workers, clinics, and a Level 4 health facility to address the needs that we must support. I am asking for your support."

Dan's strident, almost accusatory tone made us wonder if the upper-class audience would be repelled by his message. Just at that moment, Prime Minister Raila Odinga made an entrance into the auditorium, surrounded by a detail of security men. He was introduced by James Orengo and came straight to the podium. A hush fell over the auditorium as his large frame and determined, iconic face captured attention.

"I am new to this," he began slowly, "because. . . uh. . . Dan Ogola and uh. . . Gail Wagner came to my office early this week and took me through what we have seen here."

Some were surprised that the prime minister could find time to come and address a medical fundraiser, but he stood solidly and began to wave his hands—a political conqueror beholding subjects, capturing their mood. Hardly new to large assemblies, "Agwambo" would not pass up an opportunity to address a friendly crowd, and he liked the cause.

"They explained to me what the Matibabu Foundation is trying to do in Ugenya. This is a noble idea," he went on, raising one hand and then the other, "because the minister of health, he believes that the right of quality heath is a fundamental right and that every Kenyan should have a right when he or she is sick to quality health care. And there's no better way to do it. . .than bringing these model facilities closer to the village."

I looked at Amanda Schoenberg, the pediatrician sitting next to me. We were both excited by the sales pitch. But he was still warming up.

"We as a government are trying to promote what we call public-private partnership so that the government partners with the public sector. . . for functional development. So, it is generally recognized that the government alone does not have all the resources required. . . for development. So, in the field of health, we need to partner with the public sector, and this is where I give my advice to the Matibabu Foundation and this project comes in."

His words were powerful. After eight years in prison undergoing intervals of torture and privation, Raila Odinga was now dressed in suit and tie, a leader of East Africa, and he seemed to be enjoying himself.

"We will give them all the support they need as a government so that this project succeeds. And this much I assured them when they came to see me."

People blew horns. The band drummed and Gail Wagner had a smile on her face. I wanted to join the dancers, but Amanda stared me down.

As the prime minister concluded his remarks, the pledges started coming in. In harambee fashion, everyone wanted to be recognized and join the new development. Private donors raised their arms, promising fifteen thousand shillings, thirty thousand, and then fifty thousand. A Kenyan named Godfrey, one of the Matibabu Board of Directors, donated 800,000 shillings. Banks promised more hundreds of thousands of shillings—pledges went on for about an hour. By the time Raila left to make an appearance at a soccer game, the attendees had pledged more than a hundred thousand dollars.

Drums and flutes played loudly as we filed out of the auditorium and headed into a large, banquet-style restaurant. Plates filled with rice and curried chicken abounded. The gathering was mostly couples, but with more women than men. Dan gave a brief thanks to the crowd, and then a singer named Iddi took over. A coloratura soprano dressed traditionally in bright orange, she surveyed the crowd and began to sing a cappella. With no encouragement, every woman in the restaurant joined in, singing loudly and in unison. Raila had been right when he said, "This is a noble idea!"

Riding past the Future

Osiep maber loyo chiemo. Genuine friendship is better than food.

—Asenath Bole Odaga, *Luo Proverbs and Sayings*

A short time after attending the Matibabu Benefit, I joined up again with my friend Kevin near his home in Siaya District.

"Come with me and I'll show you the lake," Kevin tells me, as he rides up to the Mwisho Mwisho hotel where I'm staying. I climb onto the back of a weathered motorcycle, not sure where the trip will lead. From experience, I know that Kevin has barely enough gas to complete a journey, but he assures me we can make it, wherever it is we're headed. In less than ten minutes, we're outside the town of Siaya and riding past a large road sign announcing the Dominion Farm.

"You drive," he suggests, knowing I will want to go slow and look closely at the perimeter. Oklahoma businessman Calvin Burgess leased the 17,000-acre ranch in 2003 for $140,000 annual rent, or about eight dollars an acre. He was required to pay the Siaya City Council $100,000, but there is no documentation of what happened to that money. Likewise, $120,000 was paid to the local Lake Basin Development Authority. It disappeared, as well.

Burgess has a greater real estate empire in Oklahoma. His company website announces that Dominion Properties is "among the largest landlords to the U.S. Government." The farm website further boasts that "during the 1990s, Dominion developed more high-security prisons than any other privately owned company in the U.S., and its affiliate, DM Correctional, transported more inmates by air than any other private company. Several of Mr. Burgess' entities have pioneered their fields of work and have materially advanced the concept of privatization." I'm reminded of a statement by Bill McKibben—"America has twice as many full-time prisoners as full-time farmers," and wonder if Kenya might be at risk for a similar disconnect.

As we travel mile after mile around rolling fields of rice and wheat, stretching as far as the eye can see, giant harvesting machines punctuate the sky along with a thirty-foot cross erected to give notice to witchcraft practitioners—Christ overseeing agribusiness.

Some of the villagers are unhappy, because the enterprise required building a dam, draining the Yala swamp, and flooding much of their land. Those who had land titles were offered $640 for their land, but others without titles lost their means of subsistence. We pass by women pulling weeds who are earning less than two dollars a day—more than they can earn in the local market, but not enough to make them feel secure. They also feel they are working in the midst of pollutants. Burgess denies using pesticides, but I know a local beekeeper who gave up his work because his bees had a die off after a crop plane sprayed white plumes over the fields.

"Kevin," I protest, as I stop the motorcycle to check on our fuel, "we're on empty!"

"No, we'll be fine. Let's keep going so you can see the lake."

I'm not sure why he wants to show me this lake. As we get further and further from town, I know we'll have to walk for long miles to return back, and it's late in the day. Evening rains are due in an hour. As we take a dirt road that diverges from the Dominion Farm, we pass by myriad fields, small farms, and occasional villages that typify most of the Nyanza District. Kenyan farmers on average have less than a hectare of land, and the soil is less productive each year due to nutrient exhaustion. Nevertheless, families make do with what they have, relying on each other to share when harvests are good and the cattle are healthy. Perhaps Kevin wants me to see the stark contrast that is appearing all over Kenya—the interface of modern agribusiness and traditional farms—a duality as sharp as the division between Monsanto and back to earth organic farmers.

"I'm not hurting the people," Burgess has explained. "If everyone starves, there are no people to save."

I've never met Calvin Burgess. I know he spends several months a year running a farm that's a model of large-scale rice production in a country that was previously dependent on imports. Along with a fish farm and dairy industry, his mega-farm attracts investors from many parts of Africa and there's a great demand for more food production. But here's Bill McKibben again—"In the last ten years academics and researchers have begun figuring out what some farmers have known for a long time: it's possible to produce lots of food on relatively small farms with little or nothing in the way of synthetic fertilizer or chemicals." (6) And according to the United Nations Environment Programme reports: yields across Africa have "doubled or more than doubled where organic or near organic practices have been used." Burgess flies in Kenyan doctors and nurses to provide medical care to the local people, although he has never reached out to work with Matibabu for a sustainable local health solution. His motivations seem genuine, however, except that they require a large infusion of Western capital. As Kevin takes over driving and heads further into the hinterlands, I wait for the motorcycle to come sputtering to a halt.

"Look! There's Lake Kanyavanga," he proclaims, and we ride alongside a dark, expansive body of water that once provided fish for a smaller community. It's now a source of fishlings for much of Kenya, and Burgess recycles any waste back into fertilizer he uses for farming. I say a small prayer as we turn east, and miraculously, the fumes inside the gas tank propel us all the way back to Siaya. Is it an irony of fate when Kevin's motorcycle coughs to a final rest in front of the police station?

The Dangling Hive and a Nuclear Explosion

Mo ilo kich. Honey makes bees merry.

—Asenath Bole Odaga, *Luo Proverbs and Sayings*

Kevin is anxious to get started with his home apiary, so we make plans to visit his *dala* and transfer his new hives. He needs a spot where it will be safer to collect honey and manage the boxes without causing local mishaps. The usual rule is that hives have to be moved at least three miles to prevent them from returning to their original location, but these bees are newly located and we hope to get them into a shaded orchard area where they won't return to his house. Obtaining a good smoker is in order; I buy a handmade one for twenty dollars. Then, we jump on the back of the motorcycle with our suits and equipment and ride out to the family compound to survey the hanging hive.

"I think there is plenty of honey in there," he tells me, indicating the Langstroth box that dangles from a thick rope. The box is about nine feet from the ground, too far to reach and high enough that the bees mostly leave everyone alone. His home has a small front yard, fenced-in livestock, and several buildings that house his father's four wives and the rest of the family. The foraging bees are dancing and entering the bottom opening of the hive in successive waves.

"Do you want to climb or catch?" Kevin asks.

He's being courteous. It seems logical that he climb the tree and cut the rope and that I catch the hive as it's lowered down. I already know the importance of keeping a hive balanced and upright so as not to disturb the bees. What could go wrong? Buoyed by the relative success of our work at Mama Sarah's, we assume we can get the hive moved with careful orchestration. Alas, I forget a motto pounded into my psyche when I was a surgical intern: "Trust no one; assume nothing!"

The caveat to that warning is "Check, check again, and then triple-check!", but we have no way to even single-check. If you were to stand on a small wooden box and reach for it, the hive still would be a foot too high to test its weight. Kevin wisely chooses to climb the tree, untie the knot, and lower the bee-filled package into my waiting hands. Waiting just below, prepared to catch hold as the hive comes down, I stretch my arms as far as I can. Since the cut rope is too short, I plan to balance the hive in midair and guide it another seven or eight feet to the ground. How heavy can it be?

The Langstroth hive is used around the world. Designed in 1851 by an ordained minister who had rediscovered his youthful fascination with insects and begun raising bees, his hive was conceived during a Eureka moment. He figured out how to squeeze ten frames into a box, which left just enough space for the bees to move around while giving the beekeeper a way to access the honey. When full, it weighs around a hundred pounds—one hundred pounds of honey and affiliated bees that create a guided not-so-sweet missile.

Kevin climbs up the tree to release the hive, as I look around the compound. It's a halcyon day. Surrounding us are many unsuspecting spectators, along with the usual assortment of cows, chickens, and dogs. I concentrate on the arriving package. When the knot on the rope won't yield, Kevin pulls out his machete and with a sharp grunt and a rapid swing, the machete comes smashing down. A millisecond later, the box drops into my waiting hands. It's heavy! Much heavier than I had anticipated; the bees have been busy making honey for several months. In slow motion, I half-guide it, watching it tilt disastrously, and hit the ground with a massive thump.

The hive is now planted face-down in dirt, its lid knocked loose. Thirty to fifty thousand angry inhabitants explode in the air becoming a critical mass that disseminates exponentially with burning outrage, aroused by Kevin and me. Even at the height of the cold war with Russia and the apogee of MAD (Mutually Assured Destruction), when our most advanced nations struggled to outnumber each other with weapons of mass annihilation, I could not have predicted the conflagration we are experiencing. Bees smash into our veils, pinging us angrily, as they desperately try to insert stingers and venom. We scramble and retreat, but more alarming is what the poor animals endure. The cows, chickens, and dogs run in confused circles—what they did they do to deserve such hostility? Humans hide behind doors and windows.

As the blast of bees spreads in larger waves, the neighborhood empties and Kevin and I, like the last inhabitants on earth, wonder what we have unleashed. African bees are such passionate defenders of their hives that they will follow and sting invaders as far as a quarter of a mile, so we set out on what might be a long journey. Fortunately, we experience a little relief after walking a few hundred yards. The bees sense that it's futile to engage with the white suits. After several minutes, we gather our courage and a fully-lit smoker and venture back to ground zero, hoping to upright the fallen hive. It's like exploding another incendiary bomb. We succeed in straightening the box somewhat, but the intensity of the after-explosion convinces us that we should wait for nightfall.

As Kevin starts up the motorcycle, he shouts to the few remaining neighbors, "We'll be back. We're going to get some chemicals!"

6

Bees, Trees, and Hospitals

Like the volcano, Africa can stun you in an instant. It can throw floods and drought and disease at you, sometimes all at the same time. In the next moment, it will tease you with its magnificent beauty, so even if you don't forget, you can find a way to forgive. Ultimately, it keeps you coming back for more."
—Jacqueline Novogratz, *The Blue Sweater*

Post-Explosion and Relocating Bees

Kevin and I return in the evening and rig the smoker. I buy a five-dollar mosquito net from the local store. He thinks it is too expensive, but after tossing it around our tilted beehive in the dark, it seems like a good investment. The bees, still unhappy about the disruption, sting our ankles through tennis shoes and socks, but covered with the mosquito net and darkness, there are far fewer of them outside the no longer dangling box. Using a homemade wheelbarrow, we gently pick up the hive and balance it in the middle and begin a rocky journey. It leads around Kevin's *dala* to a tree-protected pasture, perhaps an eighth of a mile away, but it seems like the other side of the world as we push over rocks and dirt, foot by foot. The volatile inhabitants of the hive bounce and buzz in the darkness.

The masked light of a gibbous moon and a thin beam from our flashlight reveal more ruts and rocks ahead. I feel the ancient fear of hyenas and leopards, which once were common to this area. Kevin tries to reassure me by saying that now the hyenas only come at night. Thanks Kevin. It's night, and if they do come, I will offer them a hive of bees! At last, we deliver the two boxes to a new sanctuary and set them up on a waiting bench. Then we find our way back to the house.

Kevin's mothers and a few of his sixteen brothers and sisters are sitting inside. They welcome us with a soft drink. His biological mother is reserved and surprised by my attempt at conversation in Dholuo. Too nervous to respond, she shakes my hand but looks aside. She seems thin and wan, perhaps anxious about other things, and I hope not to seem threatening after the day's wild excursion with honeybees.

In a family this large, the challenge of obtaining education and employment is steep. Kevin began college but never finished. His entrepreneurial spirit, however, might get him through training at the nearby agricultural school and his father's connections could even help him to start a honey cooperative. When his father enters the room another exchange of greeting and handshaking takes place. Kevin's mother brings a plate of food, and we talk about the construction of the Mwisho Mwisho Tourist Hotel. Development proceeds very slowly, he explains. There are no funds, and construction requires resources—a familiar theme in Nyanza District and also for re-located bees.

Consider the process by which honeybees construct their homes. A hive can accommodate up to fifty thousand inhabitants and have up to a hundred thousand units. All the builders are females that have eight wax glands arranged in pairs on the bottom of their abdomens. The glands produce paper-thin scales of wax, and the bees further process and knead laboriously with their mandibles until the wax achieves the correct consistency. A swarm of bees needs about fifteen pounds of honey to make three pounds of wax. Starting from the bottom of a chosen surface—a tree branch, the eave of a roof, or a wooden foundation bar—they work downward as they construct segments of combs that join together seamlessly. But what makes the hexagonal pattern?

Kepler, Galileo, and Einstein marveled at the precise symmetry of beehives, but it required physicists and chemists to understand the key to six-sided cells. Beeswax has three hundred chemical components as well as the property of a liquid, but it needs the right temperature in order to assume its special shape. The bees create cylindrical, tube-like cells, and then the liquid wax produces the hexagonal shape. Bees facilitate the process using temperature receptors located in the distal segments of their antennae and also by following their sense of gravity. When the body temperature of the bees gets to 43 degrees centigrade and the wax is between 37 and 40 degrees centigrade, walls of perfect strength and thickness form together, hexagon after hexagon. The queen lays her eggs, the workers store honey and pollen—and within this geometric paragon, the bees spend the majority of their lives.

Will Kevin's hives expand and become a source of both honey and income? He could master the craft of beekeeping and make a living by connecting other beekeepers in the area. But this vision, like my efforts to see an African queen bee and to relocate Mama Sarah's bees, is elusive.

Disappearing Bees

The lives of animals are parables of our lives.

—African Proverb

Like AIDS, the disturbing acronym CCD (Colony Collapse Disorder) is well known to both the public and to the keepers of 2.5 million hives in the U.S., a number that is about half of what existed in 1980. Something is happening here, and it includes Europe, South America, Central America, Canada, Asia, and anywhere colonies have diminished dramatically. In other words, this is a global phenomenon. Many bumblebee species are gone forever. Feral bees in the U.S. have diminished by 90 percent. The most frequent question—what causes it?—reverberates through the public, in apiary forums, and in entomology research labs. Despite many reported etiologies—including the varroa bee mite, viruses, fungi, bacteria, pesticides, stress of constant transport, immune suppression, electromagnetic radiation (do bees carry cell phones?), genetically modified foods, climate change, starvation, and any combination of the above—a clear answer hasn't emerged.

What is certain is that the decline of bees in America impacts a fifteen-billion dollar enterprise and puts a canary in the coal mine of modern agribusiness, signaling a limit to what soils and farm systems can produce sustainably. There have been sudden declines in the past, but never in such volume as now. (See Appendix—Chapter 6.) Imported to America by sailing vessels during the time of the pilgrims, honeybees arrived along with plants, goats, cattle, pigeons, and mastiffs. As one unhappy Native American commented in the 1630s, while watching an apiarist work in Newbury, Massachusetts, "Huh, White men work, make horse work, make ox work, make fly work. This Injun go away." (1) If honeybees were to disappear completely, it would not affect native plants, which have stingless bees and other insects and methods for pollination. But it would set back a third of the food crops grown in the States, including almonds, peaches, soybeans, apples, pears, cherries, raspberries, blackberries, cranberries, watermelons, cucumbers, and strawberries. Perhaps Africanized bees will fill the vacuum?

The African honeybee is hardy, having evolved through millions of years of competitive existence with other insects and animals, most recently man. It is also considered resistant to varroa mite, a pathogen implicated in Colony Collapse Disorder, and that may bring some survival advantage to European honeybees as it breeds with them and continues northward through the U.S. This advantage may even mitigate their killer-bee reputation that, while fear-mongering, is still based on the fact of numerous deaths.

As I look for the African queen, hoping to see how the role of women in Kenyan society is changing, I continue encountering African bees. The queen bee, it seems, meets the criteria for maternal greatness. She can arise from any single egg, from the common wananchi of the colony, and become an exceptional mother just by being fed on royal honey. Second, she sets a leadership example by laying one to two thousand eggs a day. Finally, she contributes at least half the chromosomes for all the bees she gives birth to, including the next and future queen.

A Swarm's Immortality

We need another and a wiser and perhaps a more mystical concept of animals. . . . For the animal shall not be measured by man. In a world older and more complete than ours, they move finished and complete, gifted with extensions of the senses we have lost or never attained, living by voices we shall never hear. They are not brethren, they are not underlings: they are other nations, caught with ourselves in the net of life and time, fellow prisoners of the splendour and travail of the earth.

—Henry Beston, *The Outermost House* (2)

Simple insects do not impress us with the ability to live a hundred years, cure breast cancer, plant trees, or build hospitals, yet they have long been regarded as symbols of royalty and a natural manifestation of eternal life. In ancient times, the bee was incorporated in the pharaoh's title, representing Lower Egypt. Signifying diligence and industrious behavior, the bee was a royal emblem for the Merovingians, the Barberini, and the Mayans. Most impressive is that the queen bee has accomplished something humankind has sought since the beginning of recorded time—immortality.

How does a bee live forever when its lifespan is only six weeks and the queen survives for just a few years? The answer lies in the colony. Even Darwin was baffled when he considered the method by which bees reproduce. With all their reproductive energy dedicated to just one queen, the many thousand worker bees are unable to genetically modify and improve their survivability on an individual basis, so their strategy threatened his theory of evolution. How could bees be so successful when the vast majority can't reproduce and diversify their lineage?

Outside of honey bees, sweat bees, and ants, most insects use the strategy of producing hundreds of thousands of offspring, all capable of reproducing. Female honeybees, with the exception of the queen, are sterile. Now, here is where the superorganism achieves its long-lasting advantage. Each time a queen is produced and nurtured, she carries the colony's germline, and each time the hive swarms, usually at yearly intervals, that germline doubles. With the old queen taking two-thirds of the colony and the new queen keeping a third, the colony divides and creates two superorganisms, both consisting of the children of one queen. Therefore, her lineage can continue forever.

This could explain the process that causes the colony to continually return to Mama Sarah's mango tree. When it is trapped out and moved to a Langstroth hive a hundred yards away, it waits until the end of the rainy season. As the flowers proliferate, so do the bees. The colony grows crowded, and the message gets around to the collective that the old queen must move on and a new queen must be nurtured. The scout bees begin their search, perhaps from memory, or perhaps from leftover wax and scent on the tree branch, and find their spot back in the mango tree.

As Thomas Seeley outlined in *Honeybee Democracy*, bees know how to do house-hunting. They have at least five preferences as they explore for cavities in a three-mile vicinity. High on their list are cavity size; direction of entrance (a south-facing entrance allows for sun exposure, especially important in New England's cold winters); size of entrance (to keep out invading birds, bears, and honey badgers); position of entrance (a lower entrance prevents loss of heat from convection); and presence of comb from previous colonies to facilitate new comb formation.

Once a site is located that pleases the scouts, they ready the swarm to make a move. Scouts might investigate from ten to twenty sites before they reconnoiter at the swarm location, waggle-dancing the pros and cons of what they have seen. By quorum, the group that has the greatest number of scouts with the most energy wins the debate. With this democratic decision, flight preparation begins. Honeybees fan their wings 250 times a second, to warm up and notify colleagues that it's time to travel. The queen is slimmed down to more easily stay aloft, and the rest of the bees load up with honey. Piping sounds intensify, and the assemblage lifts off as a swirling collective.

Kenya is decidedly different from New England, however, where Seeley conducted his studies. Located exactly on the equator, Mama Sarah's mango tree represents a dilemma for house hunters because the bees have to live out in the open, hanging from a branch where they are punished by the rains. One Sunday, the massive, water-soaked, honey-filled comb broke loose and hit the ground. Panicked, the bees in turn punished every available human and animal in the vicinity and had to find another tree.

Disappearing Trees

The primary change for local people to benefit from commercial forestry is through democratization of forest governance.

—Rosemary Bargerei, Forest Landscape and Kenya Vision
2030 Symposium

Entomologists agree that loss of foraging space is one important explanation for the decline in honeybees. Trees are critical! As minister of Parliament and assistant minister in the Ministry for Environment and Natural Resources, Wangari Maathai, anticipating the needs of her constituency, continued to pursue environmental strategies. Her attention focused on the *shamba* (field) system, in which the land around Mt. Kenya, Aberdares, Mao, and other water-tower forest regions were stripped of natural forests to make way for monoculture timber crops. Started during the 1930s and '40s, the colonial plan utilized local labor to care for the non-native tree species and allowed farmers to cultivate their own crops in exchange for access to the land. The farmers were satisfied with any access, and the colonialists had timber for construction and locomotive fuel. For more than fifty years, the slash, cut, and burn *shamba* system progressed, depriving land from indigenous tribes. Kenya reduced the size of its original forests from 17 percent to 1.7 percent. A further consequence, Maathai argued in her 2009 publication, *The Challenge for Africa*, was the steady degradation of rivers and soil, which require a sustained water tower source.

> These water resources, and the forests, are essential for Kenya's agriculture, livestock, tourism, and energy sectors, as well as household water and fuel. If the mountains' ecosystems continue to be degraded, it will become impossible to achieve the MDGs in Kenya. (3)

The United Nations and twenty-three international groups defined eight MDGs, millennium development goals, in the year 2000. Today, few remember them except for the government officials and foreign aid workers who targeted their funds.

The MDGs, in order are to:

1) Eradicate extreme poverty and hunger

2) Achieve universal primary education

3) Promote gender equality and empower women

4) Reduce child mortality rates

5) Improve maternal health

6) Combat HIV/AIDS, malaria, and other diseases

7) Ensure environmental sustainability

8) Develop a global partnership for development

These goals were to be reached by 2015, but they met major obstacles, especially in Sub-Saharan Africa. China and India made substantial progress in the first goal, reducing the poverty level by 50 percent, but most countries of Sub-Saharan Africa have reduced their poverty index by only one percent, or less. While advances in global health took place (Matibabu was one recipient of the financial investment directed towards AIDS and

Malaria control), there was not an equivalent improvement in education, sanitation, or agriculture.

Wangari believed that MDG 7, the ensuring of environmental sustainability, never received adequate emphasis. By restoring the mountain ecosystem, just one part of MDG 7, the first six MDGs would all be addressed. The economy (MDG 1) would benefit from better rainfall patterns, river-dependent irrigation, and soil protection—all critical to agriculture. By stopping deforestation, girls and women would not have to search farther each year for firewood and water and could attend school and seek other employment (MDGs 2, 3). By restoring rivers, the hydropower source for electricity and power—around 60 percent of Kenya's energy—would be preserved and free up resources for health care (MDGs 5, 6). Her vision presaged the 2015 Sustainable Development Goals proffered by Jeffrey Sachs in his current book, *The Age of Sustainable Development*. (4) She was ahead of her time, and did not realize how short her time would be.

When the Kibaki government chose to ban the *shamba* system in 2002 in an effort to enhance conservation and restore natural forestation, Maathai hoped there would also be restoration of the Mao forest. The Greenbelt Movement organized planting of native trees and rewarded seedling planters—mostly women—with small but beneficial wages.

By 2007, however, the government had adopted a new program called PELIS (Plantation Establishment and Livelihood Improvement Scheme). This, according to Maathai, "opens the door to the possibility of further destruction of remaining forests." The PELIS program was a response of the government and forest department to the requests of the local population for more farming land. It was also a response to national needs for a multiple-use policy, which would allow some farming, grazing, timber harvest, recreation/eco tourism, and protection of the water tower. The pressure from many parts of the society, as well as a need to devolve management to local communities, made for an uphill battle that Wangari could only partially influence. With the country receiving 68 percent of its energy supply from wood and biomass, and with half the population living below poverty level, the need for charcoal for fuel and crops for survival put tremendous pressure on the forests. Population growth anticipated to reach 60 million by 2030 doubles the pressure.

These two competing needs, economic growth and environmental preservation, make manifest a cultural struggle in Africa and the rest of the world. In Kenya, the struggle takes place within the larger context of ethnic division and the needs of communities. During the 1990s, Wangari witnessed serious corruption in the Moi administration, including the Goldenberg scandal, in which 10 percent of the GDP was siphoned off in a massive exporting scheme. The Kibaki administration followed, when hopes for a more transparent, accountable government were constantly disappointed—the goal of protecting the country's forests and water towers was submerged in the rivalries among major tribes contesting for political supremacy and land ownership. When she pushed for a return to biodiversity, to planting native trees in the Aberdares and Mau Forest, her own constituency pushed back for a return to agriculture and jobs. Searching for a middle way, the forest service emphasized community input—also called the *social phase* of forest management. By 2008, the forest department acknowledged *future shock*—the inability of their discipline to anticipate society's expectations and the accelerating rate of change within Kenya. (5)

Kenya confronts its own version of Colony Collapse Disorder, although the disappearing species is trees, not bees. However, the two are interconnected, since the loss of forage habitat directly affects the health of bees and the honey industry. The contest between economic growth and the environment depends on government choices and the perseverance of the GBM and other environmental groups. Economic growth continues to be a priority. Uhuru Kenyatta has expressed concern for environmental protection, but the first lady, Margaret Kenyatta, has been even more outspoken on behalf of Kenya's ecology as well as for reducing maternal mortality. Hospitals are an interrelated challenge, because without them, neither the economy nor the environment can prosper.

Hospitals

If you give a man a fish, you feed him for a day;
if you teach a man to fish, you feed him for a lifetime.

—Proverb often used to refer to providing resources to foreign
countries, exact source unknown

"Oh, you must be from Doctors without Borders?" is a frequent
response when you mention to anyone in the U.S. that you do
medical work in Africa. Kenyans have a sense of the burgeoning field of NGOs, and as of 2011, more than six thousand
organizations were working in their country, about a third of
them supported by foreign countries. (6) NGOs have been increasing at a rate of 400 per year, and if this seems significant,
compare it with 1.5 million nonprofits in the U.S. While there
are more national NGOs in Kenya than there are international,
the source of international funding is much higher. Germany
accounted for 36 percent of all funds, Kenya for 7 percent, and
the U.S. for 5 percent. All told, around a billion dollars goes
toward NGO aid. When the government attempted to survey
the registered organizations, they were able to collect responses
from only 18 percent. (7)

NGOs present with an expanding list of acronyms, including the faith-based and non-faith based FBOs, RBOs, PBOs,
BINGOs, TANGOs, MANGOs, and so on.[3] In Kenya, the greatest sector of attention for these groups is HIV/AIDS, followed
closely by education and general health. Not included in the list
is the U.S. International Health division of the Department of
Defense. (Some say more special forces units are deployed in
Africa than in Afghanistan or Iraq.) The Kenyan government
and the CIA surely have lists of the illegal organizations, includ-

---

3 Faith-based organizations, religious-based organizations,
public-benefit organizations, big international non-governmental
organizations, the Association of Non-Governmental Associations, and Management Accounting for Non-Governmental
Associations.

ing underground cells of Al Shabaab and ISIS, but they're not available to the public.

Compared to Doctors without Borders or Medicins Sans Frontieres (MSF), the Matibabu nonprofit is miniscule. MSF sends around 3,000 volunteers to 80 different countries and is one of the largest independent medical humanitarian relief organizations in the world. Awarded the Nobel Prize in 1999, its doctors are noted for traveling to the toughest parts of the world, including the West African Ebola Crisis, and for being "medical mavericks, the cowboys of emergency aid" and "arguably the most effective—and inarguably the cockiest—medical-relief organization in the world." MSF early on recognized and helped control the Ebola outbreak of 2014. It was joined by Partners in Health, which has 15,000 employees globally, and The International Medical Corps, which has 5,300 staff and volunteers worldwide. National understanding of the crisis by the governments of Liberia, Sierra Leone, and Guinea allowed a combined response. They worked together to halt the spread of the Ebola using containment strategies. MSF, IMC, and Partners in Health are small compared with the 97 million volunteers in the International Red Cross and the Red Crescent Movement.

The Matibabu organization is dedicated to the Siaya and Ugenya districts, a population of approximately 180,000, and beyond into Nyanza Province—upwards of 4.5 million. While a medical clinic offering HIV/AIDS detection and treatment was an initial focus, an extensive clinical system and eventual construction of a hospital had become the goal. Would it be justified? Based on the level of human suffering we witnessed, it seemed so. Like the Russian hospital in Kisumu, the patients at Siaya District Hospital often arrive too late for effective treatment, and they can't afford it. Strong in my memory was a boy who had broken his leg, required fixation of the bone, and developed a wound infection that required skin grafting. It was a simple procedure requiring a single skin grafting blade, but none existed. When I returned to Kenya a few months later, grafting blade in hand, he had already died.

General surgeons come and go at rural hospitals and rarely stay long. No salary, no surgeon. The village chiefs had requested a new hospital, and after organizing three medical missions, Dan and Dr. Wagner agreed with the priority. As Dan had pointed out during the *harambee*, the poverty level was 58 percent, the prevalence of HIV/AIDS was 38.4 percent of the population, the maternal mortality rate was 456 per 100,000, and the infant mortality rate was 77 per 1000. With no blood bank, neonatal care, or comprehensive emergency care, only three lower-level hospital facilities existed to serve more than a million inhabitants. Dan and Gail wanted a facility that could serve as a model for the rural provinces of East Africa. It would be a women and children's hospital offering high-end medical services in an ecological, African-designed building.

"If you start building the hospital," I asked Dr. Wagner early on, "how do you manage the costs? How much comes from the Kenyan side?"

"It's not *if*," she insisted. "It's *when*."

The first strategic plan put a 7.7 million dollar price tag on five-year expenditures, of which about 20 percent would come from the Matibabu-Kenya organization. The remaining 80 percent would be funded through the American public/private donors and grants. In a time of recession in the American economy and a lagging Kenyan economy, the five-year projected budget required heavy lifting.

Significant help for the clinic came with the grant of 1.5 million dollars through the President's Emergency Plan for AIDS Relief program (PEPFAR) in 2008. Awarded to only twelve recipients in Sub-Saharan Africa and Haiti, the grant allowed Matibabu to expand its capacity by serving a community of HIV/AIDS patients. It was no longer just Dan and Gail and a nonprofit board. Matibabu collaborated with John Snow, Inc. (JSI), a public health research and consulting firm that coordinated twenty projects throughout Africa, most of them connected to HIV/AIDS work. The JSI program seemed to dovetail with the Matibabu mission as a low-budget clinic in Ukwala, and the

Western regions of Kenya moved towards a larger health care provider system.

After JSI came two consultants—experts with the goal of boosting fundraising and rendering independent advice based on experience. It was difficult to fathom which of the two men was more integrally involved. One was tall, soft spoken, and reserved. The other brought an energy that reflected his prior experience in the military. The Kenya-based Matibabu organization had already established a U.S.-based 501(c)(3) nonprofit called the Tiba Foundation. The two branches allowed both better fundraising in America and a Kenyan board to run the clinics and hospital in the host country.

But there were growing pains. Building a hospital with two cultures ten thousand miles apart is never simple.

"It's a dog fight," the energetic consultant said, trying to describe the daily challenges and competition between forces of government bureaucracy, funding agencies, local infrastructure, and the needs of an indigent population. Fueled by espressos and determined to make the project successful, he traveled to Kenya and sat through long meetings, hammering out policies, procedures, agreements, and alterations. Lean, outgoing, and boots-on-the-ground, he seemed to enjoy the pace of working in two countries, although they functioned at different speeds. After laborious discussions and policy debates, he would return to the caffeinated offices of San Francisco.

The taller consultant was philosophical but difficult to interpret. He measured his words, offering them with cautious assurance that the goals of building a hospital needed to be eminently practical. The six or seven million dollars needed to construct a modern, ecologically designed building would somehow materialize. His reputation for business skills and his ability to combine humor with a comprehensive approach seemed right for getting answers. When I asked him about more about financing, however, he became reticent. The Kenyan side would need to come forth much more, and there weren't enough examples of that happening.

One and a half million dollars comes and goes quickly. The

PEPFAR grant, supervised through the New Partner Initiative with technical support from JSI, resulted in a rapid expansion of services. The number of patients undergoing HIV counseling and testing increased fourfold, and health services reached out to referrals from seventeen government services. New laboratory equipment, supplies, and medications improved the Ukwala and Nzoia clinic sites, and Matibabu could direct more attention to building a hospital. With a sliding scale charge to patients who received services, however, returns were minimal, and the funding remained dependent on outside sources. Land donation was the community's primary way to provide help. Locals, especially women, provided much of the manual labor.

Two Ceremonies in Wananyiera

When Raila sneezes, Kibaki coughs. When Kibaki coughs he spends money, and Raila feels better.

—Mama Sarah Obama

In July of 2009, President Kibaki made a whirlwind tour of Nyanza province, perhaps deciding to build a better allegiance and coalition with Prime Minister Raila Odinga and the Luos. Targeted into the helicopter travels was a short landing in Ukwala near an open field, once called *Wananyiera* (they are laughing at me) because it had been a village market where men drinking too much beer were often observed. A red carpet was laid out on a patch of rust-colored soil, and the president and Prime Minister Odinga were directed to the ribbon-cutting. Dr. Wagner was back in Oakland, California, still seeing patients in the oncology clinic, but Kaiser doctor Bill Plautz flew out to represent the California group. Dan, as usual, took an all-night bus from Nairobi and arrived just in time to direct the event. His Cheshire smile widened as he greeted and shook hands with the president and prime minister.

The event was significant for President Kibaki, not only given the long history of Kikuyu-Luo rivalry and the "Kisumu

FIGURE 12: President Kibaki Meets with Dan Ogola and James Orengo

Incident" of 1969, but also the more recent rivalry between Kibaki and Odinga in the 2007 elections. It was equally important for Dan, dressed in a light-blue suit and colorful Kenyan tie instead of farm clothes. With a secondary school education and background as a community organizer, he had helped orchestrate a shared commitment between Kenya's foremost political leaders. Village chiefs struck a pose in ceremonial robes as Prime Minister Odinga's turn to speak came.

"I have pledged to work with President Kibaki in order to better this country, and I want us to discard politics of division and work towards improving this nation."

Kibaki cut a ribbon that led to the proposed site for the hospital.

Skeptics could say it was an opportunity for Raila Odinga to strengthen his bid for president in 2013 and for Kibaki to secure some support with the larger Luo electorate. Dr. Plautz, as the designated American Matibabu representative, felt it was a time of sincerity and goodwill. After many years in the making, a community hospital provided a healing event.

FIGURE 13: Prime Minister Raila Odinga Pointing to New Hospital Site for President Kibaki

Second Ceremony

One year later, in 2010, bids had been made, architects and engineers chosen, and another ceremony planned. I had traveled with a small group to Nyanza District to do more surgical work at Siaya District Hospital, and we were invited to Wananyiera again for the site-marking of the new hospital. We flew from California to Amsterdam to Nairobi and then to Kisumu. After thirty hours en route, we climbed into a small van and drove late into the night to a small hotel near Mama Sarah's village. A few hours later, we met up with Dan and a group of doctors before heading off to the ceremony. There were the usual time delays and confusion about where the construction would be, and finally we reached the destination—a large open field bordered by a papyrus swamp that stretched southward towards Lake Victoria.

Scattered candelabra euphorbia trees lifted cactus-like arms upwards, exuding a poisonous sap that the local women used as a medicine to clear out the placenta following childbirth. Already on-site, the Kenyan architect, Peter Sherris, the Tiba

FIGURE 14: Marking the Hospital Site – Ukwala, Kenya

Foundation president, local construction workers, and various local "opinion leaders" wandered about the several-acre clearing. Dan, bestowing his Cheshire grin, did a customary "meet and greet," but it was the young priest giving the benediction who captured our attention. His evangelic voice boomed across the barren field, alerting even the cattle.

"Lord we beseech you to place your blessing on this land!"

We looked towards the circular chalk line that indicated where the first module/hospital building would be erected. In the distance, as far as one could see, the rolling savannah and adjacent swamp gave no hint of angels or divine intervention, but small groups of villagers kept watch from a distance. The cattle and goats looked for higher grass.

"Let your hand guide us in the building and the making of this hospital that we must be servants of your will and . . . and that your love for us as we take part. . ."

Cameras clicked. Camcorders whirred. Since the first line had been misdirected, the workers continued etching out and reinforcing a new circular chalk line meant to contain the hospital building. There was a tent nursery at the bottom of a soft descent of field, and across from it, a large pond had been dug out for tilapia farming.

The priest's vision grew: "...will guide us, and your blood will be spilled unto this land, and it shall give forth, and we beseech you, Jesus, to carry us and our workers, and it is your blood that gives us life in the making of this place to heal our bodies."

Christ's blood was alluded to for some time. In the warm, peaceful day were intimations of a different kind of activity for the bucolic setting. Medicines would be given out, babies would be born, vaccines administered, and wounds healed. Imagining crowds of sick people, walking and driving from distant parts of the region to this technological miracle in Wananyiera, I wondered if they would "laugh at me."

After the priest completed his blessing, I left the construction site and mingled with several workers who were sitting by the entry gate. White skin was commonplace, but my accent and choice of Luo words were comical. There would be pilgrimages of all sorts to this remote location, bringing the diseased from each corner of the district for every medical treatment imaginable, and the locals would find opportunities to continue laughing.

7

Colonies and Communities

Life wastes nothing. Over and over again every molecule that has ever been is gathered up by the hand of life to be reshaped into yet another form.
—Rachel Naomi Remen, *My Grandfather's Blessings*

Odd similarities existed between the Matibabu hospital project and the colony of bees living high in Mama Sarah's mango tree. What had started as a small community development project in the Kibera District of Nairobi had reproduced and migrated to the Nyanza District, home territory for Dan Ogola. And it reproduced once more in the new hospital being built in the old Wananyiera market site, now part of the town called Ukwala. I was returning twice a year to work in a government hospital where conditions were challenging—no running water, unreliable electricity, and despite a dedicated nursing staff there was a shortage of surgeons. Having lost both my mother and my sister in difficult circumstances, I felt a strong empathy for the

FIGURE 15: Second Colony in Mango Tree

cancer patients, and there was an abundance of other surgical diseases. There was another process taking place, however, almost as challenging.

During this time, the large, ominous colony in Mama Sarah's front yard, relocated into a Langstroth hive, reproduced and swarmed back to the mango tree from which it originated. This process of reproduction by bees, also referred to as propagated immortality, parallels the expansion of human communities. Growth occurs based on the availability of resources. In the case of Matibabu, resources depended largely on grants, donations, and to the extent possible, payment for treatments.

Bees depend largely on pollen and nectar and reproduce as long as the environment supports them. The precursors of bees date back to the Jurassic period; they were herbivorous wasps that were thought to have evolved into carnivores, not unlike our ancestor *homo habilis*, who transitioned from consuming fruit and tubers to meat eating. As the wasps digested honeydew-filled aphids, however, it was like eating ice cream cones in a Baskin Robbins parlor. They developed a sweet tooth and became more social. Sweat bees and honeybees would begin the symbiotic dance of fertilization as angiosperms developed irresistible flower designs and colors to attract these new pollinators. In the Cretaceous period, flowers spread across the planet much faster than the conifers, cycads, and ferns, and along with the bees, they diversified the earth. Today, suburbanites pick and choose their floral garden displays and even the species of bee they want to have in the backyard.

It wasn't that simple with *Apis mellifera scutellata*, the less friendly species of bee returning to Mama Sarah's mango tree. African honeybees, as already described, like to abscond and swarm in order to reach the moving target of pollen and nectar in the fast-changing, rainy seasons. Italian bees, by contrast, tend to hang out and enjoy a stationary home, a *dolce-vita* life with a plentitude of local flowers during spring and summer. Not so the Russians, which suffer Siberian winters and, like their African counterparts, will bolt the first chance they get to find better forage. The Carniolans, from the Baltic region, are gentle to work with, but they don't like a crowd and travel fast when the hive fills up.

In America, colony migration is mostly controlled. Imagine a queen bee on a ten thousand-hive bee farm (call it a mega city). She and other queens are joined tightly with seventeen million worker bees, packed onto eighteen-wheelers, and transported from Florida to the San Joaquin Valley in California. It's a long ride. On arrival they pollinate almond trees, a monoculture target with one taste. Their work complements a seven-billion-dollar industry; more than half the bees in America arrive in the valley by January. If there still aren't enough, then honeybees from Australia are flown in on 747s to complete the work force. Several weeks later, bees are loaded back on trucks and taken north to alfalfa fields in the Midwest. After a month, they may travel to the blueberry and cranberry fields in New England, and then, assuming the queen is still healthy, she goes back to her winter home in Florida. If the hives are filled with varroa mites, fungi, or viruses, many bees won't make it back, and conditions are ripe for colony collapse disorder.

To think of a queen bee as just an enforced worker or slave is misleading, for the power of this insect to attract and influence her followers is legendary. Thomas Wildman perfected the art of queen bee showmanship in the 1870s. Like Jan Swammerdam, who a century earlier found that tying a silk thread to the leg of a queen and pulling her forward would bring the rest of the colony along, Wildman would douse his worker bees with sugar solution and then take hold of the queen for his exhibition. In public display to the nobles and royalty, he conjured the colony to his chin where the attached queen waited; all the bees amazed the audience by forming a live buzzing beard. Then, after mounting a horse, he manipulated the beard to cover his chest. On dismounting and "at his word of command," the bees would return to their hive (after the queen was slipped in first). Still, his display couldn't match Mark Biancaniello's world record in 1987, in which he attracting 350,000 bees to his body with queen power.

Social Evolution

Looking at the past history of life, we see that it takes about 10^6 years to evolve a new species, 10^7 years to evolve a new genus, 10^8 years to evolve a class and less than 10^{10} years to evolve all the way from the primeval sludge to Homo Sapiens.

—F. J. Dyson, *Time Without End: Physics and Biology in an Open Universe*

The similarity between a bee colony and a human community begs an evolutionary hypothesis. How common are the survival strategies of humans and bees? Scientists write of the integrative process that, over several billion years, has taken primordial slices of bacterial life to increasingly higher levels of cellular organization. From single cell to multicellular, from mitochondria and organelles to the thousand-gene organisms, from honeybees to human beings, life has evolved into complex, diverse superorganisms—societies that we are small parts of.

It may seem derogatory to compare humans with insects,

but beekeepers note frequent parallels. Guard bees fight defensively to protect their colony, often to the point of suicidal stinging. Is it so very different from how soldiers, guerilas, and terrorists sacrifice themselves or others in defending a nation, religion, or organization? If drone bees explore the skies in search of a new queen from a different colony, doesn't that reflect the adventures of the Don Juans of our time? Social evolution and "eusocial" behavior gives communities and cultures the capacity to be "superorganisms" that work collectively for survival. Granted, human beings can be self-sufficient and extremely independent, but acquisition of resources and reproduction are basic biological drives for both humans and honeybees. The collective behavior of the colony, tribe, state, nation, and religions has a genetic pathway. How long will it take for these social entities to work in peaceful collaboration?

Kenya's political/social fabric, whether it is considered tribal or a confluence of "micro-nations," remains complex and volatile. Like the different hive structures that contain or fail to contain African bees, and not unlike the macro-nations of Europe, the U.S., Russia, China, and others competing for global resources, there is always an ongoing struggle for survival and for affluence. For bees, the angular Langstroth hive reflects an Anglo-American ethos: it is scientifically designed to maximize honey production and growth; it is built with precise right angles, as if the Western market is exactly what honeybees want. When the right Reverend Langstroth shouted Hallelujah, upon realizing the critical dimension of "bee space," it led to a rectangular hive with detachable frames allowing bees to build honey-filled comb as easily as harvesting capital investment returns.

Likewise, beginning with Jomo Kenyatta, the English-speaking Kenyan upper-class adopted and developed a Western-based economy that emphasized labor efficiency and technology so that production and growth could be accelerated. But after half a century, the model nearly collapsed, held back by trade imbalance, corruption, poor fiscal management, and the huge disparity between rich and poor. Today, Kenya's per capita GDP climbs in minute increments from a base of $700 per year, and a quarter of the population lives on less than a dollar a day. Similarly, Kenya's bees struggle with diminishing foraging land. They are not fond of the Langstroth hive. Langstroths are easy to abscond from and often raided by beekeepers in search of honey.

Canadians adapted the Kenya top bar hive (KTBH) from an ancient Greek design. Its style is theoretically attuned to the defensive, boisterous African bee, as it can be opened without alarming and mobilizing the whole colony to attack. Moreover, it is less expensive to build. The hives can even be suspended along heavy fence wires, arranged in long lines forming a perimeter around corn fields and gardens, to keep out invading pachyderms. The bee is mightier than the elephant, or at least more agile and organized. When mobilized, they attack an elephant's mucous membranes and eyes in force, so the elephants steer clear of the crops. With the living "bee fence" for protection, the farmer can harvest honey on the side.

Surprisingly more successful are the log hives in the hinterlands. These cylindrical homes are built throughout Africa and indigenous beekeepers place them high on branches above the honey badger's easy reach. Hiking into the back mountains of the Langata plains bordering Tanzania, I watch a Maasai elder named Kitingo reach barehanded into wire-wrapped logs and pull out comb after comb of honey. His method dates back for millennia. Inexpensive log hives are placed throughout a territory so that when bees migrate from one to the next following the richer foraging sites according to rainfall, colonies are continually regenerated. Each time he harvests, Kitingo prays to the bees in four directions, acknowledging his dependence on their bounty in a dry, desolate land. He has wandered off alone since his first excursion as a *morani*, a Maasai youth sent into the wilderness for six to seven years to pass through the rites of manhood. Locating a hive with honey means sustenance with concentrated sugars and protein. It makes it easy to understand why the Maasai consider bees to be harbingers of good luck. Learning the ways of survival in a sparse pastoral land, Kitingo maintains a symbiotic existence with bees by building log hives to protect them. Besides the Maasai a host of tribes—the Ogiek,

Kamba, Hadzabe, Samburu, Tugen, and Mbeere—comb through forests and dry lands in search of honey. Unfortunately, their skills are disappearing.

Modern life and material comforts sway many tribes towards Western homogenization and consumer habits. The art of honey-hunting was discouraged by the Christian missionaries, perhaps because honey, as well as being an essential dowry item for traditional marriages, is also a key ingredient in beer-making. So many honey-hunters gave up their practice that beekeepers today attribute their skills to grandfathers, not fathers. The ability to whistle out a honey guide bird (*Indicator indicator*) and to follow or be led to different hives, is no longer common.

Mama Sarah's Colony and Footprint

"We have to slaughter a rooster immediately," my grandmother exclaimed excitedly as we walked. "The occasion must be celebrated. My grandson has come from America."

—Auma Obama, *And Then Life Happens* (1)

Mama Sarah attracts visitors from all walks of life to her *dala* and impresses me with her endurance and community commitment. Having spent seven decades within a few miles of her home-squared location, watching seasons come and go, looking after children being born, neighbors and family members dying, colonialism's rise and demise, and Kenya's successes and struggles with independence, she maintained a small carbon footprint. That changed a little after Barack Obama visited her and invited her to America. She flew into Boston in 1990 to visit him at Harvard Law School.

As she took to the skies, the fields of maize and sugarcane gave way to the desolation of Sub-Saharan African deserts and the long, blue Atlantic passage. Then the continent of North America appeared. As she flew into Boston, vast grids of electric lights revealed a network that dwarfed even the night-time view of Nairobi. Her daughter, Zeituni, accompanied her to help with translation and travel and they visited Omar, her first son, who was living near Boston. Zeituni settled in the Boston area, as well, where along with Omar she faced immigration questions that caused anger and attacks from advocates for tight immigration control. She died of breast cancer in 2014. The carbon footprint for Sarah's first trip was three tons of CO_2, the airline energy used in flying to the U.S. and back.

An energy contrast between Sarah's rural life and international travel reflects the modernizing economy of Kenya and mirrors the difference of a once rural, agricultural society moving towards agribusiness and urban consolidation. The environmental impact of "developing" versus "developed" countries comes to mind. Kenya is ninety-second in the list of CO_2-producing nations. With geothermal as well as renewable energy potential, it could be a leader in changing energy requirements for future national growth, which would incentivize East Africa and the greater continent to follow. Some government and corporate forces, however, prefer to trace the wealth and fossil fuel spiral of Nigeria and Sudan. Women and villagers such as Sarah, who have spent their lives planting vegetables and trees, actually have a negative carbon footprint. Adding her four flights to America and one to Libya, the CO_2 released by the airliners is still less than that consumed by trees she planted in the front of her *dala*. Since an average Kenyan's carbon dioxide emissions are less than a ton, compared with around twenty for an American, maybe Kenya should be regarded as an ecologically "developed" country?

Meanwhile, Sarah's step grandson was creating his own footprint. Barack graduated magnum cum laude from Harvard, and in 1992, he made a second trip to visit Sarah, bringing his fiancée, Michelle. They stayed in a small bedroom in the *dala* and Michelle was shown the Luo ways of preparing *gweno* (chicken), *ugali* (maize flour porridge), *sukuma wiki* (kale), traditional Kenyan meals. Barack received Sarah's blessing for the wedding to be and must have collected more material he needed to complete his autobiography. By 1996, he had taken on a number of projects and positions in Chicago as attorney and community leader, had finished writing *Dreams from My*

Father, and was elected to the Illinois Senate. He won two more elections, although he was soundly defeated when he ran for the U.S. House of Representatives. The upward trend continued in 2004, however, with a landslide victory to the U.S. Senate. He invited Mama Sarah and members of the Obama family to the inauguration, where Sarah met with George Bush and prominent leaders of Congress. Zeituni had to pay her own way to the celebration, Omar refused to come, and family friction was inevitable. Sarah's CO_2 airline footprint climbed to six tons.

Sarah made a third to the U.S. in 2009. As she traveled with sons Malik and Said to the Presidential Inauguration, her knees ached incessantly. A thirty-hour cramped flight from equatorial Africa into the sub-freezing temperatures in D.C. was tiring, but her discomfort lessened when she sat behind Barack and Michelle. She also sat next to Edward Kennedy: her painful arthritis from eighty-seven years of living could not compare with the impact of his expanding brain tumor. Aware of the support Kennedy had given Obama during the campaign, Sarah thanked him, and after forty-seven years in the Senate working on issues of civil rights and poverty, he told her it was a happy day.

Mary and the Angry Men

Piny luorore. The world goes round. (What is here for you today, may not be here tomorrow).

—Asenath Bole Odaga, *Luo Proverbs and Sayings*

During this time Mary Onyango was still giving advice and support to women with advanced breast cancer and tolerating metastatic disease as it traveled through her bone marrow and lungs. The pain was manageable, but as the new vice-chair of the National Cohesion and Integration Commission (NCIC), she attended to another malignant process that had again invaded the national psyche—tribalism.

Rarely are deeply rooted instincts as appreciated in tribal societies as when violence breaks out. Educated Kenyans were not expecting their country to descend into mayhem when presidential elections took place in 2007, but after two and a half months of unabated destruction, murder, and uprooting of villages and cities, the need for reconciliation between Kikuyus, Luhyas, Luos, and Kalenjins was desperate. Embers of terror still burned in the fire-charred streets, along Kisumu's black-singed buildings, behind broken windows, uprooted businesses, and destroyed friendships as an eerie calm followed the post-election violence. Like cancer cells multiplying and invading different parts of Mary's body, youths laden with gasoline cans and machetes had taken on various communities in the more densely populated regions of Kenya.

As Mwai Kibaki and Raila Odinga finally came to an agree-ment and formed a coalition government, a tenuous peace fol-lowed. Nevertheless, more than half the population was less than twenty years of age and unemployment was greater than 20 percent. Competition for resources and security continued and the youth bulge continued expanding despite better fam-ily planning, use of contraception, and decreased fertility rates. Zealots and politicians had encouraged the unemployed, dis-content young men to perpetrate the post-election violence and recognizing this Mary knew her primary work was to prevent another outbreak of violence in the 2013 elections.

"What we are trying to do," she told me during our brief meetings, "is to create a nation and have an agenda that goes beyond the individual and his or her tribe."

In a dark-red headscarf and pearls, she would enter the NCIC office with a smile and a majestic wave, greet her co-workers with a bit of humor, and set to work on the issues of hate speech and tribal dissonance. The problems of the dis-placed seeking re-settlement or reparation were still reverber-ating through the country—one and a half thousand citizens killed and two hundred thousand displaced—and as the new government struggled to find a fair solution using monetary settlements, the issues of land remained as difficult as ever.

Kenyans were dismayed that their country could not con-duct peaceful elections, so the delegation of the NCIC and Mary Onyango's role in preventing further violence and hate speeches were mostly well received. But as the 2013 presidential election approached, competition escalated between two dominant parties, Jubilee and CORD. In simplest terms, Uhuru Kenyatta and William Ruto, Kikuyu and Kalenjin respectively, represented Jubilee. Raila Odinga, of Luo stock, and Kalonzo Musyoka of the Kambas, represented CORD. Musalia Mudavadi, who pulled in a majority of the Luhya tribe, also supported Jubilee and although CORD had a strong showing in early polls, there was a frenzy of competing rallies, with helicopters transporting the candidates back and forth, and the two parties headed towards a tense election.

Wangari's Tribe

In America, tribalism is alive and well. There are four kinds—class, ideology, region, and race. First class. Pretty easy. Rich folk and poor folk. Second, ideology. Liberals and conservatives. They don't merely disagree on political issues, each side believes the other is evil.

— Chimamanda Ngozi Adichie, *Americanah*, (3)

After briefly meeting Wangari Maathai in the airport, I made repeated attempts to contact her again, hoping for an interview. I never received an answer to my emails or letters and assumed it was because I was just one more writer trying to capture her scarce time. Perhaps the problem was my nationality, that I didn't belong to the right tribe, or that I was a male. Such paranoid thinking was completely unjustified and the truth was not simple.

Wangari ran as incumbent for the position of minister of Parliament in 2007. She chose not to align herself with President Kibaki's political party, and instead represented the *Mazingira* (Environment) Green Party. She lost in both the primary and the general election.

> As a Kikuyu, I was expected to follow the party of Mr.
> Kibaki, who was, along with being president, the leader
> of the Kikuyu micro-nation. Staying with the Mazingira
> Green Party was, therefore, viewed as unforgivable by
> my constituents. (4)

The dominating role of tribe had an impact not only on her, but also the ultimate direction of Kenya. Mwai Kibaki's Kikuyu-lined State House agreed to create a coalition government with the Luo-backed party of Raila Odinga, the Orange Democratic Movement (ODM), but only after pressured negotiations overseen by U.N. Secretary-General Kofi Annan and a host of international leaders. In a country with forty-two different tribes, the largest tribe had achieved a transient balance after massive social upheaval. Would a lion lie down next to a lion?

Even as Wangari expressed the need for diverse representation, the sharing of political power in Kenya became a wrestling match. Raila Odinga, whose Nyanza estate has two stone lions at the entrance to the front door, received Wangari's support as a prime minister, which further alienated her from the Kikuyu base. Kibaki and his Party of National Unity (PNU) party retained a larger share of executive privilege, and he appointed the ministers of foreign affairs, finance, internal security, defense, and energy. The ODM took portfolios such as local government, agriculture, immigration, roads, and public works. All told, the cabinet was expanded to forty ministers and fifty assistant ministers, a move many decried as too costly for effective government. Kibaki named Uhuru Kenyatta as the PNU's deputy prime minister. (See Appendix—Chapter 7, Part 1.)

As mentioned before, the contest between Uhuru Kenyatta and Raila Odinga in 2013 was markedly tribal. Joining with William Ruto, Kenyatta secured the vote of the Kalenjins and Central Kenya. Odinga had allegiance from the Luos, some Western Kenya Luhyas, and Muslims from the Coast Province, but he lost the support of Musalia Mudavadi, who led the majority of Luhyas, thus making it a tight race to the end. Kenyatta promised economic advances and a free computer to every child beginning primary school. Odinga promised economic advances and free secondary school education. Ideology and detailed programs became secondary to the "tyranny of numbers" however, and whichever candidate garnered the most tribal votes was likely to win. There was growing uncertainty about more election violence and even political punsters were not willing to offer a prediction.

Tribes and Corruption

Indeed, the postelection violence was largely due to Kenya's particular demographic crisis—70 percent of the population is under the age of 30. . . . Compounding all these factors was the rampant distrust of government institutions among the young.

—John Githongo, *Fear and Loathing in Nairobi*

Michela Wrong, in her expose, *It's Our Turn To Eat*, portrays the insidious role of tribe and graft in government finance. Documenting the tale of a whistleblower and Kikuyu gone rogue, her story of corruption is long and perplexing. It begins with an account of John Githongo, who was appointed by President Kibaki as anti-corruption czar. Githongo, frustrated with the state of affairs and government impunity, wired his chest with a microphone to record the inside discussions of graft led by the government elite. The microphone started to screech and play back as he stealthily recorded discussions in the Ministry of Finance office. His Kikuyu government colleagues looked hard at him but didn't realize they were being taped. With this as a starting point, *It's Our Turn To Eat* relates the pervasiveness of corruption in Kibaki's government and its ethnic origins.

"If in the West," Wrong tells us, "it is impossible to use the word 'tribe' without raising eyebrows, in Kenya much of what takes place becomes incomprehensible if you try stripping ethnicity from the equation." (5)

Looking for solutions to the discord, and no longer minister of Parliament, Wangari Maathai set to work writing *The Challenge for Africa*, first released in 2009. Her book offered a different perspective on balancing tribal elements and even on the use of the word *tribe*. Eschewing negative connotations, she argued for the celebration of *micro-nations*. The forty-two tribes, or micro-nations, that made up the larger Kenyan nation would express their uniqueness, different languages, and character strengths, thereby transcending the domination of one culture and the gridlock of two opposing sides.

"Our different identities are part of a natural diversity," she said. "Instead of all attempting the impossible task of being the same, we must learn to embrace our diversity. Indeed, human beings are stronger for it."

Wangari's writing excludes stereotypes and leaves out comical references as to how one distinguishes, say, a Kikuyu from a Luo. (When two babies are found alone in a nursery, you place a coin between the two. The Kikuyu will immediately reach for the coin while the Luo is adjusting his designer diaper). The Maasai are the proud and dangerous security guards and watchmen. (Watch out for your cattle. The Maasai believe all cattle belong to them, including cows in Texas, Colorado, and California). The Kalenjins are a diverse congregation of aloof and remote pastoralists, and so on. Such stereotypes tend to isolate and minimize the uniqueness and strengths of different cultures, and Wangari's sober theme in *The Challenge for Africa* unifies these tribes into a larger nation—or what E.O. Wilson calls a superorganism.

Barack Obama's autobiography describes the ethnic tension between two larger cultures, Kenyans and Indians. When the British brought 32,000 Indians to Kenya to build the Uganda Railway, the ones who stayed eventually developed an entrenched business and trade sector that continues to be respected and sometimes resented by native Kenyans.

> "You see how arrogant they are?" Barack's sister, Auma, tells him, as they watch the interactions between an Indian woman and her black clerks. "They call themselves Kenyans, but they want nothing to do with us. As soon as they make their money, they send it off to London or Bombay."
>
> "How can you blame Asians for sending their money out of the country," Barack asks Auma, "after what happened in Uganda?" (6)

He refers to the expulsion of Indian East Africans by Idi Amin in the 1970s and tries to defend Third World solidarity. His Kenyan relatives, however, contradict him as he reports in his autobiography,

> Even Jane or Zeituni could say things that surprised me. "The Luo are intelligent but lazy" they would say. Or

"The Kikuyu are money-grubbing but industrious." Or "The Kalenjins—well, you can see what's happened to the country since they took over." (6)

Young Obama is viewed as naïve when he touches on a theme Wangari made central to her own work. While Obama stressed that we are all part of the human tribe, Wangari comes back to recognition of the distinct cultures that enrich the larger union. She stresses the critical role of family and the need for Africa's men to play a central role.

> Since the earliest days of slavery, through colonialism and beyond, virtually the entire economic system of sub-Saharan Africa has depended on uprooting the African man and forcing him explicitly or by default to seek employment away from his home. (4)

The theme of community strength and recognition of the environment, brings us to a unique tribe Wangari once worked with. Family represents the evolving strength of earliest human culture—two million years ago for Homo erectus, and two hundred thousand years ago for Homo sapiens—since 90 percent of our time on earth has been spent as hunter-gatherers made up of small groups of families. To disrupt the family unit suggests undoing genetic design and causing long-term imbalance. Wangari's work in the Kenya's forests brought her in contact with several indigenous tribes, but one in particular experienced great disruption.

The Ogieks

Merely the attempt to solve the biodiversity crisis offers great benefits never before enjoyed, for to save species is to study them closely, and to learn them well is to exploit their characteristics in novel ways.

—Edward O. Wilson, *The Diversity of Life*, 1999

As I followed the bees and Wangari's footsteps, I was also led to a hunting and foraging tribe known as the Ogiek. Dating back to before written records, the Ogieks inhabited the Mau Forest preceding the migration and incursion of the Nandi, Kipsigis, Maasai, and Kikuyus. *Ogiek* means, literally, *caretaker of all plants and wild animals.* Their early migration into the forested areas of Kenya from coastal East Africa, which was due to attacks by slave traders and various competing communities, began the pattern of displacement that currently threatens a tenuous forest existence. As hunters and foragers, they never had large numbers. After successfully fighting off and establishing a balance of territory with the Maasai in the 1850s, they were disrupted by the arrival of the colonial powers. In 1911 and 1932, the British signed agreements with the Maasai that dispossessed the Ogiek of their ancestral lands. Forced evictions from the Mau took place in successive years, and each time tribe members found their way back to the forest, they were evicted again as soon as they were rediscovered. The greatest usurpations resulted from the 1937–1938 Kenya Land Commission, when administrators evicted members of the tribe and placed them on European farms as squatters and labor camp workers. They were used to assist in their own demise by clearing the forest of indigenous trees and replanting it with exotic timber.

In the post-independence era, the Ogiek had a fifteen-year breathing period. By 1977, however, the Kenyatta government banned game hunting, and the Ogiek were regarded as trespassers and squatters. At the behest of the Rift Valley Provincial Commissioner, government forces invaded the Mau West Forest, torching homes and confiscating and arresting members of the community. The Moi government further displaced the Ogieks by not allowing them to keep livestock or to farm near the forest. Meanwhile, Kalenjin and other communities moved quickly to gain access to unoccupied land. Throughout these challenges, the Ogiek have organized a representative body of elders, currently known as the Ogiek Welfare Council, that focuses on education, on bringing national and international awareness to their plight, and on lobbying government authorities to restore indigenous land rights.

It was natural that Wangari Maathai and the Green Belt Movement would connect with the Ogiek. Their lifestyle, based on subsisting alone in the forest, made them quick to adopt a program of planting native trees. They hoped to reestablish the Mau and other forests that had succumbed to monoculture plantations. In fact, they were already maintaining the forests, despite a century of government directives seeking to displace them from one of Kenya's five water towers. Anthropologist Guy Yeoman described the Ogiek as

> Shy and diffident people, of engaging gentleness and charm, considerable intelligence, of quite astonishing technical expertise in their special arts of hunting and bee-keeping, and having a most unusual sensibility in relation to their forests and the creatures which inhabit them. (7)

Having fought off and outlasted the Maasai and the colonialists, they were not going to walk away from their land at the insistence of any government.

I wanted to know more about Ogiek honey-hunting. My first contact came through a last-minute email contact with a nonprofit called Ecoterra. The Bushman knew I had a fascination with bees and he was eager to assist in exploring a more pristine habitat. Tom and I called in Kevin to be our driver and set off to visit the top of the Mau Forest. Provided a cell phone number and a name, we left Kisumu in a white Nissan compact. Ubiquitous on the roads, these cars are sometimes referred to as "flying coffins."

Fly we did. Kevin drove over worn-down tarmac and car-swallowing potholes, weaving nonchalantly among trucks and suicidal pedestrians. Traffic was like a bi-directional meningitis, with motorists vying for any open space and Kevin risking life in order to gain a one-second advantage. The usual menagerie of herded and non-herded animals plied the roadside along with *piki pikis* (motorcycles) bearing household furniture and coffins. Bicycles were stacked perpendicularly with sugarcane and lumber, and small children walked in groups to and from school, while luckless dogs, usually the first to get turned into roadside corpses, littered the perimeter of townships. I began to understand the moniker *flying coffin*, especially when seasoned by Kevin's appetite for speed and kinship with Matatu drivers.

"Kevin," I cry out, as a lorry tries to pass us. He refuses to allow it since another truck is approaching in the lane in front of us. "Slow down! Slow down!"

The usual response follows: "Okay, you drive."

And so I do, my hair turning white as a hoary coffin on our way to the Western Mau. Meanwhile, the Bushman tells stories about the lesser and greater flamingos, soda lake algae eaters that used to fill up the sky over Lake Nakuru in numbers of a million and more. He laments their slow disappearance, attributing it to the pollution of the lake from factories and pesticide runoff. Also disturbing are the constant phone calls Kevin is receiving, one after another. He tells us he's being called back to work for his father and that he must leave Tom and I. Tom discerns a more sinister note to the conversations as we pull into Nakuru, so I give Kevin the fare to return to Siaya by bus. His life on the edge is about to become more precarious.

Guy Yeoman's observations about the gentle nature of the Ogiek is accurate. Our first contact is Leonard Midore, a field guide and social worker, at the Midlands Hotel. As we order soft drinks at a poolside table, he's so shy and soft-spoken that we have to lean forward to hear his words. He refers to the slow path of extinction the Ogiek tribe faces. He has the persona of a young man who's experienced a lifetime of disappointments, but who will never give in to them.

"We continue to live on a very small part of the forested land that once was ours," he says, sipping on a Fanta and glancing around the hotel setting. "I don't know exactly why you have come here, but I will assist you if you are willing to help us. Many groups come here. They always say they will help, and they provide funding for this help, but we never get to see where this money goes."

"How many of you are there?" I ask. The tables next to us are filled with well-dressed Kikuyus and businessmen visiting Nakuru.

"Maybe five to seven thousand here," he offers. "It is hard

to say. We are now scattered over several parts of the Mau. The Ogieks live in many parts of Kenya, including Mt. Elgon, and altogether might make up twenty thousand. Many have moved into the cities. They no longer have their language."

"I'm here to see the bees," I tell him. "It would be great if you could show me how you do your honey-hunting."

"Okay, we can start in the morning. I'll take you to the home of Simon, one of the elders. He will lead us."

After the endurance drive from Kisumu, I hope for some rest and a meal. The Bushman and I spend the night at the Egerton University, where we find clean beds, but I spend most of the time visiting the bathroom, suffering from a bout of dysentery that I hope will be gone by sunup.

A few antibiotic tablets, a little sleep, and breakfast precede our journey up into the mountains. We meet Simon, one of the Ogiek elders. He's in his sixties and has the lean sinewy features that come from a life spent in the wilderness. Now he's moved out of the high forest and built a home in the foothills, where he constructs log hives and raises bees. He leads me to a bush-enclosed bee yard where a few log hives are hidden and after crawling into the dense thicket to take photos with an iPhone, I'm quickly discovered by the inhabitants. An African stinger finds its way into my left earlobe. The bees don't like the clicking sound of the camera and rather than leaving the banana-like scent of isopentyacetate (alarm pheromone) for all the bees to follow, I make a quick exit from the enclosure and head back to Simon's house. Simon follows with a big smile.

We're joined by Leporore Mutarakwa, a younger beekeeper who, like his father, has little interest in farming. He manages around one hundred hives that are hidden throughout the forest, and his torn clothing suggests he works hard to manage them.

Like other forest dwellers, Leporore hunts for antelope, hyrax, and wild boar, using a bow and arrow. His only competition is an occasional leopard, hyena, or non- Ogiek hunter carrying a rifle. Honey remains the primary cash crop for the tribe, and honey-harvesters can collect up to sixty kilograms (132 pounds) a day when the dry season starts.

FIGURE 16: Leporore Mutarakwa with Antelope-Skin Cape and Bag

We pack the flying coffin and drive up into the forest, beginning at an elevation of four thousand feet, taking dirt roads that make Kenya's highways look friendly, and then are stopped by a felled tree in the road. The forest once was filled with cedars, blue gums, conifers, olives, and oaks. What remains are plantations of monoculture conifers. A small group of Kikuyu workers, mostly women, is cutting down firewood for charcoal. They have one burro to help carry the loads, its hide rubbed down to raw muscle from the long downhill trips.

We park next to the felled tree and set off on *waktah*, the broad paths used by outsiders. Ogiek foragers prefer to travel on the *wakta*, the indigenous pathways, and sometimes on the *irongiit*, the animal pathways, that lead away from the farms and to more pristine pastures and groves. After a few hours of hiking, we find a log hive located high in an indigenous tree (*tong 'o tuet*). It looks impossible to climb without equipment. Having spent my youth climbing trees for fun and having worked as a novice arborist, what I see next impresses me. Leporore and Simon gather liana moss and wood shavings into a small collection. Then, they take a long stick and spin it between their hands over a machete blade until friction ignites the arboreal package into a burning smoke system. This moss is tucked into Leporore's antelope skin bag. He takes the machete again and creates a bamboo ladder, using a root from the *pisinda* vine to hold it together. Within minutes, he ascends forty feet into the canopy, small branches cracking under his bare feet, and arrives next to the hive.

Wearing just an antelope-skin cape and with the bag to collect honey, Leporore begins by smoking one end of the dark, hollow log. The queen bee and her assemblage move to the opposite end of the hive, so the harvest is primarily honeycomb and grub. The bees continue to protect their bounty, however, as Leporore spends fifteen minutes pulling out golden sections containing brood and larvae, gently brushing off the attendants and setting the pieces into his bag. The bees are more submissive under a smoke blanket blown from the moss smoker, so when he finally comes down, only his face is covered with pursuers. He has lowered thirty pounds of comb and honey in the antelope skin bag to Simon, and immediately the Ogieks begin eating their prize. They pass large chunks to the Bushman and I, and perhaps the dense honey and wax does my dysentery some good. I feel stronger after a long day of hiking.

"What happens when someone raids one of the clan territories and takes the honey?" I ask.

"It is not a good thing to do," Simon explains. Because of his age, he's no longer climbing trees, but his soiled trousers and tattered jacket, like Leporore's, show that he's still active. His lean, round face occasionally frowns.

"If they are caught with the honey or trying to sell it, they will be questioned. If they are truthful and confess to the act of stealing, they will be fined and required to make a payment.

They must give up a cow or a goat. But if they do not tell the truth and conceal their act, they will have a curse put upon them. Such men will die or suffer great misfortune."

"And how might they die?" I ask, while watching water flow down a creek that joins the Njoro River, a major tributary to Lake Nakuru and Naivasha. The Mau Forest water tower provides around 40 percent of Kenya's water.

"A curse can work in many ways," Simon continues. "The dishonest man may fall victim to a bad accident, or he may just lose his appetite and wither away."

Ogieks living in or near cities have been exposed to HIV/AIDS. When their land was taken, they lost access to schools, and few of their children could afford to attend, so their illiteracy rate has been as high as 90 percent, and remains high. (See Appendix—Chapter 7, Part 2.) It would not be surprising for an individual who steals from the community to also have been exposed to HIV. But Simon's description of social justice refers to the years before the virus appeared, suggesting that the psychological impact of expulsion from the tribe can be as overwhelming as AIDS.

Although traditionally they were hunters, the Ogieks tend to be nonviolent and rarely if ever use physical punishment. While extremely agile with bows and arrows, which helped them fend off the spear-wielding Maasai, they are by nature protective, peaceful people. This became evident one night as I slept in the Mau Forest along with the Bushman and my son. The four Ogieks we visited in a makeshift shelter stayed up all night to watch over us. In the early morning hours, they prayed for the animals and the bees of the forest to be plentiful. They asked that God protect the forest and all its inhabitants, including us. I was told they have followed this tradition through as many generations as they can remember.

The Ogiek ability to follow bees and harvest honey is undisputed, so I asked Leporore and Simon, the elder, why they don't use Langstroth hives. Leporore has a hundred log hives that are spread throughout the Mau Forest, placed high in the trees where he can pull down sixty kilograms of honey on a good day. He never gives a thought to medicating or feeding his bees; he follows their natural feeding pattern and lives in balance with them. Simon, the Ogiek elder, points to a log hive he built and explains to me, "There is no need to make it more complicated. The bee is the best engineer. Her design has been around the longest."

Opening Day of Matibabu Hospital – January 27, 2012

Ng'ama dwaro ema rudo. It is he/she who searches who finds.

—Asenath Bole Odaga, *Luo Proverbs and Sayings*

The Bushman and I hike down through three hundred acres of forest that recently burned to the ground when a charcoal making operation went badly. We set off for Kisumu and Nyanza district in the flying coffin, headed for the opening of the Matibabu Hospital. Dignitaries are arriving from Nairobi and America to be part of the festivities, and we want to see it firsthand. Dan Ogola calls several times to see if I can convince Mama Sarah to attend as a guest of honor. I reach her through a distant relation, Nelson, who says she already has an important engagement and can't make the trip.

After three days of driving, hiking the Mau Forest, and resolving a bout of dysentery, it takes a single beer before I fall into a deep slumber in the country home of Wenwa Odinga, the ambassador/consul to the U.S. Early the next morning, we're pounding potholes again on our way to Mama Sarah's *dala* to pick up Nelson. We arrive midday when everyone is outside.

"*Osaore*," I greet Sarah in Luo, "*Ihde nade?*"

"*Ahde maber*" she answers, which means all is fine; it is the customary response to "How are you?" She seems comfortable as she shucks corn onto a woven mat, encircled by a few chickens and turkeys that are chasing loose morsels that roll away from the pile. She's satisfied to stay home and avoid a long drive in the flying coffin. Loading up Nelson, the Bushman, and two other passengers, we set off for Ukwala, a two-hour drive across more tarmac, dirt roads, trenches, and finally, the flat earth of Wananyiera, where the celebration is getting underway.

Seated at a table with dignitaries under one of four large

tents, Gail Wagner endures a celebrity role as benefactor. A huge, gold-colored pendant, or medal, is placed around her neck, but being the only Westerner at the front table is enough to single her out. She has flown into Kenya a day or so early, and at her side, other dignitaries, wearing suits and dresses, are thankful for the shade and fan themselves in the equator's midday heat. Ambassador/Consul Wenwa Odinga is the guest of honor and is joined by Minister of Land, James Orengo, his wife Betty Murungi, and an assemblage of national and district opinion leaders—the gatekeepers. I'm offered a chair in a nearby tent with some colleagues who have been up all night traveling from a medical mission in Rwanda.

Dan smiles, extending his hand to everyone who passes.

"Ahhh-yahh-yahh-yahh-yahh-yahh-yahh-yah-yah-yeeee!"

A woman's high-pitched ululations fill the air, her excitement uncontainable. Three other red-and-green tents fill up, and along the perimeter fence, children stand frozen, gazing at the notables and assemblage. Their cattle wander off, but it's a banner day in Wananyiera. The rhythm of drums, dancers, and voices join in chorus.

"Welcome to the Matibabu Women and Children's Hospital." Job Akuno, master of ceremonies, greets us in a flowing white gown and turban hat. "It is at this stage we roll on with the program."

He takes in the wide spectrum of people—wananchi, community workers, contributors, ministers, doctors, architects, lawyers, an electrician, nurses, community health workers, accountants, web designers, *muzungus* (White people), and prospective patients—Kenya's diverse community.

"I was telling a story while you were arriving," he goes on. "The story was about this man who had a dream." He glances over at Dan, dressed in a gray suit, restraining his Cheshire smile. "The young man, just like many other young people, traveled to the city of many lights and looked for these lights in none other than the Kibera Slums." He pauses and looks eastward, in the direction of Nairobi, then begins again.

"This young man had to make one of those hard choices —to join them or for them to join him. He had to determine

FIGURE 17: Staying Cool in the Shade

whether he was going to accept them and whether they would dictate his life or whether he had to chart a future that would be brighter for him and the community." Pause. "The young man chose to have the other young people join him, and join him they did. He formed a youth group and they began promoting education because they believed that with education at whatever stage you could actually make a difference."

Dr. Wagner looks at Job and Dan and then at the white circular building behind them, the first of the hospital's planned modules. How improbable that a local boy, with few cattle, would wear a suit and become the subject of this monologue. But she had encouraged him as much as he had conjured and inspired her to bring Western medicine to the rural edge of the country. More important, Dan's mother had imbued in him a desire to help others. He was three when his father died. His mother looked to him, as the firstborn son, to lead the family. His younger brother died of malaria a year later, and the importance of health never left his mind.

"This young man, having been part of a community initiative, met one interesting young lady."

Eyes switch back to Dr. Wagner, sitting in front of the notables and holding the medal of honor, girding herself to endure more praise.

"And this young woman whose interest in the community was beyond giving handouts—it wasn't about 'take this and go home'—having had that engagement with the young man, went on to begin what we see here."

In the stifling heat, with no breeze and beneath a small mercy of canopy shade, I think of the tensions and struggles that occurred between Gail and Dan. For five years, their synergy included a balance as well as a struggle for determining the vision and institutional development of Matibabu. Dan, close to his community and all of its needs, saw the social matrix and was an actor in its center. Dr. Wagner mobilized resources and institutional knowledge, though often from a distance. Over the years, in very simplest terms, she gave, and Dan asked. There was, of course, a give and take in hospitality and sharing of family and culture. As Americans and Kenyans come closer in their relationships, there were also inevitable strains. Dan, the master of inspiration and enthusiasm, reached a point of momentum that was difficult to slow down. Dr. Wagner, as a full-time oncologist, discerned the bottomless well common to nonprofit ventures in Kenya.

Job Akuno's expression "city of many lights" conveys hope, but this is an interface of two individuals and cultures with resources as different as the Silicon Valley and the Kibera slums. Energetic, tireless, and evangelical, Dan is on the wave of a new level of health care and education for his entire region, no less remarkable given his humble beginnings. It comes with a struggle and competition of dedicated leadership. A few months earlier, I had been in Dr. Wagner's office in California and could almost hear Dan requesting more help through his cell phone. He was calling from Nairobi, ten thousand miles away. As Gail hung up, she looked at me saying, "I want to make him go stand in the corner. If I was his mother, I would just spank him!"

Program announcements are being used as fans, and Dr. Wagner is given a chance to address the audience. Dan introduces her with the honorary surname of *Adhiambo* (born in the day), and she walks to the microphone.

"I have never met people like you before," she says to the assemblage. "You are amazing! You are proactive! And you understand what you need."

She enunciates slowly, so that her American English is easily understood. She pauses for a moment to let the words motivate and connect.

"You're not sitting there waiting for somebody to give it to you. You're doing it."

Have Kenyans previously been depending too much on the many international NGOs? In this project the builders have all been Kenyan. The architect, planners, journeymen, and construction workers are in the audience. Many of the bricklayers are women. Some of these women would otherwise have made wages with illegal beer production or even prostitution. Instead, they have earned money by doing work beneficial for their children.

"You built this hospital. We provided some resources. But the people who built this hospital with their hands are the people of this community. This is your hospital!"

The bricklayers like the statement, once it has been translated.

"And I'm incredibly proud to be able to say I'm associated with you. It's a huge honor. And like Dan said, this is the first step. We now have to figure out who will take the second step. But we took the first one, so we'll take the second one."

Gail pauses, her curly hair still wind-swept from the drive to the event. She's at home with the Luo audience and avoids eulogizing. There remains a huge funding gap to finish building the hospital and presidential elections are a year off. If Raila Odinga wins, things will be looking up. If not, who can say?

"As long as you are working for yourself," she concludes, "we will be working with you."

The speeches finish and the crowd presses into the thick-walled, air-conditioned new hospital. It's like entering a five-star hotel. Shiny stainless steel bathrooms, immaculate white toilets, electrical circuits connecting an intercom from the second story

FIGURE 18: Matibabu Hospital – First Building

nurse's station to the circumferential rooms. There's a spotless patina ready to absorb the effluents of pain, disease, and suffering, as well as the cries of newborns, and I wonder how soon the next buildings will come and how easily Dan and Dr. Wagner will work together in the financial challenges that lie ahead.

8

The Magic Window

*The relevance of aid to Africa cannot possibly be in doubt.
Indeed, it is as relevant in its own way as AIDS, civil war
and famine are in theirs: it is one of the defining characteristics
of Africa*

—Maina Mwangi, *Why Aid Has Failed Africa So Spectacularly* (1)

Who Needs the Peace Corps?

During the late 1960s, I joined an organization often attributed
to the inspiration of Sargent Shriver and JFK. Disillusioned with
a foreign policy inspired by CIA intelligence and with Cold War
competition that placed Americans in the midst of a distant
civil war, I merged with the youthful Aquarian generation of
peace and love. Instead of dropping bombs onto the rice fields
of Cambodia and Vietnam, as military training had prepared

me to do, I resigned from the ROTC, studied principles of non-violence, and entered the world of rice and wheat farming. Near the southern borderland of Nepal, known as the Terai, my status in a small village was that of celebrity and outsider. I looked different, struggled to speak four local languages, and knew little about agriculture. Like most volunteers, I was fired up with idealism.

For two years, we introduced methods of the Green Revolution—hybrid seeds, fertilizer, irrigation, and pesticides—which had boosted yields two- to three-fold in many parts of India. The villagers didn't like the taste of the new crops, and it was difficult to win their cooperation. By the second year, our group of volunteers was reduced by half, decimated by dysentery, loneliness, and the sometimes complete madness of college graduates immersed in a culture thousands of miles from home. There were, however, perks.

We struggled to make a difference in villages where an extra pound of rice could fend off starvation. In the summer months, just before monsoons, we escaped 115-degree heat spells and hitched rides up the winding Rajpath into the Kathmandu valley. Waiting in the back of a small, white, unguarded Peace Corps office, was a special-delivery point known as the "Magic Window." A petite woman, a Newari with friendly eyes, brass earrings, and a *tika* on her forehead, smiled as we handed her a requisition slip for a few hundred rupees. Conjuring up the currency, she passed it through a "magic" window on the door. It was an act based on trust, an attribute as mysterious as the idealism of volunteers.

Trust became an issue for me one morning when a young man appeared at the open window of my mud-and-wattle hut. His left eye dangled loosely from its socket and I shuddered at the prospect of trying to repair the damaged globe.

"No, no," he said, noting how focused I was on a useless eye, "My hand is caught in the machine. You are the American. You have medicine!"

He raised his right hand; it had been severely crushed between metal cylinders of a sugarcane press and stripped of its flesh until bone was exposed. It was much worse than the dangling eyeball, and with a recent degree in psychology and no medical training, all I could offer was Jungian therapy. Following his advice, I took out a tube of Neosporin from a medical kit, covered the hand with white cream, and then wrapped it up with gauze.

I didn't see the man for a few weeks. When he appeared again outside the hut window, his left eye was still dangling, but this time, he was smiling. He held up his right hand. Miraculously, it had healed. I gave him a few vitamin pills, shook his left hand, and learned to appreciate his good eye, just as he did.

Few remember Hubert Humphrey's vision, and that he first proposed a bill to the Senate in 1957, recommending the establishment of a voluntary international corps. Members of the Senate regarded it as a "silly and unworkable idea." Then, in 1960, John F. Kennedy suggested a similar concept at two a.m. to an audience of ten thousand students from the University of Michigan, and the idea was resurrected. The students had stayed up late to hear Kennedy's message while he was campaigning for the presidency. Kennedy's "ask what you can do for your country" enthusiasm was readily absorbed by the audience, who, in the next few weeks, sent thirty thousand letters supporting the idea. Richard Nixon was not impressed and derided the plan as a "cult of escapism" and a "haven for draft dodgers." He was joined by Eisenhower, who called it "Kennedy's juvenile experiment." But Nixon later came around and tried to steer the program into a more sophisticated technical support enterprise. Subsequent administrations have emphasized either the technical or social side of the organization, often based on Republican or Democratic philosophy.

The concept and development of the Peace Corps modeled earlier efforts by an African American minister, James Robinson, who had once been chased out of his Tennessee home by a lynch mob for encouraging blacks to vote. Robinson formed Operation Crossroads Africa (OCA) in 1958, based on the belief that Americans could serve in Africa in the fields of medicine, engineering, and education. Rather than using ministers, the

OCA sent students and professionals to build water systems, schools, clinics, and orphanages. Within a few years, thousands of teachers were trained, and by 1970, over four thousand students had served in the OCA. (2) Following this lead, the Peace Corps began its first assignments in Ghana and Tanzania.

What motivates young adults to travel abroad and face the challenges of different languages, cultures, and new living conditions? Since 1961, 200,000 Peace Corps Volunteers (PCV) have worked in 139 different countries. Their ventures carry risks: 284 volunteers have never returned as a result of deaths from motor vehicle accidents, falls, murders, suicides, shark attacks, elephant stampedes and other unhappy causes. Over 1,000 sexual assaults and rapes were reported in a ten-year period. Kate Puzey, a volunteer in Benin, Africa, was found dead on her porch with a slit throat after she courageously exposed a national employee who had raped and molested students. This led to a Peace Corps Volunteer Protection Act, signed into law in 2011, which required "sexual assault risk-reduction and response training" as well as policies ensuring oversight. As is often the case, politics and challenges have prevailed since then, but the Peace Corps has intensified its support system. Today, two-thirds of volunteers are women and one-third are men, exactly the opposite of the first few decades.

"The Peace Corps is stuck in a rut," notes Lex Rieffel of the Brookings Institute, who every five years issues a report on the failure of the half-century-old organization to adapt to national and global changes. While there has been bipartisan support for doubling the Corps, barely half the number of volunteers sign up today as in the Sixties, and fewer young people are applying. Given a budget that is one-tenth of one percent of the military budget, the equivalent of fifty years of service cost, compared to five days for the defense department, it might be time to improve soft diplomacy. China spends a third as much as the U.S. on defense and now has DF-21D missiles that could render our newly designed aircraft carriers obsolete in the China Sea. Were the Pentagon to cancel one new $14 billion aircraft carrier, it could increase the number of Peace Corps volunteers ten-fold for a four-year period.

Kenya's Peace Corps volunteers were withdrawn in August of 2014 after episodes of terrorism were perpetrated by Al Shabab at the Westgate Mall in Nairobi and at the coastline border with Somalia. Besides the risks of terrorism, other challenges of working in Kenya are significant. Sometimes referred to as "agents of the CIA," the volunteers spend two difficult years in villages learning new languages. They teach healthcare, science, and agriculture, and they don't always receive recognition for their effort. So how could fifty thousand Peace Corps volunteers accomplish what five thousand sailors can do on an aircraft carrier? And what motivates young women and men, either in the Peace Corps or the military, to volunteer for difficult assignments?

Accepting E.O. Wilson's concept of a superorganism, an answer lies in eusocial behavior, which gives a survival advantage to any group or colony over and above any advantage of individual competition. The multiplying organizations for international service, such as the Peace Corps, Partners in Health, Doctors without Borders, Volunteers of America, the Red Cross, Rotary International—an estimated six thousand nonprofits and NGOs in Kenya and more than fifty-two thousand worldwide—can be viewed through the perspective of biology. Wilson's concept of eusocial species, in which "the worker caste is selected to maximize colony efficiency in intercolony competition," is manifested in the altruistic behavior of young and old volunteers who travel to foreign countries, provide help and experience to different cultures, and exhibit group selection behavior by benefiting the superorganisms they represent. Military service can be seen in the same perspective.

Eusocial species are rare in the biological world. Bees, ants, termites, and wasps represent a very few species of insects that have evolved with organized brood care, division of labor, and other social characteristics promoting survival. So also, Homo sapiens represent a mammalian order colonizing the planet in an "organized" fashion that elevates the group over the individual.

"At the higher level of the two relevant levels of biological organization, groups compete with groups, favoring cooperative social traits among members of the same group. At the lower level, members of the same group compete with one another in a manner that leads to self-serving behavior. The opposition between the two levels of natural selection has resulted in a chimeric genotype in each person. It renders each of us part saint and part sinner." (3)

Peace Corps volunteers (soft diplomacy) along with international workers such as the armed forces (hard diplomacy) are prime examples of sacrifice on behalf of a larger social mission. The altruistic actions may coincide with individual motivation, fulfilling needs such as recognition, greater meaning, or the simple satisfaction of giving of oneself. So, who needs the Peace Corps? Most volunteers are quick to acknowledge that they need the opportunity to learn from other cultures as much as other cultures need their skills. So perhaps the large answer is that there is a biologic need for us to reach beyond our own cultures, developing or developed.

Soft Diplomacy

Aid won't make poverty history. Only the self-reliant efforts of poor people and societies themselves can end poverty.

—William Easterly, *The White Man's Burden*

In Kenya today, you have to struggle just to locate the well-protected Peace Corps office. Entering requires passage through metal detectors scanned by security cameras, guards with automatic rifles, and a thick, steel gate that blocks the entry of bomb-laden vehicles. The volunteers are gone for now, and twenty dollars from a magic window might purchase dinner in Nairobi, but not much more.

Meanwhile, the benevolent magic window has evolved into a global system of foreign aid that since the 1950s has distributed more than 2.3 trillion dollars to the developing world! In an ongoing debate, economist Jeffrey Sachs argues that this gargantuan donation makes a positive difference. The U.S., he tells us, and all developed countries, should increase foreign aid to at least 0.7 percent of gross national product (GNP). Then, there will be global convergence of disparate economies, the world will become safer, the bottom billion richer, and projects in Africa such as the Millennium Development Goals will be successful. It sounds straightforward.

This is "nonsense," according to free-market economist William Easterly. Centralized planning is utopian and foreign aid interferes with effective growth and development by diminishing self-reliance. Bureaucratically laden bilateral, unilateral, and multilateral systems of chauvinistic aid may boost self-esteem and self-interest for developed countries, but indigenous, grassroots solutions targeted by the people themselves are what transform society.

"It's so obvious. I'm embarrassed even to lay it out," Easterly maintains. "But it's worth laying out only because it is the opposite of the present Western effort to transform the Rest."

According to Easterly, there are six ways to incentivize the poor.

1) Have aid agents who are individually accountable for individual, feasible areas of action that help poor people lift themselves up.

2) Let those agents search for what works, based on past experience in their area.

3) Experiment, based on the results of the search.

4) Evaluate, based on feedback from the intended beneficiaries and scientific testing.

5) Reward success and penalize failure. Get more money to interventions that are working, and take money away from interventions that are not working.

6) Make sure the incentives in Step Five are strong enough to do more of what works, then repeat Step Four. If action fails, make sure incentives in Step Five are strong enough to send the agent back to Step One. If the agent keeps failing, get a new one. (4)

Numerical hopscotch? Isn't "reward success and penalize failure" the same old have-and-have-not tradeoff, with the haves being successful and getting all the benefits?

Easterly contrasts so-called "central planners" with "searchers," and gives a textbook discourse on why limited and local solutions work better than large-scale, top-down approaches. He takes constant aim at Sachs and steers away from the global perspective that massive ecological, financial, and health crises are coming too soon to ignore. Rather than large-scale solutions, he advocates targeted projects, such as Polio Plus, Matibabu, MedShare, and Preventing Cervical Cancer—local solutions to widespread health problems. (See Appendix—Chapter 8.)

A good example of large scale and also targeted aid is the Rotary International's effort to eliminate Polio: among the largest non-military projects in human history. As the widest spread service organization in the world, with 1.2 million members and 34,000 clubs, Rotary International began a limited effort in 1978 to vaccinate children in the Philippines. In 1985 Rotary pledged $120 million to the Polio Plus program and funded an expert panel to guide a global effort. Some health authorities suggested that Rotary was "just a service club"; unlikely to succeed in such an ambitious global effort. (5) But after joining with the WHO, UNICEF, CDC, and the Bill and Melinda Gates Foundation, Rotary has helped immunize two and a half billion children. There were four hundred cases of polio in 2013, compared with one hundred twenty thousand in 1964, and only two countries, Pakistan and Afghanistan, remain with uncontrolled virus. It is estimated that Rotarians will help raise $1.2 billion by the time the disease is completely gone, and as of today twenty million volunteers have helped in administering vaccines. RI works on a grass roots level through a widely connected international system and provides "service above self" where it's needed.

Bailing out the Bottom Billion:
BOPs, TOPs, and the *Wazungu*

Easterly is right to mock the delusions of the aid lobby. But just as [Jeffrey] Sachs exaggerates the payoff to aid, Easterly exaggerates the downside and again neglects the scope for other policies. We are not as impotent and ignorant as Easterly seems to think.

—Paul Collier, *The Bottom Billion* (6)

Kenya is illustrative of both successes and failures in the strange world of foreign assistance, and some failures seem to stand out more. Few have experienced or described it as graphically as Sir Edmond Clay, the British high commissioner, when he addressed a British and Kenyan audience in July of 2004.

"We never expected corruption to be vanquished overnight. We all implicitly recognized that some would be carried over to the new era. We hoped it would not be rammed in our faces. But it has."

Clay looked down before delivering his next sentence to the press and intelligentsia, as they sipped bottled water and waited for the description of the government's foreign-aid consumption habits.

"They may expect we shall not see, or notice, or will forgive them a bit of gluttony, but they can hardly expect us not to care when their gluttony causes them to vomit all over our shoes." (7)

To the shocked audience, he went on to decry the pervasiveness of non- transparent finances that were bloating higher administration officials. His visual impression was not well received by the British State Department, let alone by the Kenyans, but it was backed up with facts. An in depth investigation by Kroll and Associates (U.K.) led to reports of $3 billion disappearing during the twenty-four years of Daniel arap Moi's presidency. (8, 9) In an expose of the Moi and Kibaki government's high-level corruption, Michela Wrong points to tribalism and chronic foreign aid dependence to explain how successive regimes feel "it's our turn to eat."

Between years 2000 and 2005, four projects in Kenya worth $375 million were investigated by the World Bank. Three of the four projects had "serious irregularities," ranging from "bribing of public officials to abuse of office, inflated expenses, fraudulent claims, conflict of interest, the concerted rigging of bids, failure to carry out allotted tasks, and blatant nepotism by MPs. Two of the projects were AIDS related, and the report compilers highlighted one of the most obscenely ironic consequences of the abuse: because grant money went to bribe officials rather than being spent on orphan's school fees, many children dropped out of education and resorted to prostitution. A project intended to reduce HIV infection helped, instead, to spread the virus." (10)

Daniel arap Moi was succeeded by Mwai Kibaki in 2002, at which time Kibaki assured his country that "corruption will cease to be a way of life in Kenya." Kibaki's Kikuyu-based government, a.k.a. the "Mount Kenya Mafia," then presided over the Anglo-Leasing scandal. A decimation of government coffers took place to the tune of $600 million. Contracts for computerized passports, handcuffs, police cars, and procurements for AK 47s were provided through a firm called Anglo Leasing and Finance Company Limited. So "limited" was it that the firm never existed! Kibaki's NARC administration began buying up high-priced villas in Nairobi's upscale suburbs. Wives were handed $100,000 in spending money. A new class of government officials known as *wabenzi* (we drive Mercedes Benz vehicles) spent $12 million on luxury cars. (11)

John Githongo, the appointed permanent secretary for governance and ethics, became alarmed by high-level hypocrisy and strapped a hidden microphone to his chest. As the protagonist in Michela Wrong's nonfiction account, *It's Our Turn to Eat*, he surreptitiously taped sessions with the president and his top-level officials in the State House. Then the hidden microphone acted up, making squealing noises beneath his suit and he was almost caught, bare-chested. Githongo ended up dodging death threats, resigning, and disappearing from Kenya to a hideout in London. From there he revealed the details of Kibaki's compliance in a system that was rigged to give dominance to the Kikuyu hierarchy. (See Appendix—Chapter 8.) None of this Watergate-like brinkmanship prevented Kibaki from walking away with the 2007 election, following which the country exploded in violence.

How this relates to the pros and cons of foreign aid is obvious. Good governance is key to ensuring that financial support reaches those who need it most. In social work parlance, the TOPs (top of pyramid) have to equilibrate with the BOPs (bottom of pyramid) and the mixture of BOPs, TOPs, and *wazungu* (plural for *muzungu*, White people) makes a common formula in Sub-Saharan Africa. If the TOPs are not reliable, the *wazungu* (and TOPs) never reach the goal of helping the BOPs.

So, back to the beginning: Does aid matter? Paul Collier, in The Bottom Billion, argues that by eradicating severe poverty we improve the planet overall. It not only benefits the bottom billion, but also the five billion who are getting by and the one billion who are rich (mostly living in the U.S. and Europe) by reducing wars, famines, and political catastrophes. By understanding the politics of poverty and intensifying support for the bottom billion, it's possible to move beyond the romantic "self-flagellation" of the Left as well as the Right's simple insistence that aid creates dependence. What we need, according to Collier, are aid programs supported by free trade, security from coups, and laws and charters that enforce transparency.

Dead Diplomacy

Aid has been an unmitigated political, economic, and humanitarian disaster for most parts of the developing world.

—Dambisa Moyo, *Dead Aid*

Zambian-born economist Dambisa Moyo differs with her Caucasian colleagues. "The notion that aid can alleviate systemic poverty, and has done so is a myth. Millions in Africa are poorer today because of aid: misery and poverty have not ended but have increased. Aid has been, and continues to be, an unmitigated political, economic, and humanitarian disaster for most parts of the developing world." (12)

The Harvard- and Oxford-educated Moyo cites the bitter failures of Sub-Saharan Africa, the Democratic Republic of Congo, Zimbabwe, Malawi, Nigeria, Zambia, and others. In spite of five decades of foreign aid and a trillion dollars to Africa alone, the growth rate of aid-dependent countries has been diminishing and averages minus 0.2 per cent annum. Poverty is increasing.

An alternative formula for growth exists, she argues, as demonstrated by countries such as South Africa, Ghana, and Botswana. When they issue credible bonds at lower interest rates, stricter in compliance and shorter-term, and follow a more active policy of foreign direct investment (FDI), trade equity, and micro-loan financing, the bonds of co-dependence and foreign manipulation can be broken. She gives the example of Nobel Peace Prize winner Muhammad Yunus, who pioneered micro loans, which were given especially to women.

"What if," Moyo asks, "one by one, African countries each received a phone call (agreed upon by all their major aid donors—the World Bank, Western Countries, etc.)—telling them that in exactly five years the aid taps would be shut off—permanently?" (13)

If you closed down the magic window, she insists, economic life for the majority of Africans would improve. Entrepreneurs would rise, corruption would diminish, and the countries that are worst-off would discover the success of interdependent economies forged without a dole. Along with Rwanda's President Kagame, Senegal's President Wade, and Kenya's President Kenyatta, there exists a growing voice on the continent to cut the Western (but not necessarily the Chinese) umbilical cord. The larger question is how well they can prosper without aid or corruption.

The Chinese are Coming!

"China Shapes the World"

— *The Financial Times*, Jan 18, 2011

I tried to imagine the sensations some nameless British officer might have felt on the train's maiden voyage, as he sat in his gas-lit compartment and looked out over the miles of receding bush. Would he have felt a sense of triumph, a confidence that the guiding light of Western civilization had finally penetrated the African darkness? Or would he feel a sense of foreboding, a sudden realization that the entire enterprise was an act of folly, that this land and its people would outlast imperial dreams?

— Barack Obama, *Dreams from My Father* (14)

Moyo's most recent book, *Winner Take All*, discusses one of the larger magic windows of human history: China's foreign direct investment strategy. With a growing population that is more than four times the size of the U.S., the Asian giant needs commodities far surpassing America's or Kenya's. Its global investments extend fifty years into the future and include more than $400 billion over six years, or about a billion dollars a week, with about thirty two billion going to Africa. Many of the investment resources will come from the African continent, and China has provided cheap loans that surpass what the World Bank and beyond what Western countries offer. In exchange for petroleum, food, and water, the export market for China grows rapidly, along with the indebtedness of African countries. Kenya offers China food, minerals, and petroleum, in addition to political ties that link its resources to an expanding civilization. What do you say to 1,360,720,000 distant neighbors that offer you low-interest loans, technology, and an alternative to Western dominance? *Jambo!*

There might be reticence in Kenya's greeting, having experienced one railway that plundered successive tribes and their land during its "lunatic" extension from Mombasa to Uganda. But China, having already built a highway that spans the north-south distance of the African continent, was eager to take on a smaller project from Mombasa to Nairobi that would run close to $14 billion dollars. It negotiated contracts that guaranteed Chinese labor, capital, materials, and contract fees. It also increased Kenyan external debt by a third, the debt of GDP ratio by 9 percent, and interest payments on external debt by 50 percent. The ability of the Chinese-built railway to generate income was not only debated, but it failed to address the old "lunatic" railway or another railway project from Lamu to Sudan. Uhuru Kenyatta's goal to build an Afro-Sino partnership, however, is undisputed.

Partners in Agony

Africans want and expect to depend upon others and they want others to depend upon them. Interdependence is a high value. They fear social isolation, and the only way to avoid it is by being involved with others, and social involvement includes money and goods.

— David Maranz, *African Friends and Money Matters* (15)

Despite some economic growth and devolution (decentralization of government spending) and the current government's policy to cover hospital delivery costs, the need for a self-reliant, sustainable health system in Kenya remains. The government has yet to deliver adequate care, evidenced by one of the highest HIV incidences as well as the worst mother and infant mortality ratios in the world. (16) One in thirty-eight mothers die in childbirth and 11 percent of Kenya's children may become orphans if they don't die first from AIDS, malaria, or other infectious diseases. Up to now, some 95 percent of medicines for AIDS and malaria come from foreign donors. Kenya trains excellent physicians but still has one of the lowest doctor-to-patient ratios (1/17,000) of any continent. After three years of training, a majority of doctors leave the country in search of better wages. (17) Trauma care is unsophisticated and often non-existent, the highway accident rate remains among the highest in the world, and despite efforts to control dangerous road conditions there continue to be more passengers at risk in the city and countryside. Could a different combination of entrepreneurs, government backing, and catalyzing boost from NGOs accelerate provision of health care?

The complexity of the Matibabu project illustrates the competing interests and problems of aid programs in Africa. In Nyanza District, Matibabu's locale, the incidence of HIV and the infant and maternal mortality figures are almost double the national rate. The District hospitals in Kisumu and Siaya are overburdened, underfunded, and understaffed. When the doctors went on strike in 2014, patients were sent home to deliver their own babies. Mothers die because transfusions are unavailable, even in the largest hospitals.

Does utilizing outside aid magnify the dependence factor and does providing foreign assistance create an avenue for exploiting funds? Recognizing this dilemma, Dr. Wagner and Dan's back-and-forth discussions reflect the challenge of American/Kenyan cultures trying to build a hospital in a rural, underserved area. After working together for eight years, their relationship became strained. The years of building Matibabu's infrastructure and working off of large grants had begun to run its course and in the proverbial "tragedy of the donors" the American side was tired of escalating requests and the Kenyan side was tired of having to request.

"She isn't willing to trust me, "Dan complained. "I have to keep a staff employed, make politicians happy, and then the American management team comes and criticizes everything we have put together, micromanaging from a distance. So what should I do? I'm prepared to resign and go back to Kibera."

Dan's struggle continued. Borrowing money to fly to the U.S., hoping he would meet up with Jeffrey Sachs and perhaps obtain a grant, he attended a Global Health Conference held at Yale. Predictably, he blended in with thousands of other participants as Sachs gave his message of convergence. But hoping for Sachs and others to solve Matibabu's financial challenge was like buying a ticket for the global lottery—and the one purchased was expensive and not a winner. Without funds, Dan found his way to California, always making friends and getting help along the way. He arrived just in time to attend a fundraising benefit put together by the American nonprofit team. Not having been invited at the onset and feeling sidelined, he became frustrated with Dr. Wagner. Arguments for how to manage Matibabu took place, and the two champions of health had difficulty talking together.

"We will have to wait and see what the coming election does," Gail suggested, as Kenya approached it 2013 presidential contest.

Building a multi-million-dollar complex in the Nyanza District happens when funding from a variety of supporting sources comes together. Even with grants and philanthropic contributions, a hospital needs operating expenses covered by diversified income-generation. Dan energetically found ways to bring in outside funding, but Matibabu subsistence still depended on outside assistance. Having pioneered the Tiba Foundation and started Matibabu with Dan, Dr. Wagner knew the hosptial costs would climb, but she worked ten thousand miles away and had a demanding patient schedule. Dan, the "grassroots" community organizer and energizer, had moved the project from a dream state to one of the largest clinical providers for Nyanza District. He was overseeing the day-to-day maintenance of a large operation, but he had grown up on a farm, not in a hospital. Donor fatigue was setting in, and the magic window was closing.

Misunderstandings

African history probably has played a major role in the development of this culture trait. When people are living on the margins of existence and even survival is at stake, it is understandable that the social rules would allow people to be able to ask for what they lack in the way of essentials, and that pressure be brought to bear on those who have an excess to share them.

— David Maranz, *African Friends and Money Matters* (18)

It was easy to appreciate the back-and-forth pattern of individual aspiration and communal compromise. And perhaps it was inevitable that Dr. Wagner, as a Matibabu co-founder, would come into conflict with Dan, who wanted to continue leading the organization. The complexity intensified because there were two nonprofits, one in California and one in Kenya, and other factors weighed in.

The consultants, working as guides for the Tiba Foundation in the U.S., at first had nothing but good things to say about Dan.

"Dan Ogola is the most amazing community organizer of all time," I was told. "Barack Obama could take lessons from him!"

But after a year they maintained that Dan was useful primarily as an evangelist. They assessed his work in Kenya and insisted he was an organizational problem, too enthusiastic, and not to be trusted with executive responsibility. He lacked sufficient managerial skills, and his selfish tendencies qualified him for a pathologic diagnosis: "malignant narcissist". All this time Dan was raising a family, enrolled in business school, administering multiple programs and grants, and working sixteen hour days throughout the week. In 2013, the U.S. teams were told that traveling to Kenya was too dangerous and no medical missions should be considered until after the elections. In retrospect, tourism was so slow that foreigners were given special attention and violence was minimal.

But the consultants spent little time in Kenya and easily outsourced Dan's role. Some of the funding that might have otherwise gone to the hospital project, $250,000 a year, paid for their work which was provided mostly from a ten-thousand-mile distance. Dr. Wagner was told that "founder's syndrome" was setting in and that new leadership should be harnessed. While the consultants brought efficiency and transparency to the administrative side of a Kenyan nonprofit, they also created a blanket of mistrust between the two individuals who had worked together to create a new health system.

The Way of Trust

If you want to travel fast, walk alone. If you want to travel far, walk together.

—African Proverb

Foreign aid and eusocial behavior are interrelated. Despite a debate of how foreign aid helps and hinders development, biologic imperatives make it certain aid will continue shaping future growth; the need of humans to continue working towards larger orders of social connection. As long as there are greatly divergent levels of prosperity, aid will be sought from both the West and the East. China's recent 4.5 billion-dollar deal with Uhuru Kenyatta dwarfs the U.S. investments in energy projects. And along with convergence comes global warming. I couldn't help remembering an argument I once had with Dan about the challenges of our century.

"The real problems in the world today," I told him, "are population growth and climate change." (See Appendix—Chapter 8, Climate Concern.)

"No," Dan countered, "those are all secondary. The real challenge—it's relationship. Relationship is the number-one task. It's where all problems are solved."

We were traveling in a van across farm-lined hills of north Nyanza District. Patchwork fields of corn and sugarcane stretched to the horizon as he repeated his analogy of Kenyan-American differences.

"For you Americans, everything looks like a nail. You have a hammer, and you are quick to pound in the nail. We don't act in that way here. In Kenya, you must find the nail and then walk around it once, and then walk around again a second time. And always with others. You never walk alone. When we have walked around it twice together, we have a relationship, and only then are we ready to pound the nail in."

Looking out at the one-acre farms, no longer large enough to sustain the families that had settled the land three or four generations earlier, I saw the essential Luo, Kikuyu and "tribal" cultures—everything was related to a person's neighbors. Little changed without communal participation. This rural culture was not the quick route to an expanding GDP, and it did not build highways and bridges easily, although cell phones and computers were coming fast. I thought of my American neighborhood, where we rarely interacted. One of my neighbors, a childless woman in her seventies, had not been outside her house or seen a visitor for months. No one noticed that she was losing weight and had stopped working on her garden. I knocked on her door and when she appeared, she said she was dying, and her one hope was to make it to Halloween. Thin and lonely, she was just one of a new demographic in America, older folks without family or community support. I gave her a jar of honey, she took some thyroid medication, and she got better.

My other neighbors were busy making highways, bridges, and dams. Those things come quickly for Americans, like Calvin Burgess, whose 17,000-acre Dominion Farm covers the "unproductive" Yala swamp in Nyanza. Burgess was criticized for not doing more to assist the local villagers, but will locals develop the skills to run the farm when his 25-year lease runs out?

"So, what are Kenyans doing about the famines, right now?" I asked Dan as we continued on our journey towards Nairobi. "The ones that happen more often each decade and get worse as the weather heats up?"

Outside the van, we saw women preparing the fields with wood and metal hoes, breaking up soil a foot at a time.

"I don't think it's the Kenyans who are heating up the planet," he said, squinting through his glasses and then flashing a Cheshire smile. "And besides, you will never fix any of these problems without relationship!"

I had to pause. Foreign aid, bees, eusocial behavior: all of these concepts revolved around the idea of evolution and chromosomes shaping our future. If there are two mechanisms in which species survive on the planet, one being the individual need to dominate and the other being the group imperative to succeed together, which one takes precedence? We are pushed and pulled by these forces, but of the two, the more dominant is group pressure. The heritable traits of cooperativeness, empathy, and patterns of networking most often determine which group or species prevails.

The honeybee and the ant, from whose eusocial behavior Wilson derives his rationale, demonstrated their success more than a hundred million years ago. As Onyango, Barack Obama's grandfather, explained it to Barack Sr.: "The white man alone is like an ant. He can easily be crushed. But like the ant, the white man works together. His nation, his business—these things are more important to him than himself." (19)

Lincoln was more succinct: "A house divided against itself cannot stand."

I looked back at Dan as we rushed down the pothole-riddled road towards a supposedly brighter future. He had opened the real magic window—relationship. Our nation-building actions, not unlike tribal behavior of the past, could be altruistic and idealistic, but sometimes incredibly destructive. Peace Corps volunteers traveling off to distant countries or bomber pilots sent to Iraq or Syria represent specialized groups essential to eusocial mammals. Like the bees, we exhibit highly cooperative behavior that allows us to cover the planet. But the cooperation is balanced by our individual tendencies.

It seemed to me that what determined the success of one over the other was the elusive goal of trust. Whether individual or collective actions predominate in evolution, in both cases trust is critical. In my own mind I measured the actions of the three women—Mama Sarah, Mary Onyango, and Wangari Maathai—each working to advance causes in Kenya through countless small actions accumulated over time. A sense of trust emerged above the forces of resistance and opposition.

"Dan," I concluded, looking out the window as we dodged another crater, our driver frantically passing trucks in order to save seconds on the road, "I hope you pound that nail in!"

9

Healing Wounds and
the Sadness of Surgery

*Happiness was unthinkable, for although happiness is desirable,
it is a banal subject for travel. Therefore, Africa seemed perfect
for a long journey.*
—Paul Theroux, *Dark Star Safari*

My quest to encounter motherhood always led back to the world
of patients, as did the hope of seeing a hospital that would serve
women and children and address the health disasters of the local people. Consider two consults and the horror of Al Shabab.

Rebecca, in her late thirties, had been diagnosed with
breast cancer. On rounds with the nursing staff, I was shown
a gaping wound that was destroying half her right breast and
burrowing deep down to her rib cage. It wasn't breast cancer.
She was thin, obviously had AIDS, and an unfortunate injury
along with infection had left this gaping cavity now covered by

a rag. It had soaked with exudate, once known as "laudable pus." She was embarrassed by her condition and struggled to hide it. We spent days treating the wound, washing it with peroxide and water, cleaning out the dead tissue, filling it with honey, and after a week it became possible to apply a wound vac, a device that creates gentle suction to speed healing and allow the wound to close.

The wound improved each day but Rebecca refused to be tested for HIV, knowing the stigma would cause rejection from her family. Without a diagnosis, she couldn't receive antiretroviral treatment (ART) to rescue her immune system. Even with three children at home and an improving wound, she refused our pleas and encouragement to do testing.

The other consult, a young woman named Ellen, had been shot in the face when two thieves came to her home. Sadly, the thugs thought she had money because some cattle had been sold next to her home, and when they were unable to get through the door, they fired a pistol at point blank range. With seven children but without a left eye or nose, Ellen soon lost her husband, who couldn't tolerate the disfigurement. She was raising the children alone, reluctant to go out into public, and her earning capacity was limited to cleaning other people's houses.

Reconstructing a face requires specialists, a high-tech operating system, and a prosthesis that is difficult to come by anywhere. When I obtained CT imaging of Ellen's face and showed it to plastic and craniofacial surgeons in the U.S., they noted how difficult it would be to reconstruct. None had the time or money to fly to Kenya. The Kenyan plastic surgeons also recognized the problem's complexity, but had their hands full with similar cases. No one was able to help.

Some wounds seem beyond hope, yet most healing happens from within. Outside actions are necessary, but ultimately every wound, whether physical, psychological, or social, exists inside. With physical wounds, once you eliminate the destructive focus of the infection, the body usually repairs itself. Collective social wounds are similar, so that by correcting injustice, poverty, or any of the imbalances of a social life, people can allow for a new freedom within. *To heal* is a verb. It signifies an active process, deriving from the Anglo-Saxon root word *haelen*, meaning *whole*, or *to make whole*. Even the most difficult, sometimes fatal illnesses do not prevent the possibility of healing.

Recently, Al Shabaab created deep retaliatory wounds in Kenya. The Saturday Shopping Center massacre in Nairobi resulted in the deaths of forty-seven innocent bystanders, many of them women and children. It was followed by a series of grenade bombings aimed at churches and crowded buses and the slaughter of more than a hundred innocent villagers on the coast. More recently one hundred and forty eight students were systematically murdered in an early morning attack at Garissa University. The atrocities of the Jihad terrorists manifest a deeper wound in the Islamic civilization. Like Christianity, which went through tremendous human violence and warfare during the Reformation five centuries ago, Islam and rebellious offshoots undergo internal and external battles for supremacy that cause destruction worldwide. If E.O. Wilson is right and social movements evolve towards more balanced collectives, then a plural and more harmonious Islam may ultimately emerge. Sunnis could live with Shiites, mentally deranged terrorists and supremacy driven offshoots could be brought under control. But the wounds will need to heal from within, whatever the outside actions.

One Day in Siaya

Je le pansai, Dieu le guerit. I bandaged him and God healed him.

—Ambroise Pare, 1538

The Siaya operating room is called "the Theater." In its simple rectangular, cemented contour is a galvanized metal roof overhanging the front walkway, protecting hospital workers and patients from the torrential long and short rains that come in fall and winter months. A small wooden bench as bare and basic as the inside of the theatre leans next to an otherwise empty wall,

and during the course of a day patients with all varieties of illness find solace on this small, protected bench and its offer of
shaded rest while they wait for surgery. A nest of swallows stays
partially hidden in the crevice of the roof, but it is visible from
the bench. Perhaps it gives some temporary distraction to those
sick enough to "go under the knife." The birds fly in and out
with small pieces of grass and twigs, fastidiously strengthening
the nest while their young build up courage to take flight. The
patients go in for surgery, one after another, until the evening.
Then the surgeons take over the bench, hoping to rest and ease
their sore backs after bending over all day.

I sit on the bench, contemplating morning rounds. The
rest of our team has left, returning to the States and to hospitals
more modern and expensive while I stay with plans to work on
beehives with Kevin and to take care of any remaining patients
that are slow to recover. There are several, as well as others still
hoping to have surgery. I think about a large, open bucket that
hangs over the bed of a prostatectomy patient, supplying water
collected from the gutters of the roof for irrigation. His blad-
der is filled with blood clots from previous surgery, and during morning rounds he groaned with pain. After flushing the
catheter several times he seems more comfortable.

The list of wounds seems to get longer by the minute
as I move on through the men's ward. A full thickness skin
graft on a man's foot has healed well, but on the periphery bio-
debridement, a euphemism for larvae therapy with maggots,
takes place like a macabre circus. It's hot inside the ward. Doors
and windows are left open to allow for a breeze, and as a result
the flies are profuse. I spend almost twenty minutes treating a
teenager's massive open wound. He suffers from necrotizing
fasciitis after his broken leg ulcerated and festered beneath a
plaster cast. He moans throughout the dressing change and
bleeds rather easily. After a month in the hospital, which he
can't pay for, his spirit has turned inward, surrendering to his
disease and to the likelihood that he will die.

Henry, the Kenyan medical officer, asks me to look at another young man in a bed at the far end of the ward. I noticed

the same patient some days earlier and assumed that he was dying from advanced AIDS. He, too, will not last long, and thus there was no request for a surgeon until this morning. But now I understood the source of the strong odor that permeated the room. Henry pulls back the sheet, and we witness an advanced case of Fournier's gangrene, one of the worst manifestations of necrotizing fasciitis. The infection has taken over the groin and all the surrounding soft tissue, destroying everything in the way. It will need debridement as soon as possible, and although this wound will probably never heal, the young man deserves the dignity of an attempt. Next, I visit Samuel, a youth with advanced squamous cell cancer involving his left lower leg. For several days, I had attributed the ward's foul odor to Samuel's wound, but now I know it has multiple sources. His wound is the most haunting of all.

More wounds need changing, including an extensive burn covering the back of a man who a week earlier had become intoxicated and fell backwards onto a fire. Strangely, the burn took the shape of the African continent. "TIA," I think, a proverbial acronym meaning "This is Africa." It's so large that I have to use several rolls of gauze, first applying honey and then wrapping the man in continuous layers until the seepage stops and he looks like a mummy. Another difficult wound afflicts a four-month-old infant with burns covering her hands, arms, chest, and thorax. She was caught in the flames of a mosquito net that fell and enveloped her. The burns are deep; it seems unlikely that she will survive without a trip to Nairobi.

After imploring the nurses to give her added attention, I head off to the Theatre where I find the wooden bench. As I sit and consider the schedule—a pediatric hernia, a hydrocele, a few minor cases, the Fournier's gangrene which I have insisted Henry take part in since he watched the patient for several days without consulting, and whatever else shows up—it looks like a long day.

And now surgery is over and it's sunset. Darkness creeps over. Sitting on the wooden bench reaching out for a comforting thought, nothing returns. Light travels away without reflection, and the heart gives way to a deep loneliness. Every surgeon knows this feeling. To make human connections and battle against diseases, whether cancer, stroke, broken bones, or infection, and to lose the struggle, causes sadness. This feeling of emptiness sweeps through like a cold wind and the horizon is a darkening panorama of maroon clouds and impending rain. The sun has abandoned the earth, and my back and legs ache, as does my heart. Today's operations have gone by without major incident, but I can't keep my mind off one patient.

It's Samuel, whom I saw on morning rounds. In his early twenties, he suffers from an open wound to his left leg that for six years has gone without healing. And without the simple management any surgeon could have provided, he's chained like a prisoner to the gaping sore. He tried to ignore it and failed miserably as the inflamed tissues caused what textbooks call a Marjolin's ulcer—a cancer originating in an area of chronic inflammation. Despite occasional visits to the medical clinic, where he paid a few shillings for a salve and cheap antibiotics, the aggravated tissues mutated into an aggressive malignancy. Now, he has little choice. The cancer has expanded outward, giving off a rotting odor. It has also spread inward and invades the tibia bone, forcing him to return to the hospital to seek help for the pain. A registrar admits him, the nurses perfunctorily dress the wound, and a biopsy confirms the cancer. He refuses an amputation when it's offered, and a week later I'm asked to see him.

As I look at the x-ray, it's obvious that the bone is destroyed, which explains all the pain and his silent demeanor. Samuel lays for two weeks on a hard mattress as flies are drawn to the raw flesh, depositing eggs and causing the familiar swirling circus that cleans the wound—a poor man's hygiene.

"There is no other way to take care of this," I explain with the help of a translator. "Without an amputation, the pain will get worse. You will lose more blood and every day you wait, you get weaker."

Samuel won't make eye contact and refuses surgery for a week. Then, after his family convinces him to go ahead, he verbally consents. But the day the OR is ready, his sister calls to talk him out of the operation. That same day, after operating on the Fournier's gangrene patient, it seems as if the theatre, perhaps the whole world, is filled with the scent of gangrene. Sitting on the bench, I look up for the swallows but their nest is empty. Perhaps the odor has driven them away, too. I get up slowly and walk to the ward to make late-night rounds. Then, I walk down a dirt road that leads to the Mwisho Mwisho motel at the edge of town passing others returning from their work. In the darkness they don't recognize my white skin or sadness and for these few moments we are one, as we always are.

In the Beginning

When you are sorrowful look again in your heart, and you shall see that in truth you are weeping for that which has been your delight.

—Kahlil Gibran

Ovarian cancer begins like many others, with just a rogue cell or cells, genetically inherited or subjected to a mutating host environment over long periods of time. Strangely, one small risk factor for this disease is milk consumption, but there is no good explanation as to why. Some ovarian cancers occur in women who have a family connection, such as the BRCA1 and BRCA2 genetic linkage, or a previous cancer history, but the majority cannot be traced to any specific risk factor. Who really knows where it all begins? Science has made giant steps comprehending the molecular and genetic pathways of mutation, where viruses, toxic chemicals, and even sunlight compete with the chromosomal predisposition of our life's journey. But it's still a guessing game most of the time. Oncologists say cancers can take as long as five to twenty years to become symptomatic.

When I first met Dr. Maathai, it was unlikely that she had developed signs of bloating and abdominal pain. She was working hard to make the earth nontoxic to the humans inhabiting it. As a patient once explained to me, it sometimes helps to regard one's cancer as an uninvited guest sharing a home in which you both must live. In her case, it would be an unbearable guest, beyond surgical cure.

The first symptom might be a loss of appetite or fatigue, after the rogue cell has proliferated through continuous doublings, multiplying from one to ten thousand and so on, until billions of cells together acquire the potential to metastasize. Fatigue and loss of appetite happen for any number of reasons. For a woman in her late sixties with a whirlwind schedule requiring multiple aides and a secretary to help balance it, such symptoms were likely to be ignored for some time. Months can go by, perhaps a year. And then it's time to seek a doctor.

Besides physical exam, initial tests would include ultrasound and CT scanning, along with blood tests. The recognition of a widespread tumor would suggest treatment with chemotherapy in hopes of rendering the disease surgically treatable. To date, the ideal test for early diagnosis of Ovarian cancer remains elusive, and most patients present in their mid or late sixties with advanced disease, as did Dr. Maathai. The frustration and agony for her must have been tremendous, as well as for her family and friends. She had finally risen to a world stage with an increasingly powerful voice and the ability to make significant changes, not just in Africa, but on every continent.

Her work in the Green Belt Movement continued to expand: by 2010, the organizational grants and yearly expenditures had approached two million dollars. Four million trees were planted in Kenya alone, raising the number to forty-seven million since 1977. Thirty thousand women were trained in forestry, food processing, and other income-generating activities preserving land and resources. Her publications were coming every year: *The Challenge for Africa* in 2009, and *Replenishing the Earth* in 2010. In a tireless effort to encourage new leaders and move beyond her own legacy, she started Wangari Maathai Institute for Peace and Environmental Studies. Was she far enough along in building leadership that others could carry on her work? Was there anyone who could fill her shoes?

The deepened sense of loss, paralleling Dr. Maathai's recognition that she might not survive, was manifested in some ongoing changes in Kenya. When she first described rapid destruction of the ecosystem, with rivers drying up, species of animals vanishing, and the soils no longer supporting the farmers or sustaining the nation's food system, it was during the 1970s. Environmental movements in the U.S. were just coming alive. She had raised a green flag in Kenya, protesting a skyscraper in a public park, and was immediately denounced by President Daniel arap Moi as one of those with "insects in their heads." Four decades later, despite her successes and the work of the Kenya Forestry Department, UNEP, NGOs, and government agencies, Kenya's environmental status continued to decline.

What Wangari said forty years earlier now echoes throughout the country. And yet, population growth continues, desertification spreads south, and displaced citizens from the post-election violence remain without property titles and crowded into cities or around the perimeter of the remaining forests. The Ogiek struggle to protect the Mau Forest, a primary water tower for the country that has been their home for millennia. The Sengwar tribe watches government officials tear down and raze their homes, even though they have lived in equilibrium with the land as natural conservators.

Hiking to the summit of the Mau with the Ogieks, during a month when they should have been harvesting a bumper crop of honey, we encounter one inactive hive after another. The weather cycle has changed, and rain and hail fall out of season, leaving the bees dormant without nectar or pollen. Reports of bad crops, including corn, are appearing in the newspapers on a regular basis. Passion fruit, which depends on the bees, has fallen off so badly that farmers are clearing their fields.

Wangari continued traveling throughout the world. She wrote prolifically, and her message of the African three-legged stool—a nation supported by democratic principles; equitable, sustainable resources; and a culture of peace—seemed to gain wider support. After the electoral violence of 2007, the country settled down. The economy began to recover, and women's influence began to strengthen. The voices of Iddi, Suzzana Owiyo, and a multitude of talents resonated through night clubs, auditoriums, and radios. Charity Ngilu, Martha Karua, Sally Kosgei,

Linah Kilimo, Margaret Wanjiru, and others rose up politically. A more significant event was the 2010 vote to endorse a new constitution. Along with other democratic reforms, it determined that women must fill one-third of elected or appointed government positions.

Changes towards a more gender-balanced society were accelerating when I tried to interview Dr. Maathai, but the meeting was never to happen. During 2011, she began chemotherapy for her malignancy, and on September 25th, the public received notice that she had passed away due to complications while undergoing treatment. It was a time of mourning throughout Kenya and the world. Many trees were planted during the month of October. Wangari requested that no trees be cut or used for her casket; instead, it was made of bamboo, hyacinth, and papyrus. She received the honors of a national hero, and it was perhaps ironic that she was taken to Uhuru Park, to the renamed Freedom Corner, where she had once protested against government forces until she was clubbed unconscious. During the funeral procession, a military band played the national anthem, crowds walked alongside the hearse, singing in unison, and eulogies were given by the president and by her friend, Raila Odinga:

"All that we want to say here: Our sister, you are not dead. You will continue to live in the hearts of the people of Kenya. Your work will continue to inspire the rest of the world."

Mary's Funeral

Pon alawa. Youth is passed on to the next generation.

—Asenath Bole Odaga, *Luo Proverbs and Sayings*

Mary Onyango tried to continue her breast cancer work, counseling women who had a new diagnosis, encouraging them through their treatment, and spending time with her children in between her own courses of chemotherapy. Her primary service, however, came with an appointment to the National Cohesion and Integration Committee. Following the post-election violence of 2007, Mwai Kibaki's administration envisioned a citizen delegation that would intercept hate speeches and deter ethnic rabble-rousers to keep the country from being mired in more divisions. As it grew more active, she had less time for anything else. National tension ratcheted up, energized by the ubiquitous headlines, social media commentators, and an upcoming presidential election. In January of 2012, while returning from the opening ceremony for the Matibabu Hospital, I talked with Mary on the phone. It was apparent that she was fighting for strength. She had spent five days in the ICU and was on her third course of chemotherapy, but still she was determined.

"Breast cancer is not a death sentence," she insisted. "It's a battle to be fought. I will continue to fight and live to the day I drop."

Knowing her schedule was tight, I wanted to arrange a brief meeting with her in the Kisumu Airport. We would meet between flights for as much time as she was willing to spare. I wasn't aware of the bone pain she was experiencing, or how closely a tumor encroached on her pulmonary artery.

Kenya's political climate was an open wound of mistrust and anger. The post-election violence (PEV) had included the fatal burning of Kikuyu women and children as they huddled in a church near Eldoret; mass murders of Kalenjins, Luos, Kisi, and others; and displacement of more than a hundred thousand villagers. Since the government failed to arrange court hearings and reconciliation proceedings within a reasonable time, it was to be examined in the International Criminal Court (ICC) at the Hague. Six prominent individuals were indicted for crimes against humanity, including Uhuru Kenyatta, the current president, and William Ruto, the vice-president.

Raila Odinga, the previous prime minister, was not indicted, nor was Mwai Kibaki. Odinga was a presidential candidate for 2013, leading the CORD political party, and he was strongly supported by Luos. Kenyatta and Ruto led the other Jubilee coalition, supported by Kikuyus and Kalenjins. More ethnic divisions were predictable, and the election outcome was uncertain. As vice-chair of the NCIC committee, Mary had her work cut out on a daily basis and Kenya was described as a room full of volatile gases.

"It takes one lit match to set things off," my friend Walter told me.

Actively confronting hot heads and hostile politicians, Mary didn't shy from putting out fires. Since her diagnosis of breast cancer in 1999, she had grown accustomed to taking on authorities, including the government and the medical establishment. Perhaps the ravages of her disease provided motivation. Equally frustrating were the problems of helping women who were rejected from their matrimonial homes when they were diagnosed with cancer. Many women refused to be treated, fearing they would be divorced if they lost a breast, so Mary embraced their causes. Almost singlehandedly, she promoted national awareness of breast cancer and a larger coalition was built. Before her condition took a sudden turn, half a million mammograms had been performed in Kenya. Then, she became weaker, and her work with the NCIC became more intensive. On March 31st, she was at home in Ugenya when she began to cough blood. Her mother managed to get her into a car and took off, traversing the unpaved roads leading to Kisumu, a one-and-a-half-hour drive. On arriving at the Agha Khan Hospital, Mary was pronounced dead.

The funeral was held at Mary's home in Ugolwe, attended by admirers, friends, dignitaries, and her family. From ministers of Parliament to the poorest farm workers, they came. Purple, white, and black ribbons festooned the tent-covered ceremony. Adele, her youngest daughter, had shaved her head, and her other two sisters camouflaged their grief with exquisite dresses. A group of breast cancer survivors stood quietly in the background, a silent minority, to honor Mary. The politicians, never to be rendered silent, found a political platform and made statements about political parties, assassination attempts, and issues of importance. Finally, the women sang, led by South African singer Yvonne Chaka Chaka. Adele and her sisters, illuminated in the hot, bright sun, carried huge arrangements of white and red roses and laid them next to the coffin.

Mary was also a close friend of Raila Odinga. In his memorial address, he said,

All of us that she touched mourn her loss. In her honor, let us remain mindful that her critical work—of making Kenya a safer, unified and more peaceful place—must continue, as she would have wanted most of all. We must carry forward her legacy. In her honor we must not falter or fail in our search for unity and understanding among our people.

Prison Life

Outsiders had not the slightest understanding of what that desperation was like—of the slow, suffocating death of hope of the ghetto dweller. There was no social welfare safety net, no education without money, no way to gain qualifications and a future, no security or status. And for many, life was horribly short. Death was often the only way out of the ghetto. It was hardly surprising that so many resorted to crime, for what other options were open to them?

—George Obama, *Homeland* (1)

Kevin's phone calls to me in the middle of the night stop for several months and his attempt at beekeeping comes to an end when his hives are stolen. Then, he begins calling again, asking for financial support so he can begin a new career. His emails take on a religious tone.

> I hope that you are fine, with me am okay but life havent been a bed of roses, though i believe that someday the almighty God will open His ways.
>   once the wise men said that, in order to know life, we always have to go through it.

He wants to start over in Tanzania or Malawi. His enthusiasm is greater than his work prospects, however, so I let donor fatigue guide my response and don't send money. Each trip I make to Kenya results in five to six requests for support, almost always from young men desperate to find income. If no education is involved, I reluctantly turn them down. But

Kevin's messages come more urgently, and eventually he pins down a "delivery" job at a hospital in Malawi, which was offered by an uncle. I give in and send him a hundred dollars for travel expenses.

I miss hearing from Kevin for several more months. Then, he calls to confess—or rather complain—that the new job is not quite what he had hoped for. It consists of moving corpses in and out of the morgue, tedious work that pays next to nothing. He doesn't last long. Half a year passes, and then the calls and emails come more urgently.

> hi Richard, I hope that you are okay with me. Am not
> good, as the life here in prison is unbearable. Actually,
> since my mum died things became much tougher and
> more complicated, my elders (whole family of 6) are not
> in good terms with my father coz they claimed that he
> killed my mum.

He needs bail money. Of course, he assures me that it was a frame-up. He only used some unapproved music in a new barbershop he had started in Kericho. But he must have the money soon, if possible. His father, with nineteen children and now one wife less, is unable to help him out. I call his father and offer to cover half of the needed expenses, but he declines to meet with me.

Kibati Prison, once a colonial sisal farm, is nestled against green hills and shaded by tall jacaranda and fig trees; surroundings that are deceptively halcyon. Two thousand prisoners are packed into tight living spaces, where they experience extortion, sodomy, and few amenities beyond a meager diet. Tom, the Bushman, informs me that nine prisoners share a space ten feet by ten feet, and each has a single blanket. Tuberculosis is a frequent visitor. Tom knows from eighteen months of personal experience. An employee once saw a toolbox on his kitchen table and turned him in for theft, although he had merely borrowed it from a nonprofit organization he worked for. There was a shortage of judges, so he went without a trial for a year and a half.

The prisoners do gardening and hard labor tasks, and some make award-winning furniture, but time passes slowly. Tom was put in charge of the library, which explains some of his encyclopedic knowledge of Kenya's bird life. Without bail money, prison can be a lifetime experience, but Tom made it out. So he and I go to visit Kevin on a Monday and spend a few hours waiting for a chance to peer through a thickly barred window. We pay a small bribe in order to learn that Kevin has five capital offenses—crimes on the level of robbery with weapons and intent to commit violence. Rumors fly in prison environments, so we aren't sure of the actual crimes. Of course, he denies any guilt.

Staring morosely through a thick metal screen, he seems hopeful that we'll be his bridge to freedom. Like George Obama, the step-brother of President Barack Obama, Kevin got caught at the wrong time in the wrong place, and getting out of prison is much harder than getting in.

As one of the 22 percent of Kenyans in the age group 15–24, Kevin belongs to the "youth bulge," unusual only in that he comes from a large family with some land and money. Struggling to establish a reputation as a wage-earner and with little education to do so, he's followed closely by 43 percent of Kenyans who are aged 0–15 and who add to the bulge. They form an energetic work force, but many are disaffected and sniff glue on the streets of Kisumu, drink illicit alcohol in the makeshift bars of villages, or just lean against city walls, discouraged by their failure to find any but the most menial jobs.

Kevin's mother manages to obtain money and get him briefly out on bail. Then, after skipping bail for three months, he's re-arrested. She dies mysteriously, and he's unable to attend her funeral. The father, blamed for the mother's death, continues to say there are no family funds to bail him out. Kevin shies away from any questions about his mother. As the Bushman and I walk slowly away from the Kibati Prison, his eyes follow us from behind the metal gate.

Redemption

I am not a saint, unless you think of a saint as a sinner who keeps on trying.

—Nelson Mandela

Kevin is convinced he'll find his way out of prison. Not once in his persistent text messages and phone calls, coming from a phone lent to him by a prison guard, does he ever let on that he's discouraged. I explore different directions to seek his release, but each time I encounter obstacles. His father is unwilling to assist and still declines to meet with me, attorneys show no interest in tracking down his citations, and I'm warned that as a noncitizen, I will be seen as interfering if I pursue meetings with a magistrate. Yet, somehow I think that he will find a way to freedom. In all the unhappy events that befall patients, in the difficult deaths of Mary Onyango and Wangari Maathai, and in the challenging poverty that so many experience in Kenya, there remains human determination to succeed and to rise above daily challenges.

Even the patient who experienced a massive burn that left a map of Africa scorched on his back found his way out of the hospital, healed by sheer grit. "This is Africa," is his message as he recovers slowly, one dressing change after another, until finally, the pain subsides and he returns to his village, ready to work again. The four-month old infant that was trapped in a burning mosquito net never travels to Nairobi, but instead, heals with diligent care and also goes home.

A year and a half goes by. Kevin calls and texts me every day, hoping I'll visit and bring him some clothes, soap, and deodorant. I spend a few weeks working at Siaya District Hospital, and when my schedule allows, I hire a taxi and once more wait for an hour until the guards allow me next to the barred and screened prison window. Suddenly a windstorm sweeps across the open area, immediately followed by a cold and torrential rainfall, soaking my clothes. I see Kevin's face up against the screen. He's smiling, happy to see a visitor. He tells me he will be out, soon, but I don't believe him.

"I will be released," he assures me. "I know you will see me."

His court appearance is canceled, and his freedom seems many years away even if he survives the tuberculosis he has contracted. Our visit is over within minutes, and the guard points me away as I walk back to the taxi. Rain continues falling from the heart of Lake Victoria.

A month later I receive an email from him.

halo, richard, i hope ur fine, actualy i just wanted to let you know that i have been acquitted and i am at liberty now. i am just in a family friend's house

10

Salvation and Survival

Disappearing into the Ghetto

The sharp edge of a razor is difficult to pass over:
thus the wise say the path to Salvation is hard.

— Somerset Maugham, *Katha Upanishads, The Razor's Edge*

Traveling through Kenya takes one close to the difficult conflicts of world religions. The post-election violence of 2007 is followed by a wave of terror perpetrated by Al Shabaab, the radical terrorist sect from Somalia that joins ranks with Al Qaeda and commits repeated acts of terror on the coast and in Nairobi. While slaughtering tens of thousands of elephants for ivory, blocking humanitarian aid, and savagely killing foreigners and their own countrymen in Somalia and Kenya, the terrorists claim to be acting on Islamic faith, although they are uniformly denounced. Still, worldwide, throughout history, Christians have murdered Muslims and Muslims have murdered Christians. Now the millennia-old wars of faith have found their way into East

Africa, and competition for land, resources, and supremacy seem to be getting the upper hand. Does the biologic imperative of survival take precedence over the quest for salvation?

As survival on an individual level depends on adapting to circumstances, so too does survival of species, nations, and tribes. Some argue that reproduction gives competitive advantage to absolute numbers, but in a world of technology and nuclear weapons, large populations have fewer advantages. A few insurgents from Somalia can disrupt a city of millions, and even a small country can compete with America's Armed Forces or the collective mass of China. Will biologic imperatives messaged within our chromosomes change and transform quickly enough to adapt to diminishing resources? We are told in Genesis 1:28:

> Be fruitful, and multiply, and replenish the earth, and
> subdue it: and have dominion over the fish of the sea,
> and over the fowl of the air, and over every living thing
> that moveth upon the earth.

Have we succeeded thus far in this command?

In the case of fish—Check. Elimination of 90 percent of many ocean species is complete.

Fowl of the air—Check. Elimination of 12 percent of avian species will occur by the end of the century.

Every living thing that moveth—Check. About half of all living species will be gone by the end of the century. Our dominion has surpassed God's entreaty.

And should I acknowledge evangelists when they establish security and wealth behind promises of salvation? Or surrender intellectual rigor and common sense to the comfort of faith? Does the biblical record of immaculate conception, walking on water, casting out demons, and raising the dead fit with concepts of superorganisms and empirical science? Or should I abide with metaphoric and symbolic truth and accept the miracle of now? The teachings of Moses, Mohammed, Christ, and Gikuyu—monotheistic messages that transcend individual existence—command allegiance if I'm to rise above my animal instincts. Mesmerized by this problem, I watch a bumper sticker on a car disappear into the Kibera slums: "God is too big to fit into one suitcase," it says as it vanishes into the dense crowd of humanity.

Ponder the suitcase of Kenya's 4.6 percent fertility rate and its 2.6 percent growth rate. By 2030, the population could reach 77 million inhabitants, and much of that growth process will be the "youth bulge" with its higher expectations. Since over 50 percent of Kenyans are already less than 20 years of age, the chance of social disruption on a large scale exists. Young men like Kevin, finding no land and with little inclination to farm anyway, leave the countryside and come to Kibera, Mathare, Mukuru Kwa Njenga, Korogocho (shoulder to shoulder), and six other slums or shanty towns where they hope to make a decent living. Some, like Dan Ogola, succeed by helping others. Most do not. Given the increased frequency of droughts and the shrinkage of cultivable land, the need to adapt to available resources is great. But politicians will never showcase the need for family planning: economic growth is the holy grail of political survival. Uhuru Kenyatta and William Ruto work intensively with the West and now China in seeking prosperity and delegate a controversial task to commissions such as the Population Policy for National Development. Fortunately, the planning minister has a target of halving the number of children Kenyan women give birth to within a decade. By reducing the birthrate to 2.6 per woman through family planning, the current population increase of one million per year might be checked.

Is it ethical for a nation of Christians, Muslims, and traditionalists to encourage population control? World population is estimated to reach ten billion or more by the end of the century. Africa will be the largest contributor in the years ahead, surpassing both China and India given current fertility rates and topping off at 3.6 billion: a tripling of its current population. If this happens, God's suitcase becomes—what? An explosion of underfed and job-hungry youths? Richard Preston notes in *The Hot Zone*, his 1994 introduction to Ebola Viruses,

I suspect that AIDS might not be Nature's preeminent display of power. Whether the human race can actually maintain a population of five billion or more without a crash with a hot virus remains an open question. Unanswered. The answer lies hidden in the labyrinth of tropical ecosystems. AIDS is the revenge of the rain forest. It is only the first act of revenge. (1)

Preston's primer on the Ebola virus was prophetic, although his population estimate was widely off. Today, megacities are an end result of exponential population growth as exemplified in Lagos, Nigeria, a city expected to increase from 11 million to 19 million by 2025. Slums are doubling at a similar rate, and two billion people will live in squalid conditions as the global suitcase fills. Kenya, like the U.S., hosts a rich and poor divide that is vastly dominated by the poor. What would happen if Nairobi were to face an Ebola outbreak such as Monrovia and Freetown experienced? After considering these oncoming problems, I decide to consult a real queen.

Regal Guidance

There is only one Christ, Jesus, one faith. All else is a dispute over trifles.

—Queen Elizabeth I, responding to the Catholic/Protestant divide

According to etiquette for the monarchy, the proper way to greet the British queen is to begin with, "Madam," and to conclude with, "I have the honor to be, Madam, Your Majesty's humble and obedient servant."

Having embarked on a restricted and informal search for queens, I learn that a proclaimed queen gained her highest status after staying in a fig tree in Kenya. Elizabeth II's royal ascent happened not far from Mt. Kenya, while she was watching wildlife on a vacation with her husband, Prince Philip, Duke of Edinburgh. They were lodging in the Tree Tops Sanctuary of the Aberdares in 1951 just before the news came of the death of her father, King George VI. Her courage at the time was noted for braving a herd of wild elephants as she arrived at and climbed a ladder into the tree house lodge.

"Ma'am, if you have the same courage in facing whatever the future sends you as you have in facing an elephant at eight paces," the Tree Tops manager told her, "we are going to be very fortunate."

During her trip to Africa, she became de facto Queen of England and had to return quickly to London for the ceremonial inauguration. The tree house was burned down a few years later when Dedan Kimathi and his Mau Mau rebels set fire to the platform used by British soldiers. "Operation Blitz" and "Operation Hammer" required the military to shoot on sight any Mau Mau fighter found in the Aberdares Forest. Eventually, the revolt was contained, Kimathi was hung, and seven million acres of land were taken from different tribes and controlled for another decade. It seems unfair to hold the Queen accountable for the human tragedy and imperial domination she did not initiate. Her royal actions are well meaning, and I look to her authority for answers to my own dilemma of population control.

"Madam" my letter begins, "how may I seek guidance in the issue of overpopulation and the problem of resource availability and species preservation in Kenya. Kindly advise me in the best approach to solving these problems." The letter ends with appropriate language from an obedient servant.

Many months later, an answer with a Buckingham Palace letterhead and a queenly-stamped envelope arrives.

"Your request for the Queen's advice has been noted, but I am afraid that it will not be possible for Her Majesty to comment on this matter. I am sorry to send you a disappointing reply."

The search for motherly advice continues.

No God but God

God saith: Whoso seeketh to approach Me one span, I approach him one cubit: and whoso seeketh to approach Me one cubit, I

approach him two fathoms; and whoever walks towards Me,
I run towards him.

—*Hadith Qudsi*, an extra-canonical saying of the Prophet Mohammed

Although she has no claim to royalty, Mama Sarah impressed me deeply with her maternal qualities: humble origins, a leader of her community, and one who procreates and gives strength to new leaders. She didn't give birth to Barack Obama's father, but she helped raise him from age nine, and some biographers believe this had an indirect impact on a U.S. president's personal development. Most biographies have focused on Barack Sr.'s rise and fall. Bright, gifted, egotistical, at times self-destructive, his childhood included being left behind by his biological mother and enduring both praise and frequent disapproval and occasional beatings of his father. Ultimately, he was nurtured by Mama Sarah. Peter Firstbrook's biography relates conflicting tales of how Sarah treated Barack Sr. If one accepts the account of Hawa Auma, Barack Sr.'s younger sister, it was not easy to be a child under a stepmother's supervision. This would hold true in any rural setting, however, and particularly in Kenya, where children are expected to do farm work and help support the family.

To understand Sarah's role it is important to look at the end result of Barack Sr.'s childhood. Barack Sr. was rebellious from an early age, as is true of many high achievers, and overcame many hurdles after a rural upbringing. After being expelled from high school and sent away from home, he landed on his feet. He graduated Phi Beta Kappa at the University of Hawaii, was accepted to a Ph.D. program at Harvard, achieved a high-ranking position in the national government (from which he was fired and then hired again), and returned regularly to his family home bearing gifts for his stepmother and related family and friends.

Sarah recounts the happier moments of motherhood. When she tried sneaking into school as a child, she was punished for her efforts, so she experienced vicarious joy each time Barack Sr. succeeded in his jagged academic career. Having once provided him encouragement on five-mile bike rides to primary school, she must have appreciated his graduation from a University, and even more so his acceptance into postgraduate education at Harvard.

She made an effort to keep her stepson sincere with his girlfriends while he attended Maseno Secondary. Within a few years, she had to begin mothering the children of Barack Sr.'s first wife, as she had done for the third wife of her own husband. Ultimately, she celebrated Barack Sr.'s successes. He had many disappointments in his life, but he always returned home to show her his appreciation. While a graduation photo and doctorate diploma from Harvard were not to be, happiness came again posthumously when Barack Sr.'s son, Barack Obama Jr., attended Harvard Law School and invited her to visit the American institution. Obama strength in the face of adversity, for both Sarah and Barack Jr., may have much to do with Luo resilience, but Sarah also had another source. Raised as a Muslim, she holds the family together as it grows in number and complexity and continues to recognize the five pillars of Islam:

First and foremost is to worship Allah as God and Muhammad as his messenger.

The second pillar, the Salat, includes ritual prayer five times daily. Does she get up and pray before daylight each morning? This is hard to verify and seems unlikely given the condition of her arthritic knees. The prayer is preceded by washing (wudu), and then performed according to a series of set positions, including bowing with hands on knees, standing, then prostrating, and finally sitting in special position.

Legend reports that when Muhammad went to Allah during his renowned Night Journey to Heaven, he was "spirited on a wondrous white steed with wings to Jerusalem, and upward from there through the seven heavens." (2) He was told by Allah that Muslims must pray fifty times a day. As he returned to earth, he reported these instructions to an incredulous Moses at the sixth heaven and was told that this was not achievable. Humans would never comply. Mohammed then went back to Allah to negotiate, and over the next five visits, he reduced the number of prayers to five. Moses insisted it was still too much for mortals, but Mohammed declined to push harder and agreed. And so it is written: Prayer, five times daily. Perfect compliance is not always possible.

The third pillar is *zakat* (that which purifies): Those who have should help those who do not. I once asked her what was the most difficult, saddest thing in her life, and what makes her most happy. She answered instantly.

"This pain that I have in my knees is what makes me most unhappy. It keeps me from getting around and never goes away. What is happiest in my life is when I am helping the children. This is where I find happiness."

Sarah keeps her Kogelo home open to orphans, overseeing around one hundred. Her nonprofit institute, the Mama Sarah Obama Foundation, targets education, orphan care, and holistic community development. Reactionaries have tried to portray the foundation as an Islamic conspiracy, but a visit to the village confirms Mama Sarah's dedication. (3) Queen Elizabeth II may not hold as many public meetings as Sarah does daily in her front yard. When visitors sign in at the guardhouse, waiting in the plastic chairs arranged beneath the mango tree, she greets them with a smile, usually with children at her side. After half an hour, her expression can turn serious.

"The light makes it difficult to see," she says politely, after too many photos are taken with flash devices.

She means that the photo session is over. She will stay with guests as they converse, but then resumes her domestic work. At age ninety-three, she's more susceptible to illnesses. After a recent fundraising trip to Kisumu, she complained of a mild pneumonia and when she asked me to come by the *dala*, I grabbed a stethoscope and some antibiotics. On arrival I noted that she was as strong as ever so I asked about her quick recovery.

"I use my recognition to try to help my people," she explained, as she had once before, "because that is what a woman my age can do. It keeps me going. Helping others makes me stronger."

The fourth pillar, *sawm*, signifies observance of Ramadan

and fasting, which is not always easy to comply with. Mama Sarah fasts according to the requirements for her age.

The day that Christians and Muslims have one understanding of Christ there will be one religion.

—Mama Sarah

During November of 2010 Sarah completed the requirement of the fifth pillar of Islam, the Hajj (pilgrimage to Mecca). In the most populated annual gathering on the planet she was able to negotiate the crowds by wheelchair and with the help of her family, thus obtaining the status of *mustati*. This pilgrimage, predating Jesus and Mohammed and stretching back to the time of Abraham, represents an outward journey and an inward intention of devotion to God.

Sarah's palace is a farm, shaded by the canopy of trees Onyango planted sixty years ago. The court is attended by guests, children, cattle, turkeys, chickens, goats, dogs, cats, rabbits, and above them all, the bees. The bees serve their own queen with monotheistic dedication, harvesting a greater territory, free of human interference except perhaps my own interventions. The colony adheres to the high branch of the mango tree; after four years, I have failed to entice them away. My credibility is suspect.

Jesus Is Lord

Love is patient: love is kind: love is not envious or arrogant or rude. It does not insist on its own way; it is not irritable or resentful; it does not rejoice in wrongdoing, but rejoices in the truth. It hears all things, believes all things, hopes all things, endures all things. Love never ends.

—Corinthians 13:4–8

"Richard, you must contact Dr. Bird," Mary Onyango had told me, several times. "He is the one surgeon who has kept statistics in this country, and he really knows breast disease. He works in Kijabe." It was a year after Mary's death before I found time.

The Nairobi-Nakuru Highway runs through and along the Great Rift Valley. Towns spill onto the pavement, along with the *jua kali* (those who work in the hot sun). The merchants and pedestrians, always at risk for trauma, provide directions since no visible road signs indicate a turnoff. A small twisting road leads to Kijabe Hospital, overseen by a strong national Board of Directors and several Australians that contribute to management. The Africa Inland Church started as a missionary clinic a century ago and is now a recognized center of expertise and training, with 260 beds, a staff of 700, and multiple specialty units.

It took a day to find my way to Dr. Bird's office, and he had to pull briefly away from the morning OR start in order to meet. Tall, lean, with greying sideburns and an imposing gaze that takes in all varieties of surgical problems, he is modest about his research and direct about religious commitment. Behind thin spectacles, his intense blue eyes regard me cautiously.

"I knew Mary and admired her work," he acknowledges.

Because of the volume of cancer surgery at Kijabe, he becomes friends with many terminal patients, but there is no sentimentality. Two-thirds of the women he treats have triple-negative breast cancer, an aggressive variant of the disease all too common in Kenya. Mary was estrogen-receptor positive, which partly explained why she was able to tolerate thirteen years of treatment and was singularly able in her advocacy work and quest to facilitate early diagnosis. We discuss triple-negative breast cancer, and I tell Dr. Bird I will be happy to volunteer as a surgical oncologist, although I'm already active in the Nyanza District.

"Our faith in Christ is as important as medical background," he responds.

The influence of Christianity in Mary's life is not difficult to find; it's in all her work, but nowhere as much as in her service to women with breast cancer. Lifting up whomever was most in need, even as her own disease progressed, she singled out physicians who said it was futile to treat late-stage disease and contrasted their words with her own example. By life's end, she had eliminated much of the culturally ingrained fear of treatment.

A decade ago, Doris Mayoli had not known about Mary. While taking a shower, she noted a lump in her breast; she thought it was just "hormonal." She waited a month before seeing a physician. At that time, a mammogram and biopsy were not favorable. She writes in her book, *Ashes to Beauty*,

> September 2, 2005 was the most difficult day of my life besides the day I was told that my mother died, or the day that my marriage came to an end. I felt as though I had been handed a death sentence.
>
> "I am so sorry, Doris," her physician told her, and she prepared to go home and die.
>
> I badly needed reassurance, but the doctor did not give me any, even though I reckon he did his professional best under the circumstances. All he attempted to do was lay the bare facts on the table for me. After that, he offered his sympathy, which was of no particular assistance to me at the time. I needed someone to hold my hand and tell me all would be well. I had no one close by my side because I had chosen to go for the check up alone—at least I thought so. I felt confused, lonely, and overwhelmed. (4)

She was unaware that a friend would be waiting for her. Warned by the pathologist that it would be good for someone to be nearby when the doctor's visit was over, her friend stood close by the door and took her hand as she came out. This support, similar to what Mary experienced in South Africa and pioneered in Kenya, helped Doris continue under the care of another surgeon. After chemotherapy, breast-conserving surgery, and radiation therapy, funded mostly through her church, she made her way back to a full life balanced by emotional support.

Martyrdom has a long history in religion, but Mary eschewed such a role in her cancer work and government role combating hate speech and ethnic rivalry. Many other women pursued government positions but were not as successful. In the 2013 elections, the women who ran for office against men won only 5 percent of the National Assembly seats. Not a single woman was elected senator or governor. Compared to other countries with gender quotas, such as Rwanda, where greater than 50 percent of parliamentarians are women, Kenya lags behind. While it is ahead of the U.S. rate of 20 percent, the country continues to suffer from acts of discrimination, including reported beatings and bludgeoning of women with assault rifles, and a recent stripping of women in public places. Esther Passaris, contesting for a Nairobi Women Representative seat, was stoned and prevented from entering indigent neighborhoods. She recounts the words of one gang member before she aborted her campaign.

"What are you doing here? You're not supposed to be here, this is our area. I'm going to rape you right now, right here."

Dorothy Onyango ran for member of Parliament in Kibera and found that her fifteen years spent working as an anti-HIV campaigner gave her no advantage. She lacked money and the willingness to go drinking with potential voters at night. Her assessment of voters was blunt:

> They're keen on supporting someone who will be giving them money. As it is, I'm really discouraged. I'm really, really discouraged. I thought, oh God, is it even worth trying?

Mary would have argued yes. As girls and women begin to fill schools and colleges, they move into positions of influence and responsibility that reflect the newly endorsed constitution. They play a stronger role in the government and are determining the size and makeup of their families, especially in Central Kenya. The 2010 Constitution, after majority public vote, mandates that women have a right to own and inherit land, to exercise joint control over family resources, and to constitute at least one-third of elected and appointed positions in the parliament. Mary didn't live long enough to witness it, but her work helped allow the 2013 presidential election to proceed without violence. Although the election results were contested and undermined by irregularities in the vote-counting machinery, the country accepted a new administration peacefully, and her earlier words were prophetic:

At the end of the day you are a Kenyan. Whether you
vote yes or no, you are a Kenyan.

Mary's work has been carried on by many, and energetically by First Lady Margaret Kenyatta, who currently hosts the
Stop Cervical Breast and Prostate Cancer in Africa Conference.
A Beyond Zero campaign provides mobile clinics that allow
screening in rural areas and promises to change the curse of
late diagnosis. While radiation, hormonal and chemotherapy
are available to only a minority of patients with cancer, early
diagnosis remains a key solution.

Is there a contradiction in the Christian belief in salvation
and the human desire for survival, both individually and collectively? Mary Onyango's life suggests not. Love manifests in the
Christian faith through a continuum of personal sacrifice. The
salvation in giving of oneself through an active life was perhaps
as consistent and essential to her survival as it was to the community she served. When she said, "Even Christ cried on the
cross," she referred to her own pain and times of despair, but
her actions revealed a faith that carried her and others through
long suffering. Like Wangari Maathai, she lived and worked in
the present.

Roots of the Fig Tree

*When, for example, I look back on the Kikuyu way of life that
existed before colonialism, I am sure that one of the reasons the
community appeared to have so much time to celebrate and
enjoy the natural world was because they weren't looking at it
through acquisitive, materialistic eyes.*

—Wangari Maathai, *Replenishing the Earth* (5)

Wangari spanned cultures and religions by creating bridges
between them. Primary school with the Consolata nuns, high
school with the Irish sisters of the Loretto order, and eventually
a Catholic college in Atchison, Kansas, all prepared her for a life
of Christian service, but after thirty years of prayer, training,
and indoctrination, she reconnected with her Kikuyu tradition.

Like Ghandi embracing peasant life or Rigoberta Menchu articulating for Mayan Indians in Guatemala, she led the forces of the Green Belt Movement by way of her rural origin and social base. It was also a return to early childhood values and a close relationship with her mother, as she describes in her earliest memories. Her mother would plant seeds, till the soil, and harvest crops, and gave Wangari her own garden of "fifteen square feet in the middle of her farm" so that she would learn how to care for crops. She also imbued Wangari with Kikuyu beliefs about trees that were central to the tenets of the Green Belt Movement.

> Kikuyu priests performed sacrifices only where fig trees stood. Once a ceremony had been carried on around it, that fig tree and its location became sacred. My mother told me very clearly when I was a child that I was never to collect twigs for firewood from around the fig tree near our homestead since, she said, it was "a tree of God" (*muti wa Ngai*). (6)

The "tree of God" meant more than just a ceremonial site for sacrifice; it stabilized soil and provided channels for underground water reservoirs to surface in streams and rivulets from deep root systems. Along with the Kikuyus and other Kenyan tribes, the fig is sacred to the Hindus, who have a tree in Calcutta that "is reputed to be a quarter of a mile in circumference, with hundreds of trunks connected overhead to form a colonnade, able to provide shelter for twenty thousand people." (7) *Ficus religiosa*, or the bo tree, gave shade to Buddha with its heart-shaped leaves as he meditated in sixth century B.C. The fig tree is regarded as a keystone species in rainforests, and if it were to disappear, the forest would also vanish, like a collapsing arch without its centerpiece. By encompassing and dominating other trees, it opens up the forest canopy and provides habitat for small animals while providing prodigious amounts of fruit to feed the inhabitants. Like the Ogiek, Maasai, Sengwer, El Molo, and other indigenous cultures, Kikuyus had a reverence for the living ecosphere. When clearing the land for planting, they preserved the larger trees and called them *murema-kiriti*, or "one that resists the cutting of the forest."

> These trees were considered the habitation of the spirits of all the trees that had been cut down. In turn, the standing trees couldn't be felled unless the spirit was transferred to another tree. This was achieved by placing a stick against the tree to be cut down and then moving it to one that was to remain standing, or by planting another tree immediately in the same place as the felled one. Clearly, such restrictions stopped wholesale deforestation from taking place. (8)

Branching Out

Guceera ni kuhiga.
Traveling is learning.
The world is a great book,
of which they that never stir read only one page.

—Kikuyu Proverb (9)

> From the moment they set foot on foreign shores, colonial forces demonized and marginalized the religious practices of those they conquered and occupied. As with the followers of Asherah, the Kikuyus were told that God could not be worshipped outdoors, in the high places or in the forest, but that he was to be found only in the building built for him, where an altar would be set up and controlled by a priest whose authority had come not from the community but from another representative who lived many miles away. (10)

Wangari describes how the colonial period eventually dominated tribal cultures and replaced traditional religious beliefs with Christian ones. By far the majority religion in Kenya, Christianity became an educational foundation for many Kenyans, and Wangari blended its strengths with her mother's teachings, ultimately believing that "society is inherently good and that people generally act for the best". Perhaps education played the largest role, as noted by Namulundah Florence in her biography:

> Maathai herself recognized the joint influences of
> cultural practices and Christianity, and questioned
> the latter for its racist undertones. However, she never
> resolved her contradictory allegiance to Western influ-
> ence. She deplored the loss of indigenous African values
> that were denigrated with the onslaught of Christianity,
> but distinguished nurturing indigenous values from
> regressive cultural rites like female circumcision. On the
> issue of identity she understood her dual provenance
> as a protegee of both Africa and the West, and tried to
> balance between local and international allegiances, her
> elite status, and her humble beginnings. She would cite
> Christian scriptures to reinforce her appeals for com-
> munity (Christian charity), servant leadership (Jesus
> Christ as model), and responsible stewardship of the
> Earth. (11)

She often expressed Kikuyu-based sentiments next to Christian ones. The press paid much attention to alleged state-ments made in Nyeri in 2004 that the AIDS epidemic was the result of a botched laboratory experiment and that "HIV/AIDS was deliberately created by Western scientists to decimate the African population." The day after receiving her Nobel Prize she was quoted in the newspaper saying, "I may not be able to say who developed the virus, but it was meant to wipe out the black race." (12) Such statements were odd coming from a sci-entist with a doctorate in biology and Wangari subsequently commented in the Green Belt Movement website:

> Like many others I wonder about the theories on the
> origin, nature, and behavior of the virus. I understand that
> there is a consensus among the scientists and researchers
> internationally that the evolutionary origin most likely
> was in Africa even though there is no final evidence. I
> am sure that the scientists will continue their search for
> concluding evidence so that the view, which continues
> to be quite widespread, that the tragedy could have been

caused by biological experiments that failed terribly in a laboratory somewhere, can be put to rest. (13)

There are ample times in her writings, however, when she questions the good intentions of Christian messages. She singles out the American Gospel song that is popular at the funerals in Kenya, "This World Is Not My Home."

> Some of the faithful tend to take these words literally, and ignore the bounty the Lord has given them on this planet. Even though they say they cannot be bothered with earthly things, they still need food, clean drinking water, and air to breathe. They are, therefore, not being honest with themselves. Surely, to be able to respond to a planet that is being destroyed and may soon not be able to sustain them, the faithful would help themselves if they were to sing: "This world is *definitely* my home," and "I'm not just passing through." (14)

Her final book, *Replenishing the Earth*, returns to Kikuyu heritage and myth. The omnipotent creator, *Ngai*, has instilled vital force into all living things. While humans have the greatest vital force, plants and animals are also imbued, and leaders may increase or nourish the vital forces of their society through working with the lower forces. To approach higher forces directly is considered sacrilege, but by working with the symbolic world, humans may strengthen their connection to God and all creation. Similar practices occur with other tribes, such as the Suba and Maasai, yet few individuals have ever taken a cultural tradition to the planetary level as Wangari and the Green Belt Movement did—40 million trees planted in Kenya and 11 billion worldwide since their early campaign.

> Sometimes we are called into action on behalf of a cause because of what might be called the god within us, the Source—the voice that we feel speaks to us, and us only, and says that a situation is wrong, an injustice has been committed, and we must do something to reverse it. Here we are in the realm of the mysterious, and in trying to suggest what causes us to act, it would be prudent

to exercise a little humility, especially since so many of
the challenges that confront us as a species are due to
our arrogant belief that we know enough not to worry
about the consequences of our actions. (15)

She capitalizes Source rather than god, suggesting that
an internalized or inner divinity guides her actions. Service
to humanity, to women's rights, and to the preservation of the
natural world formed a synthesis of beliefs. While the Kikuyu
side emphasized justice and the environment, after colonial
disruption Christianity enhanced the sense of service and the
love of all peoples and allowed for healing of a disrupted world.
Salvation was a precondition for survival.

Death without a Tree

*I have seen time and again that if you stay with a challenge,
if you are convinced that you are right to do so, and if you
give it everything you have, it is amazing what can happen
and kept going.*

—Wangari Maathai (16)

Before advanced cancer overtook her active life, Wangari set
groundwork for the Wangari Maathai Institute for Peace and
Environmental Studies. The sustainably designed building, located on fifty acres of land next to the University of Nairobi, is
set to facilitate postgraduate training and a learning center for
environmental studies.

> The potential of the WMI is to introduce a new way of
> "experiential" learning, an experience that will ensure
> there is a link between the knowledge students gain
> during their tertiary training, and their capacity to apply
> it to transform the societies in which they live.

Chemotherapy makes any planning difficult, but preparing for a transition when she could no longer serve as director
of the Green Belt Movement must have been exhausting. Her
closest family would help replace her, along with close associ-

ates and the many women of Kenya for whom she had set an example. If few could match her courage and achievements, a collective force might harness greater teamwork.

Her funeral was to be open to all of her followers at Uhuru Park. Ironically, as the first woman in Kenya to have a state funeral, only a few years had passed when she and a protest group were tear-gassed in the same park for protesting against an increase in the number of members of Parliament. Given all the times she had been arrested and assaulted, it seemed unlikely that she would receive the same protocol as that of a recently deceased vice-president, and yet, a stately carriage, a military platoon, and all the decorum of a government VIP were accorded her. She was a luminary, and some opinion leaders felt that the government was co-opting her fame and environmental status to prevent oppositional efforts.

But certainly Wangari was loved and respected in all corners. As a protector of trees, she made certain that she would not be buried in a wooden coffin. Her body was transported in a casket made of hyacinth, papyrus, and bamboo, and when the ceremony was complete, a cremation took place; an uncommon practice in Kenya. Memorials were held in cities and capitals worldwide, as well as in forests, open spaces, and backyards. In the end, no one could describe her work as well as she did.

> For thirty years, I have worked in the trenches with others to find ways to break the wall that separates the peoples of Africa from justice, wealth, peace, and respect. We have searched for a route out of poverty, ignorance, ill health and early death, violations of basic rights, corruption, environmental degradation, and many other problems associated with Africa. . . . through the Green Belt Movement we are helping communities to plant trees and to improve their livelihoods, protect their environment and, in the process, increase their commitment and persistence. (17)

With the sorrow of losing a friend, Nigerian activist Nnimmo Bassey mentioned a few other supporters. "If no one applauds this great woman of Africa, the trees will clap!"

Honeybee Democracy

The beehive is perhaps the most enduring of social utopias.
Sooner or later, wherever people have dreamed of a better
life for the oppressed, they have also considered whether the
beehive might help them in their labors.

—Bee Wilson, *The Hive* (18)

Dan Ogola is accustomed to being on time and has a low-profile,
organizational approach that complements his ability to appear
publicly, such as with CNN. In addition the Matibabu program
has a non denominational system that allows Americans to participate in medical care, but which is coordinated by a Kenyan
board of directors. Sharing medical knowledge and technology
is part of a traditional interface between Kenyans and Americans
but the economic structure of two inter-connected nonprofits
led to predictable challenges. Building high tech infrastructure
in rural Kenya came with a demanding budget. When the expanded Matibabu services concluded its $1.5 million USAID/
PEPFAR grant, the process of downsizing was necessary. Matibabu secured another grant through the International Center
for AIDS Program (ICAP), but the large staff size still had to
be reigned in. Dan faced a budgetary dilemma and the uncom-
fortable need to lay off associates. The TIBA Foundation helped
bridge an operational deficit but at one point the strain of managing a large project with insufficient local funds brought him
close to resignation. There was no one else who could carry on
with his dedication or energy.

Nonprofit innovators are sometimes associated with a
condition known as "founder's syndrome". The growth of an
organization makes it critical to adapt to new business methods and leadership, and the innovators have to bring in administrative support. As a community organizer with the goal
of wanting to build a specialized hospital, Dan had to find a
balance with his American counterparts as well as find other
grants and sources of operational support. Dr. Wagner, also a
founder and innovator, chose to hand executive authority on
the TIBA board to a new president who would be elected each

year. Dan helped recruit and shape a Kenyan Board of Directors that brought experience from diverse sectors—medical, legal, engineering, and public domain—to oversee the organization within Kenya. In his role as Country Director he was able to secure grants through a German nonprofit and Planned Parenthood. In 2014 he helped guide the formation of the Mary-Ann van Dam School of Nursing. With programs in Siaya District, Samburu District, and Nairobi, Matibabu now supports maternal child health and education in clinics, schools, and hospitals around the country.

It is worth comparing the Matibabu administrative strategy and a honeybee colony's decision-making process. The honey bee superorganism has to find and choose new locations on a seasonal basis and uses a powerful democratic method.

Tom Seeley outlines the five principles in *Honeybee Democracy.*

> 1) *Decisions are made by individuals with shared interests and respect.* Bees have shared interests in finding a new site to establish their colony whenever they swarm. In human organizations, management is facilitated by recruiting congenial members with common goals, but respect is essential.

> 2) *The leader's influence over group thought must be minimized.* Bee colonies use multiple leaders, or independent scouts. Decisions about site selection are proposed by group process. One only has to look through history to realize what happens when a single person rules. Dr. Wagner and Dan were willing to give the larger organization a voice.

> 3) *Diverse solutions should be explored.* When scout bees search for a new site, they travel in all directions and bring back as many as twenty locations to choose from. Building and running a new hospital likewise requires continuous decisions and diversity of input increases the availability of choices.

4) *Group knowledge should be aggregated by debate.* Once the scout bees have explored their territory, they begin the process of waggle-dancing; recruiting others to visit the best location.

5) *Quorum responses allow for cohesion, accuracy, and speed.* Here is where the honey bee superorganism collates thirty million years of experience into a fast-moving assemblage. Within two to three days, before the swarm has used up its stored energy, the quorum of scout bees reaches a decision and pipes signals to activate the mass.

Perhaps bees should build hospitals, but their tasks are much simpler. Dan has continued to look for revenue streams by initiating a Nursing School and pulling in a million-dollar grant from Planned Parenthood. Meanwhile, Matibabu continues to serve a large indigent community. Yet as the hospital grows the operational expenses increase.

The Fire Next Time

Someday, after mastering the winds, the waves, the tides and gravity, we shall harness for God the energies of love, and then, for a second time in the history of the world, man will have discovered fire.

—Pierre Teilhard de Chardin

The Bushman and I walk along the downtown streets of Nairobi, watching the multi-tribal flow. Men are slender, tall, and focused, wearing suits or dress shirts, impervious to the hot sun. Their long, pointed shoes step forward, headed somewhere. The women are lithe, beautiful, no longer dressed traditionally, but wearing short skirts, jeans, tight blouses, and high heeled shoes. They ambulate miraculously over broken sidewalks and squeeze between moving cars that fill the streets like herds of metal bodies. With hair coiffed in buns and intricate patterns—precise, patient, corn rows that take six to eight hours of preparation—these aren't the mothers who spend their lives bent over a hoe, cultivating fields, or giving birth to seven or eight children, and sometimes dying in the act. These women read novels, newspapers, style magazines, and create their own images. Nor are they eager to get pregnant. A few participate in "chips funga," a recent trend where women accompany men for one-night stands protected with contraception; comparable to eating greasy French fries because of the pleasures involved. Birth control is in; unwanted pregnancies are out. The high-heeled are not as familiar with the Green Belt Movement. The Kikuyu women of the countryside remember Wangari—a member of Mumbi's tribe who worked the soil, planted trees, and knew the secrets of germination. But the urban women also remember Wangari's three legged stool—stable society requires democracy, peace, and a sustainable environment. The stool collapses on two legs, with three it supports.

The 2013 elections came and went, and Raila Odinga, initially given a lead in the polls, lost to Uhuru Kenyatta by a 7 percent margin. Despite a hotly contested demand for a runoff, the Supreme Court ruled in favor of Kenyatta, and a violent upheaval never took place. Mary Onyango would have been gratified that the election transpired without violence, though as a Luo, she might have regretted Odinga's loss. Wangari Maathai, a Kikuyu, might have celebrated Kenyatta's peaceful victory. She was also a supporter of ODM and Raila Odinga.

In an odd twist of allegiances, Kenyatta switched from the Western-leaning orientation of his father, Jomo Kenyatta, and in a speech to the Organization for African Unity denounced Westerners for supporting the International Criminal Court: "Thus the imperial exploiter crashes into the pits of penury. The arrogant world police is crippled by shambolic domestic dysfunction. These are the spectacles of Western decline we are witnessing today."

Raila Odinga, on the other hand, switched from the leftist leanings of his father and aligned himself with Western interests.

While Uhuru Kenyatta established deeper ties with China, signing papers for a new national railway system and hundred billion dollar trade agreements, Raila Odinga traveled back to the U.S. for three months to reconsider political strategy, once again needing to reinvent himself. Just as the U.S. political body polarized between two dominant parties, and sometimes two dynastic families, so too Kenya divided, as if there were a biological need. Charles Hornsby, in his epic history of Kenya, writes:

> Although Kenya has become a nation-state, it has never achieved its longed-for autonomy from foreign aid, and has abandoned attempts to maintain a distinct cultural identity. It has failed to deliver adequate material living conditions for most of its people: and its politics have failed to transcend its history.

This dark view of the past contrasts with a role played by the many women working in post-colonial Kenya—and three women in particular. Ordinary in many respects, they arise from the *wananchi*, or common people, provide a special leadership, and finally, they nurture the future of an evolving nation. Each comes from a different religious background, and each plays a critical role in community development.

Mama Sarah, Mary Onyango, and Wangari Maathai are still paving the way for a eusocial society.

Moving the Bees

There's no manipulation of colonies, no renting out of bees, no colonies packed on trucks like sardines and shipped off for pollination purposes. For us, instead, it's survival for the fittest, and mother nature seems to be getting it right. She's giving us a broad genetic pool of honeybees capable of dealing with any environmental shocks on their own.

—Eliud Muli, *National Geographic* (19)

It has been four years, and I still haven't relocated all of Mama Sarah's bees. It's time to deliver, or at least divert, and having exhausted all ideas and recommendations from the U.S. bee-keepers—"Don't get near them!"—I decide to call Eliud Muli, a Kenyan entomologist. Muli, on his way to North Carolina for a national bee symposium, suggests capturing the colony and transporting it away during the night. In other words, climb a tree in darkness, transfer thirty or forty thousand bees into a gunny sack, and find a getaway vehicle. Recalling my earlier work with Kevin, it seems like another potential end-of-life scenario.

At this point, Kevin is not yet out of jail, and he's contracted tuberculosis. I thought he would be around to help and was the right person to start a honey cooperative. Like others in the youth bulge, however, he now has to compete with others to make it through his thirties, find a wife, and earn a living. Is this oddly similar to my task of moving wild bees? Thousands of females will sacrifice their lives to defend the home colony from a testosterone-driven, male invader. Perhaps like Kevin, trying to gather resources in a nation of forty-seven million, I'm just one more male chasing forty thousand bees, and they won't give in without a fight.

An idea comes to mind. Why not bring in someone who really knows how to handle bees in high places and who has had decades of experience? The answer is simple enough—contact the boys from the Mau Forest, the Ogieks. They're comfortable high up in trees and have worked with wild bees for hundreds if not thousands of years.

I call Leonard. He agrees to meet me as I travel from Nairobi to Kogelo, where Mama Sarah lives. He'll bring along one of the beekeepers from the forest, younger and more confident in high places.

I choose the cheapest route and a half-dollar motorcycle ride to the Nairobi Matatu station at six a.m. leads to a three-dollar ticket on a cramped seat in a stripped-down *matatu* (minibus). Destined for Nakuru, where Leonard is waiting, we head into thick city traffic. The driver honks and steers intrepidly, finding invisible openings and forcing small gains through the urban logjam, and finally we reach the open road. On the Naivasha/Nakuru Highway, we get as far as Naivasha when we're pulled over by a policeman. I guess that a *kitu kidogo* ("something small") will exchange hands, but instead, the van is taken to an open-field police station and we're told to step out. Abandoned buses, cabs, and *matatus* are parked haphazardly, and a crowd of passengers waits impatiently, shouting for refunds as the hours go by. Eventually a mechanic arrives with a crowbar and hammer. With no explanation, he wrenches off our van's license plate.

I have arrangements to meet the Ogieks and travel to Kogelo by the afternoon, and it's now clear that the *matatu* will never make it. Then, by fortune or just clever anticipation, I'm approached by a taxi driver. I hire him for the next three days ($45), and we're on the highway again, headed east along open fertile land, observed silently by sullen troops of baboons. As we drive past the Soysambu ranch and conservancy, the driver tells stories about Lord Delamere's family and Thomas Cholmondeley, a great-grandson who shot and killed two Kenyans that were trespassing on his land. Thomas was convicted of manslaughter but, perhaps a little more fortunate than Kevin, he was released on good behavior after serving five months.

At last, we reach Nakuru and pick up Leonard and his partner, Nicholas Kausa, a thirty-year old honey hunter. Sitting quietly in the back of the car, Nicholas responds to questions in Ogiek and smiles, showing two large front teeth.

"*Ipwote tot gemuch geuyisted segemchoon iih?* (Have you traveled outside the Mau Forest before?)"

"*E'eey.* (No.)"

"*Giiwe ot imangde saang en tim po moow?* (Do you think we will be able to capture the bees?)"

"*Ooh.* (Yes.)"

The road from Nakuru to Kisumu passes through the western Rift Valley, flanking just above the Mau escarpment, one of the five forest water towers of Kenya. In thirty million years, all of East Africa may slide eastward through tectonic forces until it becomes another continent surrounded by water and rising volcanoes—a miniature Africa; but for Nicholas, on his first trip outside the Mau Forest, the savannah provides enough fascination.

We buy gigantic carrots and roasted corn from roadside stands while Joseph, our driver, relates more stories about the Delamere ranch and the days of "White mischief." Early British settlers indulged in escapades of alcohol and promiscuity, and Lord Delamere, who was a spiritual and political voice for British settlers, owned as much as 250,000 acres. He pioneered Kenya's modern agriculture for crops and livestock in the face of repeated failures and difficult odds. He was also famous for riding a horse into the Nairobi Norfolk Hotel while wearing full evening dress, shooting out chandeliers and whiskey bottles, and jumping over restaurant tables.

Traveling through another hundred miles of unfinished roads, we pass only one major bus accident. Forty passengers have died. We speed through the lush tea plantations of Kericho, have a quick lunch in Kisumu, and are finally off the highway and headed for Mama Sarah's home. Using a pocketknife and rope, I weave a purse string around the gunny-sack that was purchased back in Nairobi.

Traffic thins as the tarmac accommodates herds of goats and the ever-present potholes, and then we're onto rust-red dirt and arriving at the Obama homestead. Evening is approaching, and by the time I talk with the family and say hello to Mama Sarah, there's little time to prepare. Nicholas wears jeans and a thin shirt and is ready to climb the tree. But first, we have to bring down a swarm "catching box" with a new colony buzzing inside. It's been up in the tree for three months, and the bees are excited when they're lowered by a rope. I cover the box with a mosquito net and carry the collection to the back of a car where the bees quiet down, allowing us to focus on the large colony higher up.

"Let Nicholas wear a veil and bee suit," I tell Leonard, who translates the suggestion. Nicholas shakes his head.

"*E'eey* (No)," Nicolas replies.

"No, it will get in his way," Leonard says.

It's dark now. Nicholas is already on his way up. I want to light a smoker, but there's not enough time. Barefoot, Nicholas disappears through the thick branches of the mango tree only to reappear briefly as the beams of torches (flashlights) catch him ascending. I remember wanting to use a rope and harness, so if he falls there will be a way to suspend him, but that plan vanishes in the darkness too. We aim our torches when he reaches the colony, far out on a peripheral limb. The bees are barely visible—tiny missiles awakening to the incursion. He begs us not to shine light anymore as he takes a knife and begins to slice thick wax away from the branch. I'm to receive the colony and wait underneath silently. It's a bit eerie as the others distance themselves. Time passes quickly, three or four minutes, and then the fat, heavy gunnysack comes very slowly down, twisting around and around, into my waiting arms. It buzzes and vibrates with all the intensity of a forty-pound animal, humming an angry protest. I pull the purse string tight as sentry bees fly out to protect their queen and like a strange wild creature, it protests the capture as honey drips through the sack onto my white suit.

The two colonies are loaded into two vehicles, and we head off for a new home, knowing that we must transport the bees at least three miles away or they will return to their previous site, guided by directional memory. Traveling to a farm five miles off, Joseph's small taxi handles the terrain, but the four-wheel vehicle breaks down. Finally, carrying the gunnysack and the "catching box" into a dense thicket, we find an enclosed space where we can locate the two new hives. There's a snake lying on the ground that makes me long for hiking boots and the Bushman. It's too late to do anything except set up boxes. Green mamba? Nicholas is no longer smiling with his white buckteeth. He sits in the car, silently pulling out hundreds of stingers from his bare arms. Surprisingly, there's little reaction or swelling.

Acquired immunity from thousands of previous stings protects Nicholas, but he feels side-effects from the venom. We joke a little now as our torches wave inside the thicket, hammers hitting thumbs, and suspend heavy wires to hold the two boxes aloft. After several stings and hammer blows, we're convinced we'll be successful. By midnight we finish and head to the Nelson's home where his mother has prepared a meal of *ugali*, lentils, and hot beef stew. Standing outside the lantern-lit compound, I look up at the night sky, awash with an endless galaxy, happy to be alive.

Immortality Again

There is nothing, absolutely nothing, like a fig.

—Colin Tudge, *The Tree*

Many months later, on returning to visit the family, I'm surprised to learn that a new colony has found its way once again up into the mango tree—and it's larger than ever! Where did I go wrong, I wonder, looking up at the massive new ball of wax covered with bees. Said Obama pulls me aside and takes me to another large tree at the edge of the *dala* that reaches towards the sky. It has a large hollow center that is packed with at least one or two separate colonies of bees. The inevitable has happened, I realize. Colony reproduction! Here is where the continuous source of new bee colonies has been coming from, year after year. After recognizing a small fruit from the tree that lies on the ground, I take a few minutes to appreciate the history of *Ficus thonningii*. Known also as *mugumo*, it is one of the sacred fig trees that Wangari Maathai described in her books, those that led to the birth of the Kikuyu tribe on Mt. Kenya.

Fig trees have a forty-million year history of symbiosis with wasps. And each of the seven hundred and fifty species of figs has its own dedicated species of wasps and a unique method of reproduction that tells us why "there is nothing, absolutely nothing, like a fig." If you look closely at a fig, you will note a small eyehole, an opening at the fattest end. This is the entry point for a black female wasp that is particular to her own species of tree. As she negotiates her way inside, she's covered with pollen from male flowers at the womb like center of the fruit. In essence, the fig is an inverted container of flowers and a sepulcher for the visiting insect, which dies a few weeks after laying both female and male eggs. A reproductive extravaganza is launched as new females are fertilized and released by the male wasps, which hatch first. The males complete their role by chewing narrow tunnels for the females to escape. Like honeybee drones, they have served a final purpose. Withdrawing back into the fig, the males die while the females fly off to look for virgin figs in the forest, recreating the life cycle.

Said Obama has led me to yet another recurring process, and at last I understand why the mango tree and bees have out-foxed me each time. The answer resonates in the middle of this fig tree—what Wangari called the "tree of God"—on the edge of the Obama compound. Deep inside, the honey bee superorganism makes its decision to divide and relocate as it has throughout the millennia. Scouts begin the task of notifying every bee, waggling and piping, pushing their way into the center to activate the swarming process. Wings whir together, the temperature rises to thirty-five degrees, the piping noise reaches a crescendo, and when all the perimeter bees have warmed up, a dark flying cloud rises into the air. Within minutes, it condenses again into a thick, trembling cluster and hangs from a nearby branch. The sentries and foragers, trained by instinct to search for the best home, set off on voyages, flying in all directions, using the rays of sunlight and the earth's magnetic field to remember their way back. The queen waits, anticipating a well-prepared comb in which to lay her eggs.

When the familiar branch in a mango tree is discovered, scented with old wax, the site is eagerly communicated. A competition of dancing scouts lets the others know of their preference, and as the largest number forms a quorum, it decides in favor of the new, or in this instance, old location. The decision is unanimous! Waggling and piping, "buzz runners" ram into the cluster of other bees, vibrating their wings faster and faster until they're ready to fly. Like an explosion, the cluster rises into a cloud one more time. They bivouac at a height of fifty feet, looking down on fields of green corn, sugarcane, and orchards of papaya, till the scouts enter the green canopy of mango trees and begin fanning out pheromones. The others follow, joining together at the base of the branch, protecting the queen as she quietly takes her place in the center.

Bees lack nerve receptors and are said to have no emotion, so as the queen re-establishes herself and the colony tends to her, there may be no sense of joy. Is this why humans have little compunction about killing off bees? Could it be why genocide is often preceded by labeling human victims as insects? Mama Sarah never asked for the bees to be destroyed and knew their value to the plants and trees in the district. She wanted only for the surrounding area to be safe. Now, we look up into the thick canopy, the orchard of mangoes, orange, and fig trees planted long ago by Sarah Obama and her husband—an oasis for attracting continuous colonies of bees. The interconnected balance of insects, trees, and mammals may have an unspoken purpose. Perhaps the African queen does, as well.

"Can you bring down some of that honey?" Sarah asks.

So here is Motherhood: a defining aspect of the mammalian species, a species that gives milk to its young via mammary glands and over the course of human development shapes our consciousness in ways that bind families together. Nourishing a human society demands feminine strength and balance, together with the masculine. Sarah, Mary Onyango, and Wangari Maathai each hold a country and its culture together—forty-two tribes and forty-seven million citizens, with a blend of religions that manifest the innumerable superorganisms of Africa. I am the smallest part of a world that cannot exist without a mother, and perhaps in the end I'm just searching for Mother Earth. And therein exists the reason why I'm climbing this tree that leads to a large colony of bees. I'm determined to get some of that honey for Mama Sarah.

FIGURE 19: Mama Sara Obama holding Community Service Award

Appendix

Chapter 2: Home Cubed – A Muslim Family

Politics and Bees – More on Raila Odinga and the Queen Bee

Although less has been written about my mother she was the most formative figure of my youth.

—Raila Odinga on Raila (1)

About a year after our first visit to Kogelo, Barack Obama won the presidential election. It was celebrated with great joy in Luo land. People watched on Mama Sarah's television in her small cement-walled building day and night up to the final victory announcement. Kenya needed a celebration, something to ease the traumatic political process that had taken place the year before. In its own presidential race of 2007, Luo candidate

Raila Odinga was predicted by many to succeed the Kikuyu incumbent, Mwai Kibaki. National tension built up precipitously around tribal allegiances.

Kibaki, born in 1931, was raised in a village where most boys herded sheep and cattle. He was instead selected to go to school and did so with success, advancing from a small-mission primary to the London School of Economics, where he graduated with distinction. At age thirty, he left academics to enter politics and help draft Kenya's independence constitution, and once more, he rose up the ranks. He was elected member of Parliament, appointed secretary for the treasury, minister of commerce and industry, minister of finance, and by 1978, he had become vice-president. Known for technocratic skills and a non confrontational style—"he never saw a fence he didn't sit on,"—he eventually fell out of favor with authoritarian President Moi and became the opposition leader in Parliament. He ran for president against Moi and lost twice in a row, in 1992 and 1997. When he finally achieved victory in 2002, it came after receiving critical support from Raila Odinga, who sacrificed his own campaign to ensure a majority vote. when he declared, "*Kibaki tosha* (Kibaki's the one)." When Kibaki was disabled by an automobile accident, Raila led a tireless, difficult campaign to ensure Kibaki's success.

Odinga, now sixty-eight years old, has followed a staggered course to Kenyan leadership. His nicknames include *Agwambo*, difficult to predict or mysterious; *Jakom*, Chairman; and *Tinga*, Tractor, symbol of the Democratic National Party. He came from a family deeply established in Kenya politics. He was arrested for taking part in a coup in 1982, tortured and placed under house arrest for six months, and then later kept in prison for six years without trial. On his release, he became involved with human rights and pro-democracy activists who were pushing for multiparty democracy and was again incarcerated. When released in 1991, he left Kenya to live in Norway, alleging government attempts to assassinate him. The push for multiparty democracy continued with his return to Kenya, and he was elected member of Parliament in 1992, assumed leadership of the National

Development Party, and ran for president in 1997. Although he was alleged to have been offered the position of prime minister when he helped Kibaki win in 2002, Odinga saw the promise of a new constitution and his own rise to prominence vanish as Kibaki consolidated power.

Africa's last fifty years has been a tumultuous history of escape from colonialism, which has given way to absolute control by the "big man," an autocratic male ruler who, through patronage, bullets, and sometimes genocide, rules his country with an iron fist for a lifetime. The names Mobutu of Zaire (previously the Belgian Congo); Mengistu of Ethiopia; Idi Amin of Uganda; Omar Al-Bashir of Sudan; Charles Taylor of Liberia; Mugabe of Zimbabwe; and Gaddafi of Libya are but a few of the recognizable names. Kenya has been associated more with corruption than with dictatorship, though Kenyatta and Daniel arap Moi had modest qualifications. After the military coup attempt in 1982, Moi allowed a torture chamber to be built in the Nairobi government building. Ironically, it was named the *Nyayo* building, a word that means "footsteps," which Moi used to frame his philosophy of peace, love, and unity," following the leadership of Jomo Kenyatta. During ten years of on-and-off imprisonment, Odinga was beaten severely, made to stand for days and nights in a room with cold water up to his ankles, splashed in the darkness to increase his exhaustion, and fed a minimal diet until his health began to falter. Other political prisoners received much worse treatment and succumbed.

Bee politics has taken almost as many forms as human politics, shifting with the changing values of different places and times. The hive has been, in turn, monarchical, oligargical, aristocratic, constitutional, imperial, republican, absolute, moderate, communist, anarchist, and even fascist. As so often in politics, we see whatever it is we want to see.

—Bee Wilson, *The Hive* (2)

Supersedure

In the spring, the honey flow is on; bees encounter ample nectar and pollen as flowers come into bloom. The queen bee's productiveness is under scrutiny, and if she's running out of sperm, laying fewer eggs, and not releasing enough pheromone, she'll be encouraged to leave the hive. In the swarming process, she's taken with a consort of about half the colony while the scouts search for a new location. By doing so, she ensures propagation of the species and, fortuitously, avoids death by the worker bees who may otherwise "ball up" to sting or crush her. The workers have already begun a few "queen cells" provided with royal jelly to produce vigorous new queens.

There's an exception to this process known as supersedure, in which a colony replaces its queen without swarming. The old queen and the new queen co-exist for a time, and beekeepers are happy because the honey production and number of bees remains robust. Supersedure is not fully understood, and efforts to encourage it aren't always successful. Normally, after queens have been productive for several years and begun to slow down, the workers prepare "queen cells" at the periphery of the hive that look like large peanut shells. Supersedure queen cells look the same but tend to be fewer and located in the center. In either case, the beekeeper knows the hive is preparing for a new queen, and the old queen, not suspecting her eventual termination, lays eggs in the queen cells without any insistence from the workers.

In the case of supersedure, she coexists with a new queen for an indefinite period until she's exhausted. By not swarming and temporarily avoiding matricide, she continues laying eggs along with the new queen. This is regarded as "efficient supersedure," as opposed to "inefficient supersedure," which occurs when the old queen is killed off by the workers and the new virgin queen still has to get mated and do catch-up work. There are differences of opinion as to how one assists the process of queen progression. In Kenya, the process of artificially replacing queens is not common, so supersedure may occur more frequently. And it did take place in a unique political situation—only it was for a president and not a queen.

Supersedure Politics

When he re-established himself in Kenyan society and politics, Luos regarded Raila Odinga as a hero. Then, essentially he was double-crossed in 2002 when President Kibaki, who had agreed to revise the constitution and offer him the position of prime minister, changed his mind. Rather than facilitate a review of previous corrupt practices and legislate the sharing of power, Kibaki ordained a constitution that further consolidated presidential authority. In 2005, Odinga split off to form a new party, the Orange Democratic Movement, which was successful in defeating Kibaki's proposed revision in a national referendum.

In response, Kibaki sacked his entire cabinet, and when it was reformed, his own Kikuyu tribe dominated the new ruling elite. Those closest to him were cynically referred to as the "Mt. Kenya Mafia." While the economy improved, it was disproportionately shared with the Kikuyu sector (a process known in Kenya as eating the government's barbecue, or *nyama choma*), and corruption continued in high places. When Odinga left the government in 2005 to create a new party, he soon became the challenger most likely to succeed against Kibaki. By July of 2007, when he held a support rally in Nairobi's Uhuru Park, an estimated fifty thousand showed up, and campaign elements were sufficient for a perfect storm.

He ran against Kibaki in the 2007 presidential race, and early polls expected him to win. Kenyan dissatisfaction with endemic corruption, landlessness, and unemployment had led the voters to desire a new start. And then, with a widely publicized series of irregularities in the voting process, the result was a split vote, with only a very small fraction favoring Kibaki. As reported by *The Economist*: "It was a civil coup. All that was needed were extra votes to squeak past Mr. Odinga in what had been among the most closely contested elections Africa had ever seen." (3)

In the midst of the election, the chairman of the electoral commission announced that delays were caused by the disappearance of senior poll officials who had gone to "cook results for people who were paying them." On December 30th, the chairman withdrew into chambers with fellow commissioners and they decided that Kibaki was the winner. The chairman rushed to the State House to issue a certificate, Kibaki was sworn in, and violence erupted.

In national contests, you can anticipate disruption when there's a fifty-fifty division between two sides and power has to be accorded to one side or the other—think of the American Civil War, the Vietnamese War, and Kenya. Of course, when Bush and Gore nearly tied in the 2000 presidential election, chaos did not erupt. When Odinga and Kibaki split the vote, however, there were a host of election-process irregularities, far surpassing the issue of Florida chads. Voter registration cards were withheld from Luos, the government created thirty new constituencies, and ballots were stuffed, probably on both sides. So when Odinga's opposition party won six out of eight provinces and the largest number of parliamentary seats and then voters were informed that he lost, the accusations of fraud were loud. Soon thereafter, some ODM supporters, particularly youths and gangs, took to the streets with guns, machetes, and gas cans. Kikuyu and Kalenjin gangs retaliated, reputedly paid by politicians, and for months citizens risked being pulled out of a car and shot or hacked to death. Many of the victims were women and children, and close to 1,500 Kenyans from all sides were slaughtered; in addition, 250,000 were made homeless. Some of this devastation took place in Kisumu, the third largest city of Kenya, next to Lake Victoria—where I passed through on my way to visit Mama Sarah.

Christmas came and went, the Ugandan ambassador congratulated Kibaki, the World Bank urged getting back to business, and violence continued. For the crisis to settle down, it took two more months as well as the eventual mediation of the former U.N. Secretary-General Kofi Annan and his panel. In the National Accord arrangement, Kibaki agreed to share power with Odinga, who finally accepted the previously denied position of prime minister.

Queen bees these men are not, although there are biologic parallels. It is infrequent, but two queen bees can exist in one hive just as two men can govern a country. While some political bodies or societies can tolerate two powerful leaders, it is not the common rule. Americans go back and forth with odd regularity between Republican and Democratic presidents, but it's difficult to conceive of the two working together in one White House. For the same reason, expecting these two opposing leaders to share power in Kenya stretched the imagination. Only the full impact of international pressure, the collapse of the economy, and a drawn-out siege of tribal murders and dislocation persuaded Kibaki and his government to compromise, although he still retained the greater power.

Odinga said, on April 18th, "My swearing in as prime minister will go further than just an entry in our history books. We will now consign Kenya's past failures of grand corruption and rampant tribalism to the history books. Kenya will no longer have a ruling class. The rulers are the people."

It was an optimistic idea. Nevertheless, the two leaders shared power for five years because the larger public (think *superorganism*) accepted the awkward arrangement for the sake of survival.

Bee Territory

From 2009 till 2011 there has not been a marked change in encounters of Africanized bees. This probably slowing down of travel is often attributed to the inability of African bees to tolerate colder temperatures. They have yet to adapt to harsh winters with tight cluster formation in protected spaces the way European bees have been able to do for eons. But as Darwin pointed out: "It is not the strongest of the species that survives, nor the most intelligent that survives. It is the one that is the most adaptable to change." We can expect that Africanized bees will continue to adapt.

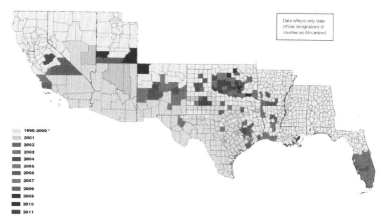

FIGURE 20: Spread of Africanized Honeybees: U.S. Distribution 2011

Chapter 6: Bees, Trees, and Hospitals

Disappearing Bees

As of 2015 the problem of disappearing bees and other pollinators has hardly disappeared. Despite improved statistics in 2012 the number of honeybee colonies are still declining at a rate close to thirty percent per year, almost twice what is regarded as a sustainable loss. The scientific-political debate over whether to ban neonicotinoids continues. Supportive and conflicting studies have yet to convince the FDA to follow the European ban. Other contributing factors including loss of foraging, nutrition, and pathogens, make it difficult to isolate pesticides as the only responsible factor.

Even if a balance between the health of pollinators and the health of the agribusiness economy still leans towards the market side, public pressure, including four million signatures and protests at the Whitehouse

In 2014 the Obama administration called for the Secretary of Agriculture (USDA) and the Administrator of the Environmental Protection Agency (EPA) to co-chair a new Pollinator Health Task Force, "responsible for focusing federal efforts to research, prevent, and recover from pollinator losses." Eleven million dollars was sanctioned by the Department of Agriculture to increase foraging for pollinators in five Midwest states where half of America's commercial honey bees are located in summer months. Seven million acres will be restored or enhanced. A further goal is to restore honeybee health to sustainable levels by 2025 and increase Eastern Monarch Butterflies to a 225 million population by 2020. (5)

Helpful Websites for Honeybees and Pollinators

www.xerces.org – bumblebees, butterflys – invertebrate diversity information

www.greatsunflower.org – keeping track of the honeybee numbers

www.scientificbeekeeping.com – one of many excellent guides to beginning beekeepers

Chapter 7: Colonies and Communities

Ongoing Contests

Part 1

Uhuru Kenyatta, who was competing with Raila Odinga for the 2013 presidential contest, traveled a sinuous course to leadership and power. The son of Jomo Kenyatta, he preferred a less public image as a youth, playing soccer for St. Mary's Roman Catholic High School and attending Amherst in the U.S., where he obtained a B.A. in political science and economics. Reportedly, he worked at Burger King while in the states and, on returning to Kenya, he served as a bank teller, though only briefly. Now considered the richest man in Kenya and the twenty-fourth richest in Africa, with a half billion dollars in assets and an equal amount of acres in family land, he clearly had advantages and skills. During the 1990s, he was primed and cultivated to continue the family legacy. Sometimes, when he was hanging out at a hotel bar with some of his drinking buddies, they would wonder why he asked to borrow their Morris Minor and leave behind his own plush Mercedes Benz. They thought he was on a wild date, but in fact he was on a clandestine trip to the State House to receive political lessons from President Daniel arap Moi.

Moi encouraged Uhuru to run for office. He lost his bid for Parliament in 1997, but Moi appointed him chairman of the Kenya Tourism Board in 1999 and nominated him for member of Parliament in 2001. He was appointed minister of local government and made his first bid for president in 2002. Finishing second, with only half the votes of Mwai Kibaki, Uhuru subsequently worked with Raila to promote a constitutional referendum that divested some of the presidential power Kibaki had enjoyed. By 2007, he switched his allegiance back to Kibaki and became a strong supporter of conservative Kikuyu policies. It was in this critical year that Odinga lost to Kibaki in an election widely considered to have been rigged and mishandled by the IEBC (Independent Electoral and Boundaries Commission). Accused of participating in post-election violence, Uhuru was indicted by the International Criminal Court. After more than seven years, his trial was dismissed for lack of sufficient evidence. Potentially damaging witnesses either vanished or admitted they had been prejudiced by the defense. President Kenyatta refused to release his financial records for deeper scrutiny.

Part 2

The education system for the Ogiek people has traditionally been through the oral transmission of knowledge. Ogiek men working with herbal medicines are highly regarded; the Maasai often hire them to perform circumcisions on their young *moranis* (warriors). While some hunter-gatherer societies are egalitarian, with balanced male-female relationships, Ogiek women are less likely to attend school or be found in a leadership position. There are exceptions, such as Agnes Salimu, an elected assembly member who works for her community. Their role of bearing children, foraging, preparing food, and maintaining the home is so well established, however, that it is difficult for them to attend and stay in school. Many of the Ogiek women I saw had an infant on their back, wrapped with a blanket, and other children by their side. As in all parts of Kenya, this role is changing.

Chapter 8: The Magic Window

John Githongo on Corruption

Kenya's problems with corruptions are not yet solved according to John Githongo. After the 2015 Obama visit and summit on African business development he states: "This is the most rapacious administration that we have ever had. Corruption in Kenya has deepened and widened." The country is slipping down Transparency International's annual corruption index and is now 145th out of 174 nations, down from 136 in 2013. (6)

Three Targeted Programs

Rotary International: Polio Plus

Confucius said, "It is better to light a single candle, than to sit and curse the darkness." The Rotary way is to light a candle. I light one, you light one, 1.2 million Rotarians light one. Together we light up the world.

—Gary C. K. Huang, Rotary International President

FIGURE 21: Rotary International's Polio Plus Eradication and Endgame Strategic Plan

MedShare

Andy Pines works for another nonprofit with warehouses in San Leandro, California, but based out of Atlanta, Georgia. Its staff and volunteers take advantage of the two million tons of medical supplies that come out of American hospitals yearly. Rather than letting it remain a haphazard collection that ends up in hospital closets and incinerators, MedShare collects and stores functional devices and equipment and delivers it to requesting hospitals based on carefully assessed need.

From its inception in 1998, the nonprofit has delivered $93 million worth—that amounts to 1,000 tractor-trailer containers to 85 developing countries. The largely volunteer effort has supplied 2,100 medical missions while also sparing two million cubic feet of landfill. Some of the supplies and equipment also goes to community-based health clinics in the U.S.

What defines MedShare's effectiveness is the requirement on the part of receiving countries to verify their need as well as their capacity to maintain all equipment and supplies that are shipped. If a hospital doesn't provide bioengineering, it doesn't get equipment. Once a container arrives, cost of delivery and permits are paid by the receiving country, and careful selection is emphasized. (7)

PINCC—Prevention International: No Cervical Cancer

In 2005, Kay Taylor, a retired gynecologist, traveled to Central America and began a unique nonprofit venture of diagnosing and treating early cervical cancer. With only acetic acid, cotton swabs, and minor surgery supplies, she and her team were able to develop a system of detecting early signs of cancer and treating it. Training nationals to master the techniques involved so as to reach out to larger populations is primary to the team mission. In ten years, the PINCC team has reduced the incidence of cervical cancer throughout Honduras, Nicaragua, Guatemala, Salvador, Peru, and multiple sites in South America, India, and Africa.

Dr. Taylor's philosophy is that host countries must show dedication to mastering and offering the diagnostic and treatment modalities. If they succeed, they are provided supporting equipment to run clinics. If they fail or do not sustain the services, the equipment is taken back. The clearly targeted goal of PINCC is to develop local expertise and to help eradicate the most common women's cancer in most developing countries. (8)

Climate Concern

Few express the challenge of Greenhouse Gases (GHG), Global Warming, or Climate Change, depending on your preferred terminology, more succinctly than Bill McKibben. Using three numbers taken from a UK group of environmental and financial analysts—2, 565, and 2,795—a disturbing scenario is summed up. (9) Two degrees Celsius is the scientifically chosen census number for the maximum temperature increase the planet will tolerate without irrevocable changes threatening all life as we

know since the rise of civilization—announced at the Copen-
hagen climate summit 2009. Five hundred sixty five represents
the number of gigatons of carbon dioxide that can be released
into the atmosphere by midcentury and leave a hope of keeping
temperature rise below two degrees. Two thousand seven hundred and ninety five gigatons is the amount of carbon contained
in existing coal, oil, and gas reserves of fossil fuel companies
globally. Simple math points out that using just one fifth of the
reserves will place the planet in extreme jeopardy. Since the
market value of the last figure is about $28 trillion, it suggests
that forcing fossil fuel companies to leave behind four fifths of
the reserves means writing off $20 trillion. The battle lines are
thus drawn between a fossil fuel driven and a renewable energy
economy. The stage for World Wars is giving way to a massive
competition of technologies and human choice.

Chapter 10: Another Monotheistic Religion

All gods are better than their reputation

—Mark Twain, *A Chosen People*

*Compared with the histories of Assyria, Babylon, Egypt, and
Syria, Jewish history is strictly minor league. What lifted the
Jews from obscurity to permanent religious greatness was their
passion for meaning.*

—Huston Smith, *The World's Religions* (10)

Mumbi's tribe, the original nine Kikuyu clans descended from
Gikuyu and his wife Mumbi, has similarities with another tribe
that has shaped Western history for several millennia. From the
most natural of settings, a peaceful and plentiful garden, with
trees of fruit and a special tree of "good and evil" came Adam
and Eve. They, in turn, give birth to Cain and Abel, a farmer and
a shepherd. Cain killed his brother, setting the stage for more
human struggle, but Adam and Eve had another son, Seth, and
after many generations his offspring generated Abraham ("father

of many nations"). The land of Abraham is less alpine and forested than that of Gikuyu, and Abraham also has the problem of begetting a son. God tells him: "Know of a surety that thy seed shall be a stranger in a land that is not theirs, and shall serve them: and they shall afflict them four hundred years: And also that nation, whom they shall serve, will I judge: and afterward shall they come out with great substance."

Abraham, at age 86, along with Hagar, the servant of his wife, gives birth to Ishmael. As foretold by God, Ishmael gives birth to princes of twelve Arab tribes. Still fruitful at age 100, Abraham and his wife Sarah then give birth to Isaac, who averts being sacrificed on Mt. Moriah as a result of his father's faith in God. Isaac's progeny, through Jacob, lead to the formation of the twelve tribes of Israel. Biblical history within the Torah and Pentateuch spans from creation through Revelation and relates the experience of the Hebrew tribes as Moses guides them to the Promised Land. The Kikuyus certainly suffered under the yoke of the colonial period, but the time was relatively less than the 420 years of captivity faced by the Jews in Egypt. It seems almost inconceivable to later generations that during the Holocaust of the last century, before a million of the Kikuyu people were interred by the British, six million of the nine million Jews of Europe, including the elderly, women, and children, were systematically murdered in crematoriums and prison camps by an educated Christian nation. The struggle for freedom was intense, the injustices great for both Kikuyu and Jewish cultures, and the sagas continue.

Huston Smith describes Jewish history as minor league, but only in the context of population size and territory during the Sumerian Age. By contrast, the numerical size of the Jewish culture had an extraordinary impact on Western history and the ethical foundation of civilization. Tracing back to the prophets of Israel and Judah, who cried out for justice and for God's deliverance, the trajectory of Western thought in many ways begins with Jewish culture. Smith defines the prophetic principle: ". . . the prerequisite of political stability is social justice, for it is in the nature of things that injustice will not endure." He notes that, "the prophets enter the stage of history like a strange, elemental, explosive force. They live in a vaster world than their compatriots, a world in which pomp and ceremony, wealth and splendor count for nothing, where kings seem small and the power of the mighty is as nothing compared with purity, justice, and mercy. So it is that wherever men and women have gone to history for encouragement and inspiration in the age-long struggle for justice, they have found it more than anywhere else in the ringing proclamations of the prophets." (11)

But the essence of Judaism is almost impossible to define. David Ariel, in his book, *What Do Jews Believe?*, describes the complexity: "Judaism is not a religion of fixed doctrines or dogmas but a complex system of evolving beliefs."

Central to the faith is a universal search for meaning that evolves from the sacred myths common to all religions. There is one God, Yahweh, transcendent and immanent, all-powerful and personal, just and gentle, who creates and loves mankind. All that is created is good. And yet, Adam and Eve fall from paradise as they partake of the serpent's forbidden fruit and the knowledge of good and evil. Noah must rise above the incestuous behavior of his sons and all of man's sins, so Yahweh provides him with an Ark to survive the flood. When Yahweh calls Abraham out of the darkness of the Sumerian Age, a pilgrimage of the first Hebrew people takes place—a chosen people who will serve God. Their extraordinary march through human history reflects the disproportionate impact Jewish people have had upon it. A population of only 15 million Jews still shapes our civilization in remarkable ways.

> How odd
> Of God
> To choose
> The Jews

So says a quatrain identifying the exceptionality of Judaism. (12) That one culture would be given special divine intervention contradicts a more universal notion of the Deity. More comprehensible to the uniqueness of Judaism, however, is the belief that Jews have a historically developed role—not of privilege, but to provide service to humanity and suffer the trials that such service implies. In his book, Ariel asks the question of why one should be Jewish and answers it himself, saying: "I believe that Judaism is the longest continuous tradition in Western civilization to ask fundamental questions about life, its purpose, and human destiny."

Karl Marx may have disparaged religion as an opiate of the masses, but he was a product of his culture. So was Freud, who tended to see God as an Oedipal transference of man's need for a father figure. Einstein, also a Jew, defined laws of physics and energy and stated that God did not "throw the dice." Nonetheless, as in monotheistic Christianity, Islam, and Kikuyu, there are not yet as many quotes, announcements, or prophesy from the feminine side.

Real History of The African Queen – by C.S. Forester.

The African Queen, first published in 1935, was perhaps Cecil Scott Forester's most famous book, an adventure and love story matching the evangelical purity of an English spinster with the lonely prowess of a gin-drinking merchant adventurer. As the two unlikely lovers steam down the Ulanga river in the African Queen they encounter multiple rapids and cannon fire from a German fortress, but they survive all challenges until their "tramp steamer" sinks and they are captured by the Germans. What becomes of Rose Sayer (Katharine Hepburn) and Charlie Allnut (Humphrey Bogart) is dependent on which ending you choose from Forester's writing and John Huston's movie production. Hepburn endured bouts of dysentery while filming the blockbuster, but Bogart avoided illness through dietary restriction: "All I ate was baked beans, canned asparagus, and Scotch whisky. Whenever a fly bit Huston or me, it dropped dead." The original African Queen survives and can be seen today in Key Largo, Florida, where it was restored, made seaworthy and steams along after more than a century.

FIGURE 22: The *African Queen* in Key Largo, Florida

Endnotes

Chapter 1

1. Barack Obama, *Dreams from My Father: A Story of Race and Inheritance*, New York: Random House, 1995, 397.
2. Maurice Maeterlinck, *The Life of the Bee*, 1901, 3–4.
3. Bert Holldobler and E.O. Wilson, *Superorganism*, New York: W.W. Norton & Company, Inc., 9.
4. Francois Huber, *New Observations on the Natural History of Bees*, Letter 1: "The Impregnation of the Queen Bee," 1806.
5. Charles Butler, *The Feminine Monarchie or the History of Bees*, 1623 edition, RareBooksClub.com, 2012.
6. Barack Obama, *Dreams from My Father: A Story of Race and Inheritance*, 394.
7. Ibid., 405.
8. Ben Macintyre and Paul Orengoh, "Beatings and Abuse Made Barack Obama's Grandmother Loathe the British," *The Times*, 2 December 2008.
9. Peter Firstbrook, *The Obama Family: The Untold Story of an African Family*. London: Preface Publishing, 2010, 190.

Chapter 2

1. Barack Obama, *Dreams from My Father: A Story of Race and Inheritance*, 377.

2. Asenath Bole Odaga, *Luo Proverbs and Sayings*, Kisumu, Kenya: Lake Publishers & Enterprises Ltd., 1995, 33.
3. Peter Firstbrook, *The Obama Family*, 158.
4. Sally H. Jacobs, T*he Other Barack: The Bold and Reckless Life of Barack Obama's Father*, Philadelphia: Public Affairs, 2011, 20–21.
5. Daphne Barak, *Mama Sarah Obama: Our Dreams and Roots*, Beverly Hills: P.I. Publications, Inc., 2012, 9.
6. Peter Firstbrook, *The Obama Family*, 177.
7. Ibid., 178.
8. Ibid., 178
9. Daphne Barak, *Mama Sarah Obama*, 15.
10. Peter Miller, *The Smart Swarm*, New York: Penguin Group, 2010, xx.
11. Thomas D. Seeley, *Honeybee Democracy*, Princeton, Princeton University Press, 2010.
12. Sally H. Jacobs, *The Other Barack*, Philadelphia: Public Affairs, 2011, 29.
13. Caroline Elkins, *Imperial Reckoning*, New York: Henry Holt & Company, 2005, xii.
14. Ibid., xiv.
15. Ibid., 241.
16. Ibid., 238–240.
17. Mark L. Winston, *Killer Bees*, London: Harvard University Press, 1992, 3.
18. www.ars.usda.gov/research/docs. htm?docid=11059&page=6
19. David Maraniss, *Barack Obama: The Story*, New York: Simon and Schuster, 2012, xvi.
20. Daphne Barak, *Mama Sarah Obama*, 22.

Chapter 3

1. Lawrence Packer, *Keeping the Bees*, Harper Collins Publishers Ltd., 2010, 227.
2. Hattie Ellis, *Sweetness and Light: The Mysterious History of the Honeybee*, New York: Three Rivers Press, 2004, 19.

3. Lawrence Packer, *Keeping the Bees*, 227.
4. David W. Roubik, *Ecology and Natural History of Tropical Bees*, Cambridge: Cambridge University Press, 1989, 367.
5. Peter Firstbrook, *The Obama Family*, 58.
6. Ibid., 53.

Chapter 4

1. E.O. Wilson, *The Social Conquest of the Earth*, New York: Loveright Publishing Corporation, 2012, 8.
2. Wangari Maathai, *Unbowed: A Memoir*, New York: Anchor Books, 2007, p.58.
3. Terry Bridges, Wangari Maathai Quotes, Oct. 2011, www.ecology.com.
4. Stuart Jeffries, Planting the Future, *The Guardian*, February 16, 2007.
5. Wilson Odero, et al, "Road Traffic Injuries in Kenya: Magnitude, causes and status of intervention," *Injury Control and Safety Promotion*, 2003, vol. 10, no. 1, 1–2, 53–61.
6. Tijs Goldschmidt, *Darwin's Dreampond: Drama in Lake Victoria*, MIT Press, 1996, 231.
7. Charles Hornsby, *Kenya-A History Since Independence*
8. Wangari Maathai, Speak Truth to Power, Speech, May 4, 2000, www.greenbeltmovement.org.
9. Ibid.
10. Namalundah Florence, "Wangari Maathai: Visionary, Environmental Leader," *Political Activist*, New York: Lantern Books, 2014, 109.

Chapter 5

1. Michael Harrington, *The Other America*, Touchstone, Simon and Schuster, 1997, 7.
2. IRIN, Humanitarian News and Analysis, www.irinnews.org, Oct 22, 2008.

3. E. S. Atieno Odhiambo, "Ethnic Cleansing and Civil Society in Kenya, 1969–1992," *Journal of Contemporary African Studies*, vol. 22, no. 1, 2004, 29–42.

4. Cindi Brown, *Poverty and Promise: One Volunteer's Experience of Kenya*, 2008.

5. Hanna Rosin, *The End of Men and the Rise of Women*, New York: Riverhead Books, 2012, 5.

6. Bill McKibben, *Oil and Honey: The Education of an Unlikely Activist*, New York, St. Martin's Griffin, 2013, 168.

Chapter 6

1. Hattie Ellis, *Sweetness and Light*, New York, Three Rivers Press, 2004,120.

2. Henry Beston, *The Outermost House*, New York: Henry Holt and Company, 1928, 24–25.

3. Wangari Maathai, *The Challenge for Africa*, New York: Anchor Books, 2010, 240.

4. Jeffrey Sachs, *The Age of Sustainable Development*, New York: Columbia University Press, 2015, chapter 14.

5. Moses Imo, et al., "Professional and Societal Mismatch in Kenyan Forestry: Is There a Right Way to Manage our Forests?," *Nairobi: Forest Landscape and Kenya's Vision 2030*.

6. NGOs Co-ordination Board, *Report on the National Validation Survey of NGOs*, 2009.

7. Executive Summary, *Report on the National Validation Survey of NGOs*, 2009, 16.

Chapter 7

1. Auma Obama, *And Then Life Happens: A Memoir*, New York: St Martin's Press, 2012, 196.

2. Chimamanda Ngozi Adichie, *Americanah*, New York: Anchor Books, 2014, 227-228.

3. Wangari Maathai, *The Challenge for Africa*, 197.
4. Wrong, Michela, *It's Our Turn to Eat*, Harper Collins, 2009.
5. Barack Obama, *Dreams from My Father: A Story of Race and Inheritance*, 348.
6. Wangari Maathai, *The Challenge for Africa*, 275.
7. G.H. Yeoman, 1993: "High Altitude Forest Conservation in Relation to Dorobo People," *Kenya Past and Present*, 3.

Chapter 8

1. Rasna Warah, *Missionaries, Mercenaries and Misfits: An Anthology*, Excerpt: Maina Mwangi, "Why Aid Has Failed Africa So Spectacularly," AuthorHouse, 155.
2. James Albins, "James Herman Robinson: Historical Note," Amistad Research Center, www.amistadresearch-center.org.
3. E. O. Wilson, *The Social Conquest of the Earth*, New York, Loveright Publishing Corporation, 2012, 289.
4. William Easterly, *The White Man's Burden*, Oxford: Oxford University Press, 2007.
5. Cliff Dochterman, *Rotary's Involvement in Polio Eradication*, www.rotaryfirst100.org
6. Paul Collier, *The Bottom Billion: An Agenda for Action*, Oxford University Press, 2007, 175–92.
7. Michela Wrong, *It's Our Turn to Eat*, New York:Harper Collins, 2009, 202.
8. Philip Mwakio, *East African Standard*, May 19, 2005.
9. https://wikileaks.org/wiki/The_looting_of_Kenya_under_President_Moi.
10. Michela Wrong, *It's Our Turn to Eat*, 208.
11. Ibid., 79–80.
12. Dambisa Moyo, *Dead Aid: Why aid is not working and how there is a better way for Africa*, Farrar, Straus, and Giroux, 2009, 144.
13. Ibid.

14. Barack Obama, *Dreams from My Father: A Story of Race and Inheritance*, 555.

15. David Maranz, *African Friends and Money Matters*, Dallas: SIL International, 2001, 144.

16. Peter Ouma, et al, "Antenatal and delivery care in rural western Kenya: the effect of training health care workers to provide 'focused antenatal care.'" *Reproductive Health* 2010, 7:1 doi:10.1186/1742-4755-7-1.

17. Daniel Okoth, "Why Doctors' flight is a growing concern in the ailing healthcare system," *Standard Digital*, May 31, 2013, http://www.standardmedia.co.ke/?articleID=20 00084831&story_title=why-doctors-flight-is-a-growing-concern-in-the-ailing-healthcare-system&pageNo=2.

18. David Maranz, *African Friends and Money Matters*, 144.

19. Peter Firstbrook, *The Obama Family*, 185.

Chapter 9

1. George Obama, *Homeland*, New York: Simon and Schuster, 2010, 184.

Chapter 10

1. Richard Preston, *The Hot Zone*, New York: Random House, 1994, 289.

2. Huston Smith, *The World's Religions*, Harper Collins, 1961, 245.

3. www.MSOF.org

4. Doris Mayoli, *Ashes to Beauty*, Nairobi: Aura Creations, 2009, 8.

5. Wangari Maathai, *Replenishing the Earth*, 101.

6. Ibid., p.78.

7. Colin Tudge, *The Tree*, Three Rivers Press, 2005, 191.

8. Wangari Maathai, *Replenishing the Earth*, 78.

9. Betty Press, *I Am Because We Are*, Books for Africa, 2011, 80.

10. Wangari Maathai, *Replenishing the Earth*, 95.

11. Namulunday Florence, *Wangari Maathai: Visionary, Environmental Leader, Political Activist*, New York: Lantern Books, 2014, p. 40.

12. Amos Kareithi, "Kenya: Disease 'A Weapon to Wipe Out Blacks'", *East African Standard*, Aug 31, 2004.

13. Namalundah Florence, *Wangari Maathai: Visionary, Environmental Leader, Political Activist*, New York: Lantern Books, p.197.

14. Wangari Maathai, *Replenishing the Earth*, 123

15. Ibid., 183.

16. Wangari Maathai, *Unbowed: A Memoir*, New York: Anchor Books, 2007, p. 194.

17. Wangari Maathai, *The Challenge for Africa*, 3.

18. Bee Wilson, *The Hive: The Story of the Honeybee and Us*, New York, St Martin's Press, 2004.

19. Jennifer Holland, *Honeybees in East Africa Resist Deadly Pathogens*, News.nationalgeographic.com.

Appendix

1. Babafemi Badejo, *Raila Odinga: An Enigma in Kenyan Politics*, Lagos, Nigeria, Yintab Books, 2006, p. 345.

2. Bee Wilson, *The Hive: The Story of the Honeybee and Us*, New York, St. Martin's Press, 2004, p. 109.

3. "Twilight Robbery: Ethnic Violence Comes to Kenya," *The Economist*, January 2, 2008.

4. http://www.ars.usda.gov/research/docs.htm?docid=11059&page=6

5. www2.epa.gov/pollinator-protection/federal-pollinator-health-task-force-epas-role

6. AFP, "Corruption in Kenya is 'worse then ever' says veteran campaigner John Githongo," *The Nation*, Sunday August 2, 2015.

7. www.medshare.org

8. www.pincc.org

9. Bill McKibben, *Oil and Honey: The Education of an Unlikely Activist*, New York, St. Martin's Press, 2013, 141–153.

10. Huston Smith, *The World's Religions*, Harper Collins, 1961, p. 272.

11. Ibid, p. 292–293.

12. Ibid. p. 307.

Photo Notes and Credits

A majority of photos used in the text are from various trips to Kenya beginning in 2006 and the resolution and choice of images a due entirely to my own limitations. Thanks and acknowledgement for the following photos:

cover:
Fig tree photograph © Steve Heap/Depositphotos, Inc.; Mama Sarah Obama's portrait courtesy of Mama Saraha Obama foundation; Wangari Maathai's portrait courtesy Paul Ng'auru Mugoro; Mary Onyango's portrait © Copyright 2015 The Standard Group, www.standardmedia.co.ke; author photograph courtesy of Steven Godfrey.

frontispiece and chapter opening illustration:
Courtesy of Steven Godfrey.

Figure 2: Map of the Distribution of Bees; base map courtesy Creative Commons License, TUBS, August 18, 2011.

Figure 4: Spread of Africanized Honeybees: U.S. Distribution 2009. Courtesy of Agricultural Research Service, United States Department of Agriculture.

Figure 6: Family portrait in Mama Sarah Obama's home. Photographed by the author with the gracious permission of Marsat Obama.

Figure 7: Gathering Honey: Mesolithic rock painting of a honey hunter harvesting honey and wax from a bees nest in a tree. At Cuevas de la Araña en Bicorp. (Dating around 8000 to 6000 B.C.). Drawing courtesy of fr:Utilisateur:Achillea; GNU General Public Licence.

Figure 9: Wangari Maathai – Winning the Prize; courtesy Paul Ng'auru Mugoro.

Figure 10: Dan Ogola in Kibera; courtesy Matibabu Kenya.

Figure 11: Miriam Odhiambo; courtesy Norma Bozzini and Dick Thompson.

Figure 12: President Kibaki meets with Dan Ogola and James Orengo; courtesy Matibabu Kenya.

Figure 13: Prime Minister Raila Odinga pointing to new hospital; courtesy Matibabu Kenya.

Figure 20: Spread of Africanized Honeybees: U.S. Distribution 2011. Courtesy of Agricultural Research Service, United States Department of Agriculture.

Figure 21: Rotary International's Polio Plus Eradication and Endgame Strategic Plan; Global Polio Eradication Initiative.

Figure 22 (top and bottom): The *African Queen,* the original vessel from director John Huston's classic 1951 film by the same name, sails on a Key Largo, Florida, canal Thursday, April 12, 2012. The vessel is steered by Steve Bogart (third from left), son of actor Humphrey Bogart. Built in 1912, the 30-foot boat that carried Humphrey Bogart and Katharine Hepburn has been refurbished to provide Florida Keys visitors an opportunity to ride the cinema icon. The *African Queen* has been the pride and joy of Key Largo since 1982, where she is registered as a National Historic site and in 2012 celebrated her centennial year. © Key Largo Sightseeing Canal and Dinner Cruises; http://africanqueenflkeys.com/index.html. Permission for use graciously granted by African Queen Trust LLC. Photos courtesy of Newman PR.

Acknowledgements

It took Kogelo town, Siaya city, several hospitals, long flights, and many families to write this book. Most of all, I thank my own family for allowing the time, and can only begin to recognize all the assistance provided in setting words and fingers to the digital universe.

Deep thanks to the Kenya Obama family for their support, especially Mama Sarah, Said, and Marsat Obama, and all those who patiently answered my questions and watched a comic struggle to change an apiary environment that changed me instead.

I am indebted to many authors—Wangari Maathai, Barack Obama, Peter Firstbrook, Daphne Barak, E.O. Wilson, Namalundah Florence, and Thomas Seeley are but a few. If I have recorded the smallest part of what Mama Sarah, Mary Onyango and Wangari Maathai have inspired and achieved, then my own efforts are rewarded. Help and encouragement came from Edward Wageni and Njogu Kahare of the Greenbelt Movement. Njogu can teach anyone how to build a Kenya top bar hive, and his passion for raising bees is endless. Ed Bacardi (Mr. Bee) has been a continuous source of apiary teaching and experience. Eliud Muli is a brilliant, devoted entomologist that fielded questions with a beekeeper's patience and understands bees and ecology with profound insight. Salaton and Kitingo Ngutu showed me the wonders of the bees of the Maasai Mara. Their camp at Maji Moto, organized through Nariku Travel Experiences, is a full experience of wild bees and the Maasai culture.

Special appreciation goes to Kevin Simbi and Tom Mboya (a.k.a. the Bushman), my partners in crime and adventure. Although Tom tried to educate my tongue, I will remain a student under both him and Martina Akinyi forever, *erokamano*!

Dr. Walter Adero helped inform this book more than any other and never gave up. A friend and partner in medicine, he is becoming a teacher to many.

I mention only a few of the providers who have made several trips and devoted innumerable hours of good medicine: first and foremost Gail Wagner, along with Mike and Terry Dunn, Amanda Schoenberg, Ram Ramachandra, Monica Odero, Sakti Das (known to me as The Guru), Sami Dughman, Peter Sherris, Norma Bozzini, Dick Thompson, Linda Waters, Sue Jacobson, Margaret Hegg, Gary and Linnette Clark, Hernando Garcia, Elena Skovorodnikov, Julie Green, Jana Ametshpavic, and so many more—most from Kaiser Permanente, along with the UCSF - East Bay Surgery residents, that have made trips remarkable. Roland and Ellen Bunche provided meals, a hideaway to read, sleep, and write in Nairobi, as well as good advice on life and agriculture in Africa. Roland's books, *Two Ears of Corn*, and *America in the Crosshairs*, are an education on global service. And thanks to the many volunteers from around the world that have shared in the medical work.

My experiences in the land of the Mao Forest was possible thanks to Leonard Mindore, Simon Konana Konin, Leporore Uteraqua, Nicholas Kausa, and the Ogiek community. They share their extraordinary knowledge of the natural world as if their lives depend on it, which is critically true.

Special thanks to Suresh Nehra, Peter, Simbi, and for their stellar anesthesia. Thanks to Dr. Fred Okango, Esther, Carolyn, Pascaliah Odango, Tony, and all the staff of Matibabu for their leadership and support. The opportunity to work with Kenyan patients was due to the hospitality of Siaya District Hospital and a hard-working staff, including Granville, Maureen, Neim, Yano, Odombo, James, Agnes, Peter, Ruto, Philip, Dr. Omoto, and so many others! Nyanza District Provincial Hospital and Dr. James Otieno were always accommodating, providing the residents and me valuable lessons. Thanks to Mwisho Mwisho and Namsagali hotels for accommodating countless volunteers.

I am remiss if I don't thank one who introduced me to Kenya and the incredible world of insects. I am indebted to all the early readers who suffered unguided explorations: Juliane Godfrey, Tim and Ilka Barnes, Paul and Wahu Oseso, Sakti Das, all the Dunn family, Marcia Lansford, Dexter Newton, Gail Wagner, Julie Green, Ameena Saeed and many others. Mike Veronin has graciously provided his graphic skills to this book cover and others, and Steven Godfrey did all drawings and art illustrations.

Patient and forgiving editors Isaac Mayo of The Mighty Pen and Sarah Aschenbach of Inspired Solutions gave life to a struggling manuscript. Thanks to Kris Weber of I Libri Book Design for unending encouragement and book design. Thanks to Jane Mueller of Well Chosen Words and Alyssa Palmer who also contributed. It remains a work in progress—all errors and rambling, inconceivable adjectives are my own.

Those who guide most are mentioned last. Dan Ogola and Dr. Wagner, may you share your work with all humankind and may we have an ounce of your dedication and energy!

Most importantly, I offer my profound gratitude to my wife, Nancy, for being my source of love and family—a mother, a queen.

About the Author

Richard Godfrey is a surgical oncologist whose international work includes Nepal, Nicaragua, Guatemala, Kenya, Tanzania, and Sierra Leone. He participates in a hospital-building project with Matibabu Foundation-Kenya and TIBA, two NGOs that are striving to empower rural, hard-to-reach, and vulnerable communities. With friendships in rural communities including the Mau Forest and the Maasai Mara, he has enormous respect for the Kenyan people, and their fortitude and resilience in facing challenging health-related conditions.

Proceeds and royalties of this book will be donated to Matibabu Hospital and to the Mama Sarah Obama Foundation.

If you wish to support medicine and care for orphans in Kenya, please consider a donation to the following organizations:

www.matibabukenya.org

www.msof.org (Mama Sarah Obama Foundation)

www.tibafoundation.org (501(c)(3), USA-based

Made in the USA
San Bernardino, CA
09 February 2016